REDEEMING CAPITALISM

REDEEMING CAPITALISM

Kenneth J. Barnes

WILLIAM B. EERDMANS PUBLISHING COMPANY
GRAND RAPIDS, MICHIGAN

Wm. B. Eerdmans Publishing Co.
2140 Oak Industrial Drive N.E., Grand Rapids, Michigan 49505
www.eerdmans.com

27 26 25 24 23 22 21 20 19 18   3 4 5 6 7 8 9 10

ISBN 978-0-8028-7557-0

Library of Congress Cataloging-in-Publication Data

Names: Barnes, Kenneth J., 1957– author.
Title: Redeeming capitalism / Kenneth J. Barnes.
Description: Grand Rapids : Eerdmans Publishing Co., 2018. |
   Includes bibliographical references and index.
Identifiers: LCCN 2017060601 | ISBN 9780802875570 (hardcover : alk. paper)
Subjects: LCSH: Capitalism—Religious aspects—Christianity.
Classification: LCC BR115.C3 B38 2018 | DDC 261.8/5—dc23
   LC record available at https://lccn.loc.gov/2017060601

The author is represented by MacGregor Literary Inc.

To Steve and Diane Eyre

CONTENTS

FOREWORD

This book matters because capitalism matters. Arguably, global capitalism is among the most pervasive and most powerful forces in the world today, and it is a force for good and for ill—for much good and much ill. This is why capitalism needs reforming, or "redeeming," as the title of the book puts it, using a favorite Christian metaphor for overcoming sin and its consequences. *Redeeming Capitalism* is a nuanced and critical Christian procapitalism voice in the important debate about the future of capitalism.

Very few people today would contest the claim that capitalism needs reforming, but increasingly many are questioning whether capitalism *deserves* reforming. One pillar of Barnes's argument is his claim that no economic system today represents a better, workable alternative to capitalism. It is important to note this right at the outset, for much of the book depends on this claim. I don't read Barnes to say that a better alternative to capitalism cannot be *imagined*. It would be strange for a Christian to argue that capitalism is unsurpassable in principle. Christian hope for the "end of history," to use the phrase popularized by political scientist Francis Fukuyama, is not the victory of capitalism, not even the victory of some superefficient, eco-friendly, and humane form of capitalism. Christian hope is for *the new world* that comes from God, a world that John the Seer describes as "the home of God among the mortals." According to the first two books of the Bible (Genesis and Exodus), the goal of the creation is the establishment of the "tabernacle," God's dwelling place among the people of Israel. The last two chapters of the last book of the Bible (Revelation 21–22) record a broadening of this vision: the entire world, nature and culture, is God's holy of holies, the place of flourishing life, justice, abundance, and security that God indwells.

From the perspective of this grand vision, all economic systems, capitalism included, are interim arrangements. But as an interim arrangement, capitalism is irreplaceable, at least it is so in today's globalized world. Loosely using some terms from soteriology, the branch of theology that explores the nature of salvation, you might say that capitalism is justified not so much by the goods it helps create but by its irreplaceability, by the facts that better alternatives are unavailable and that, in any case, the abolition of global capitalism would require something like a worldwide revolution and therefore cause more harm than good. Justified in this twofold way, capitalism remains a sinner. That's why it both deserves and needs reforming. In soteriology, the process of reform is called *sanctification*. Capitalism is badly in need of sanctification. That's one of the main points of *Redeeming Capitalism*.

To know that capitalism *needs* reforming we don't need to appeal to the lofty perfection of the eschatological vision! Simple moral convictions will suffice, convictions formulated with the view of the world as it presently is, inhabited by finite and fallible beings living in fragile environments. To illustrate the need for reform, take just one Christian conviction. Christians have always believed that the poor are "God's first love," to use a felicitous phrase of Pope Benedict XVI, not known for his radical politics. For the capitalism of today, however, the poor seem to be the last concern. True, unprecedented economic growth over the last half century or so has lifted many out of poverty. Still, a long, dark shadow of growing disparity in wealth and power has trailed this stunning economic growth, with opulent and powerful elites living alongside an underclass made up of millions upon millions of hopelessly poor, overworked, and disenfranchised people. The sufferings of the poor are an indictment against current forms of capitalism; their groaning, like the groaning of the Jews in the ancient Egypt of the great pharaohs, is a cry for redemption and therefore reform. (A parallel line of argument for the reform of capitalism, the one that concerns its relation to the entire ecosystem, could start with the biblical statement, "God saw everything that he had made, and indeed, it was very good" [Genesis 1:31].)

It isn't only on account of its effects that capitalism needs reforming, however. Many students of capitalism have noted inner tensions and inherent instabilities in the functioning of capitalism itself, the most famous—not necessarily the most compelling!—among them being Karl Marx, who argued that capitalism's inner tensions will inevitably lead to its eventual collapse. Barnes is much more nuanced; he is no Marxist. In *Redeeming Capitalism*, he highlights two related tensions within capitalism. One is between the kinds of structural interventions capitalism needs to function well and the resistances to these interventions that the inner logic of its operation generates. The other is a tension between the moral ecology presupposed by a responsible capitalism and the kind of amoral world in which it operates today and which it in fact helps to generate.

Barnes's main concern is the second tension, the "moral vacuum at the heart of capitalism," as he puts it. For without bringing a moral vision to bear on capitalism, the first tension cannot be addressed and its deleterious effects cannot be remedied. Three central claims give *Redeeming Capitalism* urgency:

- no good substitutes for capitalism are available;
- capitalism is self-undermining and destructive without moral convictions to regulate it;
- capitalism has insulated itself against these convictions.

The book is a call to reimagine and reform capitalism as a moral enterprise so it can become a morally steered servant rather than a cruel, amoral master. Subduing global capitalism is a difficult mountain to scale, a Mt. Everest of social engagement. But climb it we must. And climb it we can, even if it is one step at a time and only part of the way.

Redeeming Capitalism isn't just about bringing morality to capitalism, though. It's also, and below the surface perhaps primarily, about the place of economics in who we see ourselves to be as humans and about how we understand the basic orientation of our lives. It's an endeavor to align capitalism not just with common morality but with our very humanity. The very first words of the book, a quotation from Jesus's Sermon on the Mount, are meant to set the direction for the entire project: "For where your treasure is, there your heart will be also" (Matthew 6:21). Note the relation between the treasure and the heart: the heart doesn't determine the treasure (as Christian champions of unredeemed capitalism have often insisted); it's the other way around: the treasure pulls the heart to itself. Where should human treasure be so that the heart would end up in the same place as well? In the same sermon, Jesus gives the answer: "But strive first for the kingdom of God and his righteousness, and all these things will be given to you as well" (v. 33). For Christians, the great challenge behind the moral challenge is to reform capitalism so that, "sinner" that it will always remain, it can still be integrated into the striving for the "kingdom of God" as the true "location" of human hearts and the true goal of our lives.

Consider the first temptation of Jesus in the light of the need to reform capitalism. "Turn these stones into bread," the Tempter taunted Jesus, famished after a forty-day fast in the wilderness. Jesus resisted, responding, "One does not live by bread alone, but by every word that comes from the mouth of God" (Matthew 4:4). Jesus was quoting the Hebrew Bible. Moses, the great deliverer and lawgiver, first uttered these words to the children of Israel as a summary of the main lesson they were to have learned in the course of their forty years of wandering in the wilderness before entering the promised land. Bread was what they needed in the wilderness; that much was never in doubt and that trite truth, as insistent as a growling stomach, they didn't need to learn. But they needed more than bread, and that truth, not as obvious as the hunger, but as real as the possibility of losing our very humanity, they did need to learn. All humans do, perhaps especially we moderns.

In the course of modernity, we have made our greatest temptation into the chief goal of our lives and the main purpose of our major institutions (that is, the state, the market, science and technology, and education). Modernity isn't just an age in which people believe that "only the world can be the case" (Peter Sloterdijk). More significantly, it's also an age in which *people act as if* only the world were the case, whether or not they believe in transcendent realities. Most of our social and individual energy and imagination revolves around turning stones into bread. And yet we, both the rich and the poor, are still in the wilderness, plagued by hunger and thirst. Once we are convinced of the *deep poverty of living by bread alone*, we'll be ready to start the great endeavor of morally taming capitalism so as to push it into being less of a master and more of a servant.

Redeeming Capitalism is an important resource in helping Christians engage in a serious debate about how best to undertake an endeavor critical for the future of our world: how to reform capitalism both by lessening the importance in our lives of the goods capitalism can deliver and by bringing moral conviction to bear on its functioning.

MIROSLAV VOLF
Henry B. Wright Professor of
Theology, Yale Divinity School
Founder and Director of
Yale Center for Faith & Culture

ACKNOWLEDGMENTS

Writing a book is a team effort and this project is no exception. I could never have done it without the support and encouragement of my colleagues at Gordon-Conwell Theological Seminary (especially Dennis Hollinger, Richard Lints, Tom Pfizenmaier, Jeffrey Arthurs, and Svatia Mueller), at Oxford University (especially Paul Fiddes, Nicholas Wood, Isabella Bunn, Robin Gibbons, Peter Tuffano, John Hoffmire, the Reverend Joe Martin, and Jonathan Brant), and at Ridley Theological College, Melbourne (especially Brian Rosner, Tim Foster, and Kara Martin).

Countless other friends and associates have been mentors, confidants, informal editors, and prayer warriors and whose contributions are lovingly and seamlessly woven into the fabric of this book. They include Stuart Judge, who was the first person to read and comment on the opening chapter and whose positive words encouraged me to complete the rest of the book; Donald Hay; Peter Heslam; the Very Reverend Martyn Percy; Peter Barnett; Os Guinness; David Miller; Wendy Simpson, OAM; Ian Harper; Jim Longhurst; Ted Malloch; Fr. Richard Wilson; Lord Brian Griffiths; Miroslav Volf; Laszlo Zsolnai; Bob Doll; Lindsay McMillan, OAM; the Right Reverend Colin Fletcher, OBE; the Reverend Canon Chris Neal; the Langs; the Newtons; the Broadways; the Adamses; the Eyres; the Galvins; the Fishers; the Sandforts; the Holdens; the Smiths; the Cabajs; the Pecks; the Wisniewskis; the Furbushes; and countless others whose names do not appear but whose influence is writ large on every page.

I must also thank my publisher, Wm. B. Eerdmans (especially the tireless Linda Bieze, whose attention to detail saved me many an embarrassing typo, and the extraordinary Lil Copan, whose patience as an editor is matched only by her encouragement as a friend); my literary agent, Chip MacGregor; and the person who guided me through the earliest stages of this project and in many ways made this book possible, my friend, renowned author, Davis Bunn.

I must, of course, thank the Kern Family Foundation for their generous support of this and other projects at Gordon-Conwell Theological Seminary and the very gracious benefactors who have endowed the Chair I am privileged to occupy, Mrs. Joanna Mockler and Tom Phillips (not to mention my predecessors David Gill and William Messenger). Thanks to their vision and their faithfulness, we are able to continue our work in the critically important areas of faith, work, and economics.

Last but not least, I must thank my family, who have not only journeyed with me for a lifetime but have made it all worthwhile. My parents (Frank and Mary), who taught me right from wrong; my brothers (Frank and Tim) and my sisters (Connie, Anne, and Bette), who taught me that the whole is greater than the sum of the parts; my amazing children and their spouses (Bernadette, Christian and Serafina, Julia and Joe—plus two grandchildren on the way as I write this!), who have always been my inspiration; and my beautiful, loving, and long-suffering bride of nearly forty years, Debby, who has modeled every virtue mentioned in this book, but especially faith, hope, and love.

To all of you, I give my sincerest thanks—and to God be the glory.

KENNETH J. BARNES

INTRODUCTION

For where your treasure is, there your heart will be also.

Matthew 6:21

Capitalism is a subject, not an object. It possesses no *hypostasis*, no human essence, and imposes no will, but it does reflect the values of the culture in which it resides. Capitalism is nothing more than the result of countless individual and corporate decisions, and for good or ill, the capitalism we have is the capitalism we have chosen; its *redemption* rests on the choices we are yet to make.

The global financial crisis of 2008 was not the near miss some would have us believe. It was the first shot in a battle for the very soul of capitalism, and it scored a direct hit. Governments and central banks across the world took unprecedented measures to stave off complete economic meltdown, and while they have succeeded in avoiding economic Armageddon, for now, the long-term effects of recent monetary policies remain unknown, and regulatory responses to the crisis are already under threat.

Of still greater concern is what those measures did not achieve or even address and that is the *moral vacuum* at the heart of capitalism. If that issue is not addressed, history will not only repeat itself, but it will magnify itself, and the results will be catastrophic.

Fortunately, this is not an unalterable prophecy. Despite capitalism's inherent limitations and the moral failures that led to the global financial crisis, there is still hope, but only if individuals, businesses, civic leaders, and religious institutions address the cultural and moral malaise that has infected our overall economic health.

The devastating effects of the recent crisis strengthened the voice of those who believe capitalism is inherently evil. Their remedy is the wholesale reconstruction of our economic system. In this book, I argue against this approach and expose the folly of seeking an alternative economic utopia. I propose instead that capitalism, once rooted in a particular religious ethic and long since lost to the moral relativism of the modern era, need not be replaced, but needs instead to be *redeemed*.

After tracing the evolution of Western economics from precapitalist systems, to the traditional capitalism observed by Adam Smith, to the critique of capitalism of Karl Marx, to the modern capitalism observed by Max Weber, we will examine the unique relationship between economic activity and religious belief, especially the influence of Judeo-Christian teachings on work, worth, wealth, and business ethics. Since we cannot simply turn back the clock to a time of religious hegemony, we will look instead at the universal truths, sometimes known as *common grace*, at the heart of the Judeo-Christian tradition that guide society today. In doing so, we will explore the relationship between wisdom and ethics, unpacking the so-called *cardinal virtues* of prudence, justice, courage (that is, fortitude), and temperance (that is, moderation) and the *theological virtues* of faith, hope, and love as they relate to this question: is capitalism redeemable?

I hope to challenge you to imagine what capitalism would be like if individuals, companies, communities, and policy-makers made economic choices consistent with those universal truths. Also, I aim to challenge you to imagine *virtuous capitalism*: an economic system with all of the wealth-generating possibilities of the capitalism we have, plus the social benefits of the capitalism we desire—a system that consciously embraces and enthusiastically employs *common grace* for the *common good*.

I

Capitalism—
What Went Wrong?

For what will it profit them, if they gain the whole world but forfeit their life?

MATTHEW 16:26A

In September 2008, the world was shaken by an economic crisis that few saw coming and fewer still knew how to resolve. The US presidential campaigns were temporarily suspended and crisis talks were held in New York, Washington, London, Frankfurt, Hong Kong, Tokyo, and other global financial centers. The opinions of pundits commenting on events ranged from calling the crisis a mere financial "blip" to an economic Armageddon, while the rest of us looked on helplessly, wondering what it all meant to us, our children, and our children's children. We simply did not know how it would all shake out and we still do not. The immediate crisis may have passed, but its medium- to long-term effects are still being felt around the world.

The crash of September 2008 was not so much a malady in itself as it was a symptom of a much more serious disease infecting global capitalism. It exposed deep structural and moral fault lines that many people both within and outside the financial sector knew about but chose to ignore. As the billionaire investor Warren Buffet once quipped, "You only find out who's swimming naked when the tide goes out."[1] As it turns out, an awful lot of economic skinny-dipping has been going on for a long time. In September 2008, the tide went out.

As with previous market crashes, this one seems to have started with the collapse of a single financial institution, the New York investment bank

Lehman Brothers. Prior to its spectacular failure, it had been the fourth-largest investment bank in the world with twenty-eight thousand employees and nearly $700 billion in assets under management. It was a colossus, and its chairman and CEO, Richard S. Fuld Jr., was one of the richest and most powerful people on Wall Street. He was also one of the most feared—as his nickname, the "Gorilla," suggests. Prior to June 2008, the company reported fifty-five consecutive quarters of profit, and Mr. Fuld received nearly a half billion dollars in total compensation; yet within three months, the company went bankrupt, triggering a near-meltdown of financial markets around the world.

Since the bank's failure, much has been written about how events unfolded, who was responsible, and what the effects have been on both Wall Street and Main Street. After summarizing the salient points of others' assessments,[2] I will look specifically in this chapter and generally in this book at why these and similar events have transpired at all, what *motives* drive individual and corporate decision-making, and what role *culture*, both corporate and civic, plays in economic activity.

Most know that those who invest aggressively in markets are known as bulls and those who are more cautious, bears. An old saying on Wall Street once warned newcomers about the dangers of greed: "bulls make money and bears make money, but pigs get slaughtered." The events of 2008 suggest that this saying has become out-of-date.

Structural Failures

So, how did a bank the size of Lehman Brothers fail? Who was responsible for its failure, and what does it all mean to the banking sector, the financial sector, and the economy in general? The simple answer can be found in three words: deception, debt, and derivatives. Let's start with the latter and work up the list.

Derivatives are financial instruments that, as their name implies, derive their value from other underlying entities. They are not individual assets per se but payment contracts predicated on the anticipated performance, or cash flow, of their underlying assets. Derivatives are very clever devices that, if constructed and managed properly, have the potential to generate high rates of return while dispersing and, in theory, mitigating risk. They take many different forms and have been around since the 1980s, yet one particular type of derivative, known as a collateralized debt obligation (CDO), is a relatively recent innovation. CDOs were the instruments at the heart of the Lehman Brothers collapse.

Collateralized debt obligations are tradable derivatives that use various debt instruments, such as loans and mortgages, as collateral or security against potential default. As with all derivatives, they are payment contracts, and their source of revenue is the cumulative payment of interest and principle on the underlying loans that constitute a derivative's pool of assets. In short, collateralized debt obligations promise to pay investors a return based upon the promises of borrowers to pay back their loans. Assuming that the loans in question are themselves secured by tangible assets, such as personal property or commercial real estate, and that the borrowers have been properly vetted and are likely to meet their debt obligations, one could argue that CDOs carry no more risk than any other investment. But if the underlying loans themselves are not sufficiently secured by substantial equity on the part of the borrowers, or if the buyers have not been properly vetted and are less likely to meet their debt obligations, CDOs then become extremely risky investments. This became evident during the so-called subprime mortgage crisis that immediately preceded the global financial crisis.

Subprime mortgages, as the name implies, are mortgages carrying greater risk than conventional mortgages. The additional risk comes from several factors, including the credit-worthiness of borrowers (that is, their previous credit history), potential volatility in the repayment terms of the mortgages (such as variable rate or "teaser rate" mortgages), and historically high loan-to-value ratios. Traditionally, when a person wanted to take out a mortgage on a home, he or she needed to demonstrate three things to the bank. First, the borrower needed prove that he or she could afford the home in the first place, which was determined by combined factors including evidence of annual earnings equal to no less than 30 percent of the value of the property. Then the borrower needed to demonstrate credit worthiness by providing a history of uninterrupted repayment terms on other debts, such as credit cards or car loans, usually in the form of a credit score provided by an independent credit rating agency. Finally, the potential home buyer needed to raise enough money on his or her own (that is, without having to borrow from other sources, including friends and family) for a sizeable deposit, usually a minimum of 20 percent of the value of the property. All this vetting was done to protect both the borrower and the lender against the ravages of default. Defaulting on any credit obligation is a serious thing, but defaulting on a mortgage is especially disastrous for both bank and borrower, as the former stands to lose a very large sum of money and the latter, the family home.

In the late 1990s and early 2000s, all that changed. Because of a long period of economic expansion and an influx of foreign investment, the US financial system was flush with cash that needed someplace to go. The US housing market seemed the perfect place, not only because house prices were rising and real estate seemed like a sound investment, but because CDOs would theoretically mitigate the risk for lenders by allowing them to sell their mortgage liabilities to third parties. That sparked an exceedingly high demand for mortgages that could be met only if the number of high-risk or subprime mortgages increased significantly. From 2002 to 2006, subprime mortgages tripled from 7.4 percent to 23.5 percent of the market, with an approximate value of $2.5 trillion, most of which was sold off by the actual lenders and sold on to investors in the form of CDOs.

So desperate were lenders to create mortgage products that they abandoned the traditional lending models described above and offered mortgages to people regardless of their ability to repay them. In some cases, people were given mortgages although they had no income, no job, and no assets—so-called NINJA[3] mortgages. In addition, individuals were enticed to take out mortgages on homes they could not actually afford by "teaser" rates of interest. Teaser rates are artificially low, offering monthly payments that initially seem to be affordable with the caveat that the rates would adjust over time, possibly resulting in higher monthly payments down the road. In theory, this should be manageable, as long as interest rates remained generally stable, the borrower's income increased, and/or the value of their property increased. However, in reality things proved to be quite different, and when the real estate bubble burst and the housing market went into decline, and as interest rates subsequently began to rise, people found themselves with mortgages they could no longer afford, on homes now valued lower than the amount they owed on their mortgages (so-called negative equity). As one might expect, this resulted in loan defaults on a massive scale, and the economic ripple effects caused a financial tsunami.

Economics is considered a predictive science. It is not. At best it is an indicative science. That is to say, while historical data and computer modeling are helpful in trying to predict future economic events, there is no guarantee that people will continue to behave in a certain way. This was the case with the subprime mortgage crisis and the accompanying CDOs. Historically, mortgage failure rates are very low, around 2 percent, and while the computer models that were developed to calculate the risk of mortgage-backed derivatives factored in the possibility of a slight increase in mortgage defaults, they never anticipated an exponential increase in them. Consequently, as the defaults increased, confidence in the CDOs that held those mortgages decreased. To make matters worse, because mortgages were divorced from their original lending sources and bundled together, no one could be sure which CDOs were most exposed. Instead of mitigating risk by spreading it, the CDOs actually had the opposite effect of contaminating good loans with bad loans.

The effect of the subprime mortgage crisis was felt across the entire financial sector as banks were forced to write down, or lower the value of, billions of dollars of assets. And the contamination was not limited to the residential mortgage market; it was also felt by the commercial real estate market. It was time for the big investment banks to get out of CDOs—except for Lehman Brothers; they had a different strategy. Instead of getting out of CDOs, they saw the exodus of other banks as an opportunity to fill the void and chose instead to increase their exposure by acquiring more CDOs, exceeding their own internal risk limits in the process. It was a colossal gamble, and while the decision to do so may have fallen within the generally accepted parameters of the business judgment rule,[4] it failed spectacularly and ultimately resulted in the company declaring bankruptcy.

The word *gamble* here is critical. One may argue whether gambling is or is not a virtuous activity. What people do with their own money is largely their business. The problem is, investment banks deal with *other* people's money, and the morality of gambling in this context is at best, questionable. The business judgment rule is a legal standard, not a moral one, and a virtuous economic system would logically be based on a higher standard than merely that which the law permits. That said, CDOs were only part of the problem. An even greater problem for Lehman Brothers was its debt-laden business model, excessive leverage, and lack of liquidity, the combined effects of which were unsustainable when losses began to mount and confidence in the company began to wane. It was this constellation of threats that led to an even greater moral dilemma: the use of deceptive, albeit legal, accounting practices, to present an inaccurate picture of financial health to the markets.

Before 2008, most investment banks had business models similar to that of Lehman Brothers, which consisted of acquiring high-risk investments that were heavily leveraged, that is, bought with borrowed money. The near-collapse of Bear Sterns, another investment bank, in 2007 brought to light the problems inherent in this model, and soon both regulators and markets realized that Lehman Brothers, with its aggressive growth strategy and commitment to CDOs, was in a particularly precarious situation. As the Valukas Report notes, while Lehman Brothers had $25 billion in capital, it held approximately $700 billion in long-term assets against a similar amount of short-term liabilities. Consequently, it had to trade nearly $200 billion of assets on the repo market[5] every day just to meet its daily cash requirements. Since a large proportion of the asset base of Lehman Brothers was in CDOs, the value of those assets came under intense scrutiny, and the repo markets became reluctant to lend to Lehman Brothers. Their mountain of debt, or leverage, secured by another mountain of debt, CDOs, simply became unsustainable, and when the repo markets refused to support them anymore, they were in trouble.

Ironically, the instrument of deceit used by Lehman Brothers involved an accounting method, associated with the repo transactions themselves, known simply as Repo 105. Under normal circumstances, when a bank makes a repurchase agreement on the repo market, the transaction is treated, for accounting purposes, as an instrument of finance, that is, a short-term loan. Even though temporary ownership of the assets involved transfers between the two institutions, the value of the assets themselves remain "on the books," that is, the balance sheet, of the borrowing bank. But, when the value of assets traded during the transaction is equal to 105 percent or more of the cash value received, accounting rules allow the transaction to be treated as an actual sale, thereby removing the assets from the borrowing bank's balance sheet. Lehman Brothers would use this accounting device at the end of a reporting period for the sole purpose of reducing its leverage ratio "on paper."[6]

In the strictest sense, this was a perfectly legal activity, but the bank and its auditors, Ernst and Young, had a fiduciary responsibility to disclose its use of Repo 105 to its stakeholders, including the regulators, shareholders, Board of Directors, and investors—which it did not do. Consequently, Lehman Brothers led stakeholders to believe that the bank's financial position was less precarious than it actually was.

Lehman Brothers also deceptively reported the value of its liquidity pool.[7] Despite having a pool of approximately $45 billion on paper, the vast majority of the money was pledged as security elsewhere or was otherwise too difficult to monetize (that is, turn into cash). Consequently, when the bank went to the market to raise money with a public offering in June 2008, it presented a deceptive picture of financial health to investors. While Lehman Brothers succeeded in raising $6 billion in that public offering, it failed to substantially improve the bank's financial position or, more importantly, the bank's reputation on Wall Street.

Once the repo markets lost confidence in Lehman Brothers and its own liquidity was insufficient to fund its daily operations, management realized that the company was in serious jeopardy of insolvency. Despite desperate attempts to sell the bank at the eleventh hour, or to secure emergency funding from the Treasury Department, Lehman Brothers ran out of cash, ran out of accounting tricks, and ran out of options. At 1:45 a.m. on September 15, 2008, Lehman Brothers Holding, Inc., filed for Chapter 11 bankruptcy protection. Their high-stakes game was over and the losers were legion.

Moral Failures

In an article published by the *New York Times Magazine* on September 13, 1970, economist Milton Friedman famously stated that the primary responsibility of a corporate executive is to "make as much money as possible while conforming to the basic rules of the society, both those embodied in law and those embodied in ethical custom." This, along with various precepts laid out in his 1962 book entitled *Capitalism and Freedom*, became known collectively as the Friedman doctrine.[8] The notion that business is amoral and that companies have no social responsibility other than the maximization of profits has been the generally accepted mantra of business schools and boardrooms for a generation. Yet, there are obvious flaws in the logic of Friedman's argument.

First, curiously, Friedman's formula gives no consideration to the variable of time. "Make as much money as possible" over what period of time—the next day, the next month, the next quarter, the next conference call with analysts, the next year? As demonstrated by the actions of Lehman Brothers, a company could make a great deal of short-term profit while creating a medium- to long-term existential threat to the business. Surely, investors expect executives to maximize their return on investment, but that does not preclude the executives' duty to act responsibly and with consideration given to short-, medium-, and long-term horizons. Some investors may be short in the market and others long; some may be interested in dividends, while others merely share value. All executive decisions have consequences, and making "as much money as possible" is simply an insufficient metric for measuring the success of a business, much less the morality of its actions.

Second, we have seen that obeying the "rules of society [as] . . . embodied in law" does not guarantee responsible behavior either. Using Repo 105 to manipulate the balance sheet of Lehman Brothers was technically legal but morally irresponsible; and what, exactly, is the "ethical custom" Friedman was referring to? If it was the custom of investment banks to employ high-risk/high-leverage business models and trade in complex derivatives whose underlying assets are either unstable or untraceable or, in the case of some CDOs, both, is that ethical? Obviously not, yet according to the precepts of the Friedman doctrine the executives of Lehman Brothers did exactly what was required of them—they were simply trying to "make as much money as possible while conforming to the basic rules of the society, both those embodied in law and those embodied in ethical custom."

It would seem the prosecutors agreed. Despite the catalogue of errors, misjudgment, and even deception highlighted in the Examiner's Report, none of the senior executives of Lehman Brothers went to jail or even faced criminal charges, because prosecutors concluded that they had not actually broken the law. That being the case, one could be forgiven for thinking that the legal system failed spectacularly in its duty to protect investors from malfeasance. Of greater concern to us as we look at this portrait of a particular time in the history of capitalism is the catalogue of *moral failures* that led to the downfall of Lehman Brothers—and the downfall of many world-renowned companies in recent years.

The Cardinal Virtues

What do I mean by the term *moral failure*? For our purposes, I turn to the great moral theologian Thomas Aquinas, who defines a moral failure as any action or policy that is inconsistent with the moral virtues, or cardinal virtues, noted in his seminal work *Summa Theologiae*, namely prudence, justice, courage (or fortitude), and temperance (that is, moderation). Why speak to the Thomistic model in an economics context? For several reasons, actually. Aquinas himself identifies these virtues as being common to humankind regardless of one's religious beliefs or lack thereof. Also, for our purposes, this definition spares us the ethical gymnastics of consequentialism.[9] Finally and importantly, the cardinal virtues and their subsidiary virtues, along with the Decalogue,[10] have been at the heart of ethical and legal thinking in the West for centuries.

Some may argue that such a definition is impractical, unworkable, simplistic, or even naïve. I contend, however, that its beauty is in its simplicity and that its practicality demands neither superior intellect nor an in-depth knowledge of complex principles, requiring instead only the unfettered exercise of one's conscience. In light of this functional definition of morality, let us view the decisions leading up to the collapse of Lehman Brothers through the prism of the cardinal virtues.[11]

Prudence

Aquinas did not invent the cardinal virtues. He built upon the ancient Greek understanding of them, particularly that of Aristotle and the Stoics, as well as those of the early church fathers, especially Gregory the Great and St. Augustine of Hippo. But Aquinas's combination of theology and philosophy has produced definitions of virtue that are neither overtly religious nor unduly esoteric. They are, in fact, exceedingly practical and rooted in both reason and experience. This is demonstrated by his affirmation of St. Augustine's simple yet profound definition of prudence as "the knowledge of what to seek and what to avoid,"[12] or more simply put, "what to want and what not to want."

Augustine's truly sublime definition indelibly links virtue with values, actions, and motives. In this regard, prudence is far more than mere caution, as it is commonly understood in contemporary culture; it is the subjugation of desire, or motive, to the principle of goodness, or value, thereby producing actions that are virtuous.

This, of course, begs the question "what should one want?" While there are many schools of thought in this area, the traditional view of virtually every faith tradition and many secular philosophers as well, from Plato to Cicero, Augustine to Calvin, Muhammad to Gandhi, Kant to Hegel, is that people of good character should seek the common good, above all else. According to Aquinas, the idea that human beings only seek their own personal welfare "is opposed to charity . . . [and] is contrary to right reason, which judges the common good to be better than the good of the individual."[13] In other words, the only "reasonable" behavior is that which "prudently" considers the impact of one's conduct on all of society.

This, Aquinas logically concludes, must involve the "reasoned regulation of conduct," not merely as a "general rule" but in "particular cases."[14] That is to say, when making decisions that could affect others, which is true of most business decisions, virtue requires us to "think forwardly," using our cognitive abilities and such tools as "memory, insight," our ability to "learn from the experience of others," and "soundness of judgment" to ultimately determine "the best course to follow" without resorting to "imprudence," which consists of "willfulness, headlong haste, and negligence," the latter leading to "guile and fraud."[15]

With this definition of prudence it is easy to see the moral failure inherent in both the Lehman Brothers business model and in the decisions its senior executives made leading up to its collapse. In the first place, what the management of the firm desired was clearly not the common good but the maximization of its own profits, regardless of the risk to shareholders and investors alike. Senior management knew of the problems associated with CDOs and further knew that every other major investment bank was exiting the business. That arrogance and hubris led them to believe that they alone could buck the trend and profit from their "counter-cyclical strategy." Their decision to violate their own internal risk limits by more than $700 billion was shockingly imprudent as well. The very purpose of a risk limit is to guard against reckless behavior and prolonged downturns in the market. When a business exceeds its risk limit, the normal response is to take corrective action, that is, either balance the risk or cut one's losses. But in the case of Lehman

Brothers, the bank decided to continue with its high-risk strategy in the hope that conditions would swing in its favor. One of its board members used the term "double down"[16] to describe the strategy, which you may recognize as a term normally used in casino gambling.

All business decisions involve a risk/reward calculus, and responsible executives gather as much data as possible before making those decisions. Sometimes they get it right and sometimes they get it wrong. That is not what we are referring to in this instance: in the case of Lehman Brothers, their gambling involved making business decisions either without sufficient data or in the face of overwhelming evidence that their course of action represented an inordinate amount of risk for their stakeholders. Of course, such behavior is not uncommon just before a financial collapse. In 1995, the actions of a single derivatives trader, Nick Leeson, famously brought down Barings Bank, one of the oldest and most respected merchant banks in the world. While Mr. Leeson was involved in a series of frauds, for which he was ultimately convicted and imprisoned, it was his constant "betting" on a recovery in the Japanese stock market that finally caught up with him. Had he cut his losses early, the bank would probably have survived. Similarly, had the Lehman Brothers executives not acted with such guile and bravado, they too might have been able to avoid destruction. They did not, however, and countless others have suffered as a consequence, which brings us to Aquinas's next virtue, justice.

Justice

Aquinas defines justice as "a stable and lasting willingness to do the just thing for everyone" and injustice as "unfair discrimination." That is to say, the virtue of justice demands that people are treated equitably "in proportion to their social worth" and not according to their associations. He further distinguished between "distributive justice" (that is, dealings that are communal) and "commutative justice" (that is, dealings between individuals).[17] While Aquinas was suspicious of business and commerce, he never condemned it. He did not object to private property, nor did he espouse equal distribution of wealth regardless of one's contribution to society or the creation of that wealth. He *did* however, condemn any "practice enabling one to sell a thing for more than its real worth," and he specifically stated: "when there are hidden flaws in something offered for sale and the seller doesn't disclose them, the sale is fraudulent and illicit."[18]

Obvious in the sale of CDOs, especially those backed by subprime mortgages, was their suspect value, but the more egregious violation of this particular virtue was the public offering of Lehman Brothers stock when their balance sheet and their liquidity position were both misrepresented. Yet the company took these actions despite having both actual and constructive knowledge of their impropriety. It is no accident that among the "subordinate" virtues Aquinas aligned to justice is the virtue of truthfulness.[19]

Without a presumption of truthfulness, basic human intercourse cannot take place. Contracts, pledges, vows, and promises all presume truthfulness; it is this virtue, along with the other subordinate virtues of loyalty, respect, obedience, gratitude, and honor that make commercial transactions possible at all.[20]

Yet the motive for deception was strong, not because the penalty for failure was severe—as we have seen all of the Lehman Brothers executives survived its collapse—but because the financial reward for success was extreme (a situation we will consider later in this chapter). The company's executives were rightfully concerned about their own survival, but their actions demonstrated a complete disregard for anyone else, and while the demands of the law may not have required greater transparency, the demands of justice did.

Ironically, the company had other options. They could have come clean with their customers, shareholders, analysts, and others, admitted the failure of their counter-cyclical strategy, and reversed course. They could have cut their losses and worked to rebuild their business and their reputation, but they did not. Instead, it seems the company's executives considered admission of error and a change of direction too humiliating to contemplate, and so they continued headlong into the abyss and brought countless others down with them. What they thought they needed most at the time was cash, when in fact what they needed most to survive was courage.

Courage

People in positions of power and authority rarely find it easy to admit mistakes. When they do, they are often accused of weakness or indecision. Interestingly, history has offered some counterpoint observations: sometimes the bravest decision a leader can make is one of retreat. George Washington was famous for his use of strategic withdrawal during both the French and Indian Wars and the American Revolutionary War, recognizing it is better to change course and live to fight another day than to continue down a path of obvious destruction. Winston Churchill, renowned for his dogged determination and fighting spirit, oversaw the retreat of Allied forces at Gallipoli during the First World War and delivered his famous "we shall fight them on the beaches" speech on the very day in 1940 that the last British troops were evacuated from Dunkirk during the Second World War. The executives of Lehman Brothers could have learned from those and countless other examples, and they might have avoided their ignominious fate in the process, but as we have seen, courage at the company was in very short supply.

When speaking of courage in the context of virtue, Aquinas made clear that he was describing "spiritual bravery," not "physical bravery." "Courage of spirit," he wrote, "keeps the will steadfastly attached to the good."[21] To remain steadfastly attached to the common good one may add, in consideration of Augustine and Aquinas's aforementioned definition of prudence, the willingness to take a virtuous stand in the face of great peril.

That is why Aquinas defined martyrdom as a virtuous act: it requires someone to make an extreme sacrifice for the benefit of others. Quoting the words of Jesus in the Gospel of John, he reminds his readers, "No man has a greater love than this, that he lays down his life for his friend" (John 15:13). Sacrificing one's own pleasure or comfort, one's own liberty or reputation, or even one's own life for the benefit of others calls for true courage. It is not merely a case of standing firm in the face of adversity—this, as we have seen from history, may in fact prove to be folly. It is about resisting and even opposing those things that are at enmity with virtue itself.

Courage, according to Aquinas, is also about being purposeful in the use of our time, our talents, and our treasures in such endeavors as "enterprise" and "munificence."[22] There is no sin in seeking to do great things including, one might surmise, building a great business, assuming of course the ultimate purpose of that business is, once again, the common good and not merely personal gain; but to do so in a virtuous manner requires great fortitude in the face of adversity and, above all, moral courage in the face of temptation.

This kind of courage was seemingly lost on the executives at Lehman Brothers. They prized only their own power, their own reputations, and above all else, their own material wellbeing. At the end of the day, Lehman Brothers executives made exorbitant amounts of money and did not want the gravy train to stop; so instead, they drove it over a cliff. Not surprisingly, then, we meet the last, and in the context of the great financial crises of 2008, perhaps the most important, of the cardinal virtues, temperance (or moderation).

Temperance and Moderation

Aquinas's discussion of temperance is especially useful because he was not an ascetic. He understood the value of pleasure, not only in terms of its utility (such as the role of sexual desire in propagation of the species and taste-sensation in our quest for nourishment), but in its ability to give one rest from the burdens of life. In fact, he was scornful of those who avoided pleasures needful for survival, unless of course such abstinence served some other utility such as dieting for health reasons or penitential fasting. And derided those he called "wet blankets" (that is, people lacking a healthy sense of humor).

Aquinas also understood that while desire for pleasure was both natural and useful, if left unchecked it had the potential to wreak havoc physically and spiritually; hence he defined temperance as "a special virtue of restraint operating in fields in which we find ourselves specially and exceptionally attracted."[23] That is, because our natural desires are hardwired into our DNA as part of our survival instinct, their power over us can be overwhelming, requiring us to use our other uniquely human powers of will and reason to moderate them for our own benefit.

Aquinas provides numerous examples of the dangers associated with excess and immoderation in things that would otherwise be beneficial to us, such as drinking in excess, eating in excess, and sexual immorality. He also addressed other natural impulses such as hatred, anger, vengeance, envy, and pride. To combat those negative emotions, Aquinas emphasized the need for the exercise of various subordinate virtues, such as mildness, clemency, and most of all, humility.

Humility is chief among the subordinate virtues because it keeps our pride in check, and our pride, Aquinas rightly notes, "can give rise to every other sin,"[24] including greed. An especially perilous vice, greed at its core is a rejection of God and God's values. That is why the apostle Paul states categorically: "greed is idolatry" (Eph. 5:5). It is no coincidence that the first four commandments of the Decalogue deal with our responsibility to God as sovereign and the requirement that we reject any and all competing idols. Throughout the Hebrew Scriptures, God is described as a jealous God who suffers no rivals and demands total fidelity. Greed and love of money can easily become competing idols, as their pursuit requires an inordinate amount of one's time and attention.

While it is true that money cannot buy happiness, it buys things that bring pleasure; and pursuit of wealth itself easily becomes both a means and an end. Spurred on by an insatiable appetite for stimulation, or for a desire to escape reality through the self-medication of pleasurable experiences, or for the power and self-aggrandizement that often impel the rich, "the love of money" can in fact become the "root of all kinds of evil" (1 Tim. 6:10).

Many suspected that greed overwhelmingly motivated the executives of Lehman Brothers to make decisions to construct the high-risk, heavily leveraged business model they employed. Missing in their model was an interest in the common good and an interest in their employees, their shareholders, and their investors.

Consider the personal compensation of Lehman Brothers CEO Richard Fuld: in hearings before the United States Congress in the wake of the collapse of Lehman Brothers, Mr. Fuld complained that Congressman Waxman's figure of approximately $500 million in compensation was exaggerated and that between 2000 and 2007 he had "only" actually earned $310 million. For argument sake, assuming Mr. Fuld's figure is correct, he was still paid over $44 million per year in compensation as one of dozens of Lehman Brothers executives whose annual compensation exceeded $10 million per year[25]; and Lehman Brothers was only one investment bank. A recent report by the Brookings Institution[26] revealed that investment banks distribute approximately half of their firms' annual earnings to their employees in bonuses. It also revealed the huge commissions traders make on the profitability of their accounts, approximately 30 percent. Is it any wonder that compensation of this kind and at this level encourages the kind of reckless behavior we have recently witnessed on Wall Street?

Wall Street's justification for such obscenely high salaries is the notion that these "masters of the universe"[27] are the architects of wealth creation without whom capitalism would fail to function. But is it true that Wall Street actually creates the wealth it purports to create? It certainly makes a lot of money, but that is not the same thing.[28] Yet no one on Wall Street, or in the halls of government for that matter, talks about that difference; it is just too scary for the politicians and too inconvenient for the "suits." While it is beyond the scope of this book to explore this more deeply, consider the fact that since the United States unilaterally abandoned the Bretton Woods agreement and converted from the gold standard to fiat currency, the country has amassed a national debt in excess of $20 trillion. Since the start of the global financial crisis alone it has added $10 trillion to its national debt and "printed" $4.5 trillion in "new" money through its program of quantitative easing.

Is that wealth creation or the creation of an illusion of wealth? It is a bit like the band playing on the deck of the Titanic, keeping the music going to keep people's minds off the fact that the ship is sinking. In the case of global capitalism, the ship is not sinking quite yet, but if we fail to change course soon, it will hit an iceberg, and we all know that story does not end well.

Postmodern Capitalism

The maladies affecting global capitalism are not confined to the financial sector; they are endemic to the entire system and reflect the West's abandonment of its historic ethical norms. The Judeo-Christian ethics of which Aquinas's cardinal and theological virtues[29] are a part, have been replaced by postmodern relativism. Observers such as Adam Smith and Max Weber, whose work we will examine in more detail in later chapters, would be shocked to see capitalism no longer undergirded by faith in a higher power or to observe commerce failing to assume commonly held beliefs about right and wrong, morality and immorality. A mutant, postmodern capitalism has begun to define our culture: devoid of a moral compass and resistant, if not impervious, to ethical constraint. Left unchecked, this form of capitalism will continue to produce the behavior responsible not only for the collapse of Lehman Brothers, but for such scandals as Enron, WorldCom, Barings Bank, Parmalat, the subprime mortgage crisis, the LIBOR scandal, and the ticking time bomb of national debt.

Recalling that capitalism is the result of countless individual and collective choices and that all choices are ultimately moral in nature, reflecting our beliefs and values, the work of this book is to explore what capitalism requires most: a moral compass. While my particular understanding of that moral compass comes through a Christian perspective, my hope is that those of other faiths, or no faith, will find important common ground in these discussions.

For centuries in the West, Christianity has been the guardian of Aquinas's cardinal virtues, whose universality is generally accepted. While it may be the duty of Christians to seek the redemption of capitalism, it is not a parochial activity. It is an inclusive mission whose participants are simply those who reject the widely-held narrative of naked self-interest and who seek instead an economic system that rewards the individual while, first and foremost, seeking the common good.

This, of course, begs the question "how can we turn capitalism around?" To answer that question, we must first consider where capitalism came from, where it is headed, and who is at the helm. In the following chapters, I will attempt to do just that and then begin the exploration of how people of goodwill, regardless of their religious beliefs, can set about the redemption of postmodern capitalism.

Opinions vary on this matter from the very start. Some people believe the answer lies in government regulation. While we certainly need regulations in place to guard against the dangers of fraud and recklessness, if history has taught us anything, it has taught us that legislation is usually one step behind the offenders. It might even be argued that most regulation is born of unethical behavior or the assumption of unethical behavior. Historically, as legislators and regulators establish fair and reasonable rules of engagement, those rules are quickly followed by the clever work-arounds of lawyers, accountants, and others determined to be above or beyond the law. Furthermore, technology is moving at breakneck speed and products are introduced to markets before their ultimate impact on society can be properly assessed, making it virtually impossible to legislate against their possible effects. We need another approach.

Others believe the answer rests with ethical decision-making on the part of senior executives. While that is certainly a step in the right direction, it simply is not good enough, not when people across organizations are empowered to make high-impact decisions, as was the case with the aforementioned Barings Bank or more recently, Barclays Bank and the LIBOR scandal, where the activities of relatively low-level employees had catastrophic consequences for millions of unsuspecting people.[30] Ethical businesses require ethical business cultures, not just ethical executives.

Rather than rushing into solutions, I argue that the only effective way society can overcome the corrosive effects of postmodern capitalism is to consider how we got here in the first place; to celebrate what we got right; to fix what we got wrong; and then set out to redeem capitalism—from the bottom up *and* from the top down.

2

Economics:
A Very Concise History

*And ye shall dwell with us: and the land shall be before you; dwell and
trade ye therein, and get you possessions therein.*

GENESIS 34:10 (KJV)

Capitalism is not an artificial construct devised by clever minds but an economic system that has evolved over centuries. It is the cumulative effect of countless individual and corporate decisions, a multitude of effects brought about by a multitude of causes, a complex constellation of institutions, organizations, and processes devoid of a master plan. As such, no moment in history stands as the beginning of capitalism. While there have been watershed events and defining moments for the phenomenon we now know as capitalism, for the purposes of this chapter, I want to review instead several major eras in what historian Joyce Appleby refers to as a "relentless revolution."[1]

Precapitalist Commerce

Capitalism has not always existed, but commerce, or trade, in one form or another has. For millennia the primary driver of trade was the universal challenge of human subsistence. The story is told of two men who go down to a river; one has wheat, the other wool. The man with the wheat is cold and the man with the wool is hungry. The two exchange their surplus goods for the mutual benefit of both parties and there exists, in its most basic form, a market. For as long as humans have attempted to feed, clothe, shelter, and

21

protect themselves from the elements and other animals, including at times their own species, they have found it necessary to share scarce resources and recruit the assistance of others in their efforts to survive. The cursory review of several economic epochs that follows will give you a basic understanding of capitalism in historic context.

Prehistoric Economics

Anthropologists and sociologists generally agree that all hominids, including early Homo sapiens, survived simply by eating and drinking whatever they could find. While this may have included the flesh of other species, their diet consisted primarily of whatever fruits and vegetables could be easily gathered; hence, some prefer to call these early humans foragers rather than the traditional hunter-gatherers, but in either case, the picture of prehistoric human activity is one of scarcity and subsistence without any notion of surplus or plenty. This changed, though, during the Neolithic period, when humans began domesticating both plants and animals, developing basic tools, and forming agrarian societies.

For the first time in human history, communities were formed around what we may accurately call economic activity.[2] Farmers could plant seeds that produced crops, sometimes to surplus levels, and animal husbandry provided the resources necessary for both food production and secondary products such as clothes and more advanced tools. Because of various external factors, not the least of which were meteorological, communities often found themselves with a surplus of some commodities and a scarcity of others. This created opportunities for exchange with neighboring communities, and while the primary form of exchange was simply bartering, it was not long before precious metals such as gold and silver became de facto currencies.[3]

Early agrarian societies were also seminomadic, and their constant migrations brought them into contact with other civilizations whose goods and artifacts were often both useful and interesting. Improvements in farming techniques, the further development of tools (including the tools of war), the establishment of migration paths, the use of animals for transport, the mining of raw materials, the development of creative skills, and the emergence of markets[4] meant that for the first time, humans could create wealth[5] on a measurable scale.

Economics of Empire

In the second and first millennia BCE, the emergence of dynastic empires brought new opportunities for the creation and distribution of wealth, especially in the ancient Near East, the Mediterranean, and the Far East. They included the Akkadian, Babylonian, Persian, Macedonian, and Greco-Roman empires, as well as the Qin Dynasty, to name just a few. While each empire was unique in countless ways, they all shared certain characteristics that impacted economic life.

For instance, they were all expansionists and stretched their borders through a variety of military activities and suzerain-vassal treaties. As they expanded, they demanded tribute from the inhabitants of the lands they conquered, and those tributes involved everything from forced labor, to livestock and produce, to finished goods, to precious metals and stones. Payment of tribute necessitated complex hierarchies to facilitate both the creation of wealth and the transfer of wealth from the bottom up.

Greco-Roman Economics

The economic system of the Greco-Roman period is of particular interest to our study as it provided the foundation upon which later Western civilizations would build models of economic activity based largely upon the exploitation of natural resources, the movement of labor, technological development, industry, international trade, common law, and widely accepted currencies. It would be incorrect to refer to these economies as capitalist, but they do represent a kind of protocapitalism that clearly demonstrates the evolutionary nature of the phenomenon.

As with all cultures, the economic system of the Greco-Roman period both reflected and informed the sociopolitical realities of the time. The means of production and the instruments of commerce, trade, and taxation were all indelibly linked to the established structures of empire, including language, government, military rule, religion, and local custom. For instance, the official language of the Roman Empire and the language of the governing elite was Latin, but the *lingua franca* throughout most of the empire remained Greek; economic activity was largely determined by one's social class or rank within society, and political influence was directly related to either one's wealth or military prowess. Despite an engrained class system, a primitive road network, tribal resistance to central authority, cultural differences, and a realm that covered a geographic area stretching from the Iberian Peninsula in the west to Babylonia in the east, Britain in the north, and Egypt in the south, the Romans created a system of government that allowed commerce to flourish and wealth to be created on a previously unknown scale.

As one commentator described it:

> In Republican Italy, empire created capital inflows, checks on natural growth that were counterbalanced by slave imports, and novel opportunities for commercial exchange, elite enrichment, and violent redistribution of assets to commoners. In the long run, empire also yielded benefits for subject populations: peace reduced transaction costs, turned the entire Mediterranean into an "innersea," and improved the ratio of natural endowments to labor; tributary integration mobilized resources and enabled portfolio capitalism; knowledge transfers improved productivity; and previously underexploited mines produced bullion that not only supported monetization but also enabled imports from beyond the empire. All these developments coincided with a climate optimum that sustained production and productivity growth and, at least for a while, with an absence of pandemics that might have weakened state power or commercial connectivity. In view of all this, it is hard to see how a substantial economic expansion could possibly have failed to occur.[6]

As long as emperors ruled over a *Pax Romana*, the empire and its inhabitants generally prospered; however, with the threat of invasion from abroad, dissent within the corridors of power, military coups, threats to shipping and transport, and the exorbitant costs associated with rearmament, the empire soon faced economic as well as social decline. Periods of hyperinflation and currency devaluation, coupled with the breakdown of civil institutions and civil society, saw once-vibrant market economies turn away from trade and commerce, back to a time of subsistence farming and general scarcity. The so-called Dark Ages[7] were a time of want, not plenty, and it would be several hundred years before a socioeconomic system developed that could rival the economic success of the Roman Empire.

Feudalism

As often happens with language, terms like *feudalism* are artificial designations developed by historians and sociologists writing many centuries after a period in question in an attempt to define, in a single word, a complex web of economic and social systems. Debate rages as to the usefulness of such designations, but for our purposes we will use it to describe, in general terms, a socioeconomic model that was prevalent during much of the Middle Ages (ca. the ninth through fifteenth centuries CE).

Feudalism, also known as the manorial system, was not the only socioeconomic model in use during that timeframe, but it was dominant in the British Isles and other parts of northern Europe from whence capitalism would eventually evolve. It was a system designed to entrench the power of both church and state while maximizing the use of arable land for the purpose of mass subsistence. It has been estimated that in 1000 CE, 90 percent of all European inhabitants "were country dwellers who drew their livelihood from farming, herding, fishing or the forest,"[8] much of it within the context of the manorial system. The laborers themselves rarely ever owned the land in use; instead, it was owned by either the church or the landed gentry, who served as both lord (that is, protector) and landlord (that is, collector of tax, tithe, or tribute).

From this constellation evolved the three estates of clergy, nobility, and commoner, whose roles and responsibilities would become codified in various institutions across Europe. The British Parliament, with its Lords Spiritual, Lords Temporal, and House of Commons, and the French *ancien régime*, prior to the revolution of 1789, were both political manifestations of the same phenomenon. While the feudal system worked relatively well as a mechanism for maintaining the status quo, it was not particularly effective as an engine of wealth-creation for several reasons.

First, the system was a highly insular, land-based economy where the production of food primarily benefitted a particular fiefdom. There was little trade and, therefore, little opportunity for capital increase. Second, it was a bartering economy with little monetization outside the highest echelons of society. Third, it was a subsistence economy with little technological development and scarce opportunity for wealth-creation beyond the production of surplus goods that could be sold in local market towns. It was the expansion of these towns, though, that would eventually transform the economic landscape into something that resembled a market-based economy.

The greatest beneficiaries of the feudal system were at the top of the pyramid. Clearly defined nation-states began to emerge and the High Middle Ages saw European kings and nobles solidifying their power and exporting their influence around the world. Unfortunately, this also led to internecine wars in Europe, such as the Hundred Years War between England and France that decimated both countries militarily and economically. The Crusades in the Middle East were also major drains on the economies of these nations.

At the same time, the world was experiencing unprecedented periods of famine and disease. The Black Death killed up to half the population of Europe in the middle of the fourteenth century alone. By the end of the period, depopulation, the rise of mercenary armies, the replacement of vassal servitude with a system of rents, and the emergence of tradespeople operating in the towns, independent of the manorial system, put an end to feudalism and gave rise to a confraternal system of interconnected merchants and artisans known as guilds.

While guilds existed throughout the medieval period, their numbers and influence grew exponentially with the end of the manorial system. As populations decreased due to wars and plagues, so did demand for food, thereby driving down prices and forcing landowners to sell or lease their land to those who would work it on a freehold basis. With restrictions on the storage and resale of commodities lifted, merchants were able to earn small profits on their produce, expanding the base of potential consumers beyond the landed gentry. Cities such as London had dozens of guilds regulating every aspect of nonagricultural life from the training and certification of various artisans to the setting of prices and times of trade. As populations began to grow in the seventeenth century, improved agricultural techniques ensured sufficient means of production for general subsistence, stabilizing both supply and demand for food while increasing the demand for luxury items. These factors, combined with the exploitation of resources from the New World, including the introduction of sugar and spices into the European diet and the discovery of gold, set the stage for a new economic system that would forever change the socioeconomic order of the West.

Mercantilism

As with terms like feudalism and capitalism, *mercantilism* is a name created by later historians to describe the socioeconomic phenomenon that dominated the political and economic landscape of Western Europe between the sixteenth and eighteenth centuries. It was none other than Adam Smith (1723–1790) who first coined the term "mercantile system"[9] in his magnum opus *An Inquiry into the Nature and Causes of the Wealth of Nations* (1776). In this book, Smith derided the strictly controlled mechanisms of economic exchange as being both unnatural and the source of many unintended negative consequences. To consider Smith's critique of the system, though, it is important to understand the basic principles undergirding it.

Smith wrote at the cusp of the decline of the manorial system and the rise of the nation-state as a political and military entity. In order to consolidate power, sovereigns employed costly standing armies to defend their holdings against foreign invaders, usurpers, and rogue colonies. It was widely believed that a nation's wealth was determined by its gold reserves, so sovereigns sought to increase their nations' wealth without reducing the amount of gold in their respective treasuries.

As a result, a complex web of privately owned, state-protected trading companies—monopolies—arose, aimed at increasing national income while ensuring the maximization of domestic labor. People thought that by controlling trade through various means, including leveeing punitive tariffs on imported goods and restricting the exportation of gold itself, the resulting balance of trade would guarantee an international balance of power. But people also assumed that if a nation-state could achieve a surplus of wealth in what was largely seen as a zero-sum game, it could potentially achieve a political or military advantage over its neighbors. It was this desire for political dominance that drove the thinking behind the mercantile system.

As Smith and others have noted, some of the logic behind the mercantile system was sound. Certainly an increase in a nation's gold reserves had some value. For Smith, though, the real folly of the mercantile system was the naïve belief that a highly regulated, closed system would eventually produce more wealth than a less regulated, open one, where innovation, risk, the specialization of labor, and the sublime power of the free market would increase both personal and national wealth without the "unfortunate effects of all the regulations of the mercantile system!"[10]

While the mercantile system worked for a small group of people, namely the merchants themselves and their sovereigns, it failed to generate sufficient wealth across large sectors of the population. Eventually mercantilism would crumble under the weight of its own inefficiencies, but not before giving birth to many innovations that continue to be fundamental to our current economic system. These include the concept of incorporation (from the Latin *corpus* or "body") whereby a business enjoys many of the rights and responsibilities of a person, under the law; publically traded shares and exchanges where those shares could be bought and sold; an increase in the monetization of economic activity; and the development of global trade routes on both land and sea. These elements, along with Smith's widely held views concerning the power and efficacy of free markets (which we will explore in the next chapter), would become the breeding ground for what we now know as free-market capitalism.

Common Threads

While the various systems just described differ in many ways, we also find striking similarities among them, especially as they pertain to the motives behind the development of those systems and the relationship between societies' values and their economic activities. Recall that the primary driver behind all economic activity was, at its most basic level, survival, although economics itself was not considered at all. Individuals, tribes, communities, estates, and even nation-states did whatever was necessary to withstand the harsh realities of human existence, leaving the study of political economy to later generations. Capital existed in various forms but was still largely unmonetized, and economic activity was subjected more to the vagaries of weather, war, and pestilence than to what we might call market forces today. With the exception of a few professions, such as the law, military service, and the priesthood, work itself consisted primarily of physical labor and was largely seen as a necessary evil with no purpose beyond its obvious utility as a means of survival.

Methods of production and distribution were more the result of external influences than of any notion of planning or organizational efficiency. Similarly, no overarching ethic constrained the affairs of people beyond the blunt instruments of law and martial coercion. People were largely accountable only to themselves and their groups, whether tribal, regional, or national, and the influence of religious belief, while significant, ranged from pagan superstition to unquestioning obedience to the pope.

Society as we understand it today was of little concern to either the peasant laborer or the sovereign. Economic activity merely kept the former alive and the latter in power. Beyond the halls of power and the majestically adorned palaces and cathedrals of the ruling classes, no one thought that economic activity, business, trade, commerce, and technology could actually serve a higher purpose; no one imagined that it could promote human flourishing on a grand scale, liberate the masses from bondage and oppression, promote the common good, and even glorify the Deity. This would all change, though, with the astute observations of the Scottish moral philosopher and father of modern economics, Adam Smith.

3

Adam Smith—
Morality, Money, and Markets

It is not from the benevolence of the butcher, the brewer, or the baker,
that we expect our dinner, but from their regard to their own interest.

ADAM SMITH

For centuries, critics of free-market capitalism have taken the quotation above from Adam Smith's *Wealth of Nations* as evidence that it is a system rooted in selfishness and therefore is essentially morally corrupt. For some, the statement is the smoking gun that confirms their worst suspicions about the very nature of capitalism. Adam Smith, critics claim, was a typical Enlightenment materialist, whose reductionist tendencies drove him to codify a heartlessly immoral economic system, the fruits of which could only be the excesses and corruption so evident in today's corporate scandals and the gross economic inequalities that permeate our culture.

This is a perfectly reasonable, even logical, conclusion to reach. It is also false. Throughout this chapter, I aim to dispel these misunderstandings and offer a very different view of both Adam Smith and of capitalism, revealing the underlying religious and philosophical beliefs foundational to both Smith's thinking and the ethos of traditional capitalism.

Adam Smith was indeed a towering figure of the eighteenth-century Scottish Enlightenment. At the tender age of fourteen, he entered the University of Glasgow, where he came under the tutelage and influence of none other than the famed moral philosopher Francis Hutcheson. Hutcheson had a significant impact on Smith's life. Smith was fatherless from birth, and no doubt the "never to be forgotten"[1] Hutcheson, as Smith liked to call him, was more than just an academic tutor; he became a great friend and a trusted mentor, so much so that Smith would eventually assume the venerable professor's chair some years later.

Hutcheson, in fact, had a tremendous influence on many bright young students. It was said he very successfully combined his intellectual vigor with the oratorical skills of a seasoned preacher, making him popular among students at the university and beyond, including one young Scottish intellectual with whom Smith would have an enduring relationship, the famed skeptic and later avowed atheist David Hume.

While it is true that both men were strongly influenced by Hutcheson, Hume broke from the old master in several significant ways. For instance, he rejected the truth claims of Christianity and ultimately all Theist claims—something his mentor never did. He also rejected benevolence as a motive for moral action in favor of a strictly utilitarian notion of self-love or self-interest.

Owing to their close friendship, many assume that Smith acceded to Hume's beliefs on both counts, but Smith continued to hold views much closer to Hutcheson than Hume in both arenas. Regarding religion, while it is clear Smith disbelieved the metaphysical claims of Christianity, historian John Rae notes that, "Smith was [still] certainly a Theist,"[2] and Smith's own writings confirm that conclusion. Eventually, he broke from Hume over the second issue as well, concluding that benevolence and self-love were not mutually exclusive but worked in tandem in the development of moral reasoning and action.[3]

This lingering and misguided presumption that Smith shared the radical skepticism of Hume and the fact that many have failed to harmonize Smith's moral reasoning with his economic thinking have led to a gross distortion of the latter. And accurately understanding Adam Smith and the ethos of traditional capitalism begins with first understanding his foundational work, *The Theory of Moral Sentiments* (1759), also referred to as *Moral Sentiments*.

The Theory of Moral Sentiments

Smith wrote *The Theory of Moral Sentiments* after he assumed the chair at Glasgow once held by his mentor, Hutcheson. In the book, Smith relies heavily on the latter's work. "It is most probable," Rae suggests, "that [Smith's] whole theory of moral sentiments was suggested by the lectures of Hutcheson."[4] While this may be an overstatement, there is no question that Hutcheson's hand can be seen throughout *Moral Sentiments*. Smith's intention was to explore the range of motives for good conduct, beyond just benevolence, including what he called human sympathy.[5]

Moral Sentiments was widely read and highly acclaimed even during Smith's own lifetime, and he appeared to be as interested in influencing the public square as impressing his contemporaries, who included Voltaire and François Quesnay in France, Jean-Jacques Rousseau in Geneva, Thomas Reid in Scotland, Edmund Burke in England, and Benjamin Franklin in continental America, to name just a few.[6]

A basic understanding of his moral reasoning is paramount to our understanding his later view of economics. The following is a cursory review, but I trust it provides a helpful frame and a starting point for our exploration.

In Part I, Smith maintains unequivocally his belief that human beings are motivated by *more* than just naked self-interest. In his opening lines he clearly states:

> No matter how selfish you think man is, it's obvious that there are some principles in his nature that give him an interest in the welfare of others, and make their happiness necessary to him, even if he gets nothing from it but the pleasure of seeing it.[7]

Smith's belief that compassion, pity, sympathy, and empathy (both positive and negative) are hardwired into our human nature is fundamental to his understanding of morality and proper conduct. This belief would color his thinking in all areas of inquiry, including economics. Smith vehemently rejects self-interest as the primary motivation for our feelings of sympathy. He notes, instead, what he calls a "fellow-feeling" (4) that unites human beings in a way that transcends mere utility.

Such thinking directly contradicts those who argue that Smith delighted in capitalism because it supported his predisposition toward radical utilitarianism. On the contrary, Smith rejected such an ethic as insufficient, and while he believed that utility had a place among the motives for moral behavior, he viewed it as a secondary factor, not a primary one.

Smith also contradicts in no uncertain terms yet another fallacy that is often leveled against him, one that does far more harm to his reputation as both a moral philosopher and an economist than accusations of overarching utility. That fallacy is the suggestion that free-market capitalism is built not only on selfishness but also on greed. Smith argues forcefully that excessive admiration for the rich and powerful and disdain for the poor are, in fact, corruptions of sound moral reasoning and in direct opposition to wisdom and virtue:

> This disposition to admire—and almost to worship—the rich and the powerful, and to despise or at least neglect persons of poor and mean condition, is . . . the great and most universal cause of the corruption of our moral sentiments. Moralists all down the centuries have complained that wealth and greatness are often given the respect and admiration that only wisdom and virtue should receive, and that poverty and weakness are quite wrongly treated with the contempt that should be reserved for vice and folly. (33)

Smith goes on to criticize not only the motives and the actions of the rich themselves but also the misdirected admiration of the masses for those who achieve excessive wealth. He clearly calls readers to reject the temptation to achieve social status and admiration through the accumulation of wealth and to prefer, instead, the admiration and social standing that rightly accompany the pursuit and attainment of wisdom and virtue. This is a far cry from the objections of Smith's more ardent critics.

Smith then turns his attention from the causes of right conduct to their effects, the gist of which may be summed up in the following statement:

> Man has a natural love for society, and wants the union of mankind to be preserved for its own sake, independently of whether he himself would get any benefit from it. . . . He does also realize that his own welfare is connected with the prosperity of society, and that its preservation is needed for his happiness and perhaps for his survival. So he has every reason to hate anything that can tend to destroy society. . . . So every appearance of injustice alarms him, and he rushes to stop the progress of anything that would quickly put an end to all that is dear to him if it were allowed to continue unchecked. (49)

Here Smith establishes a clear hierarchy of moral concern in the relationship between individuals and society. He states unequivocally that human beings enjoy a love for society that is an indelible part of our human nature and that the benefits individuals may enjoy as a result of society's greater good are of secondary concern to the good of society itself, that is, the *common good*.

In Part III Smith examines not only the cause and effect of right conduct, but also the indelible *sense of duty* that should impel us to right conduct. He explores several factors that are universally applicable to the development of one's sense of moral duty, such as reason and philosophy, but he gives God most of the credit for our moral compass when he states:

> Nobody who believes that there is a Deity can doubt that the supreme rule of our conduct ought to be respect for the will of the Deity. The very thought of disobedience seems to have the most shocking wrongness built into it. How pointless and absurd it would be for man to oppose or neglect the commands laid on him by God's infinite wisdom and infinite power. How unnatural, how impiously ungrateful, not to reverence the laws that were prescribed to him by the infinite goodness of his Creator, even if there weren't to be any punishment for violating them. (89)

Smith goes on to note that reverence for God and a healthy concern for one's own wellbeing are not mutually exclusive, and in defense of his position, he notes that in most religious systems,

> after the first precept, to love the Lord our God with all our heart, with all our soul, and with all our strength, [there is a] second precept to love our neighbour as we love ourselves—because we love ourselves, surely, for our own sakes and not merely because we are commanded to do so! Christianity doesn't teach that the sense of duty should be the only driver of our conduct, but only that it should be the dominant one, which is also said by philosophy and indeed by common sense. (90)

While Smith was not a theologian himself, it seems that without attempting to do so, he makes a very strong theological argument in defense of his thesis. His thinking is not far from the teachings of the sixteenth-century reformer and theologian John Calvin, whose theological principles influenced the Scottish landscape for centuries and, it would seem, the thinking of Adam Smith.

Despite the protestations of his friend Hume, Smith held firmly to his belief that mere utility cannot explain genuinely selfless acts or our innate ability to discern right from wrong. That said, Smith does acknowledge that there are external factors that may also influence our moral reasoning, such as "fashion and custom":

> In addition to the ones I have listed, there are two other considerable influences on the moral sentiments of mankind; they are the main causes of the many irregular and discordant opinions that become dominant in different ages and nations concerning what is blameworthy or praiseworthy. These two sources of influence are custom and fashion—forces that extend their sway over our judgments concerning beauty of every kind. (105)

Smith contends that despite the universality of certain aversions, how one is raised, the cultural norms of society, the generally agreed practices of certain groups, the expectations of age and rank, and the development of manners all impact what individuals and cultures view as acceptable or unacceptable behavior. But he insists that these differences of opinion about what is or is not proper conduct tend to involve minor perversions and do not constitute the normalization of widespread moral turpitude. He clearly believes that any widespread rejection of our naturally endowed sense of propriety would lead to a complete and utter breakdown of society.

Next, Smith gives us his unique take on the cardinal virtues outlined by Aquinas (see chapter 1), and in doing so he reinforces his thesis that benevolence and self-love work in tandem to encourage moral behavior. Smith sees the application of prudence, for example, as a series of concentric circles, emanating first from one's personal needs, to that of the immediate family, then to the extended family, to peers and colleagues, to the wider community, and ultimately to the nation and the world. He professes a belief in a "universal benevolence" rooted in our mutual position as children of God:

> This universal benevolence, however noble and generous it may be, can't be the source of any solid happiness for any man who isn't thor-

oughly convinced that all the inhabitants of the universe, low and high, are under the immediate care and protection of the great, benevolent, and all-wise Being who directs all the movements of nature, and who is determined by his own unalterable perfections to maintain in it always the greatest possible amount of happiness.... The wise and virtuous man is always willing for his own private interest to be sacrificed to the public interest of his own particular order or society. He is always willing, too, for the interests of this order or society to be sacrificed to the greater interests of the state of which it is a subordinate part. So he should be equally willing for all those inferior interests to be sacrificed to the greater interests of the universe—of the great society of all sentient and thinking beings whose immediate administrator and director is God himself. (125)

This statement alone puts the lie to those who would paint Smith with the same atheistic brush as David Hume.

Finally, Smith completes his thesis by setting out his own "system of moral philosophy." Here he builds on the work of his mentor, Hutcheson, and considers the pros and cons of various commentators from across the ages. Smith's own views are best represented, though, by his affirmation of the following position:

The whole perfection and virtue of the human mind consists in its having some resemblance to, some share in, the perfections of God, and therefore in its being filled with the same drive of benevolence and love that influences all the actions of the Deity. The only actions of men that were truly praiseworthy, or could claim any merit in God's sight, are ones that flowed from benevolence. It is only by actions of charity and love that we can suitably imitate the conduct of God, expressing our humble and devout admiration of his infinite perfections. Only by fostering in our own minds the divine drive towards benevolence can we make our own affections resemble more closely God's holy attributes, thereby becoming more proper objects of his love and esteem; until at last we arrive at the state that this philosophy is trying to get us to, namely immediate converse and communication with God. (159)

Understanding the philosophical and theological underpinnings of Smith's thinking is essential to understanding and appreciating his theory of economics, and I hope that the misconceptions about Smith's view of economics might begin here to find a corrective. In light of Smith's moral reasoning, explored above, we now turn our attention to the work for which he is more widely remembered: *An Inquiry into the Nature and Causes of the Wealth of Nations*. By viewing the latter through the prism of the former, we'll begin to see the endemic relationship between economics and moral reasoning, and specifically the foundational nature of morality in a properly functioning economy.

Highlights of *Wealth of Nations*

Despite popular thinking to the contrary, Adam Smith is not the father of capitalism; in fact, he would have been totally unfamiliar with the term. He might, more accurately, be called the father of "economic liberalism,"[8] which became the bedrock for the later development of free-market capitalism. Even though it was written some two hundred forty years ago, *Wealth of Nations* remains one of the most influential and important works of the modern era, alongside such tomes as Newton's *Principles of Natural Philosophy* (1687) and Darwin's *On the Origen of Species* (1859). Smith's book offers an exhaustive review of what his generation called "political economy," and it gives us more than a casual glimpse into a time when the world was experiencing a seismic shift in political, philosophical, and economic thinking. A classic text, it is also one often misunderstood and taken out of context, often to support anti-capitalist views. It is very dense in parts and difficult to read, but for anyone wanting to truly understand economics, even on a rudimentary scale, reading and understanding the content of *Wealth of Nations* is essential.

Smith's impetus for writing *Wealth of Nations* is primarily intellectual curiosity. He is totally fascinated by the fact that some nations consist of people barely able to survive while others, in comparison, thrive. He examines the conditions that make people thrive in order to assess and ultimately to codify those practices for posterity's sake. He sees political economy as a logical extension of his theory of natural philosophy and his interest in the material benefits of a civilized society.

In Smith's mind, developing a just society necessitates developing mechanisms for the protection of one's rights and property, and if this society is properly administered, it makes the creation of wealth possible. He professes that economic activity is a naturally endowed pursuit and that societies that embrace peace and justice should logically benefit economically from the systemization of those virtues.

His second book is not a work of philosophy but one of social science. He presumes that readers are familiar with his previous work or are so naturally endowed with their own sense of propriety that no repetition of his moral reasoning is necessary. *Wealth of Nations* itself is somewhat technical in nature. When viewed through the prism of *Moral Sentiments*, it becomes more than a commentary on political economy—it becomes a credo for what might rightly be called "economic naturalism."[9]

Even the book's title makes some assumptions, so before delving into *Wealth of Nations*, it may be helpful to define what Smith means by the word *wealth*. At its most basic level, wealth is nothing more than the delta between the amount of labor and resources necessary for subsistence and everything else. That is it. As we will see below, Smith understands this definition intrinsically, especially the contribution of labor to the formula; yet it is not a definition that most of his contemporaries would have recognized. They, like most of society today, would equate wealth with money, particularly gold. They would fail to recognize that money is nothing more than a mutually agreed upon measurement of wealth. Actual wealth, both that which has been realized and that which is dormant, rests not in an instrument of measurement (that is, money), but in the agency of wealth creation itself. Consequently, Smith begins his inquiry into national wealth, not by considering gold reserves or even natural resources, but by examining the availability and organization of labor.

Smith's entire thesis begins with what he himself calls the "division of labor": the foundational principle upon which Smith's assumptions rest, as he writes, "The greatest improvement in the productive powers of labour, and the greater part of the skill, dexterity, and judgment with which it is any where directed, or applied, seem to have been the effects of the division of labour."[10]

To support his thesis, Smith tells how a divided labor force, engaged in mass manufacturing, with each laborer responsible for his or her particular part of the manufacturing process, can produce many times more finished products than the manufacturing capabilities of a single artisan. He notes that this is due to a combination of factors, from the improved skills of individual workers, to the implementation of time-saving processes, to the use of new technologies. The combined effects of these improvements do not merely create wealth on their own; they create wealth by employing more people, who eventually become consumers of the goods themselves, which in turn spins off the new businesses necessary to serve those new consumers, and on and on it goes. If one applies those principles across an entire economic area, such as a nation, the result will logically be an increase in that nation's overall wealth.

This simple formula speaks to additional considerations beyond a country's ability to make things; a country also needs people to purchase and consume things; that is, there is a need for markets. As Smith puts it, "As it is the power of exchanging that gives occasion to the division of labour, so the extent of this division must always be limited by the extent of that power, or, in other words, by the extent of the market" (18).

So while improvements in economic output may generally increase wealth and the potential for consumption, they do not, in and of themselves, produce demand. Therefore, new markets must be regularly sought in order to expand the distribution of manufactured goods, and new technologies and processes must continually improve in order for wealth to expand.

Next, Smith delves into the mechanisms that produce variations in the costs and prices of commodities, such as the availability of labor, product scarcity, rents, and any number of other factors that may influence what he calls the "nominal" price of a product (also known as the price that something will cost in a given place at a given time). The nominal price may, from time to time, vary from its so-called natural price, but Smith sees these variations as brief aberrations ultimately corrected by market forces, particularly by competition.

Competition and the market rule are both key for Smith, because he sees them as the most natural way for economic forces to balance each other out over time. Generally, he is correct; however, Smith makes a significant exception to the market rule when it comes to the question of wages, and his position may surprise both critics of capitalism and neoliberals today.

He disagrees with and even has contempt for those who do not recognize the sinister efforts of some owners to secretly fix wages, a common practice at the time. And he points out the hypocrisy of using the force of law against workers who organize a higher fixed wage. While he believes industrial actions, such as strikes, are of limited usefulness, mainly because owners have greater staying power than workers, he steadfastly believes that:

> A man must always live by his work, and his wages must at least be sufficient to maintain him. They must even upon most occasions be somewhat more; otherwise it would be impossible for him to bring up a family. . . .(57)

Further, Smith maintains that a nation benefits in the long run from a well-paid labor force. In support of this thesis, he cites the situation in the American colonies at that time, where the relative cost of goods was lower than those in England, but where wages were considerably higher. The net result, according to Smith, was that while the colonies were not yet as rich as England, they were "more thriving, and advancing with much greater rapidity to the further acquisition of riches" (59).

Harming the benefit of having a well-paid labor force, Smith asserts, are those merchants who seek exorbitant profits and in doing so raise both inflation and interest rates, causing hardship on everyone. As Smith puts it:

> The rise of profits operates like compound interest. Our merchants and master-manufacturers complain much of the bad effects of high wages in raising the price, and thereby lessening the sale of their goods both at home and abroad. They say nothing concerning the bad effects of high profits. They are silent with regard to the pernicious effects of their own gains. They complain only of those of other people. (85)

These conclusions may seem at odds with the picture of Adam Smith that is often presented by critics of free-market capitalism; they are equally at odds with the opinion of many of neoliberals who suggest excessive profits are somehow good for society and that a living wage is not economically viable. Smith would suggest that the opposite is true on both counts, and his thinking reflects not only the sober judgment of a critical observer but also the heart of a moral philosopher whose commitment to virtue—particularly prudence, justice, and temperance—is paramount.

As his book progresses, Smith considers other aspects of labor-related costs, including the free movement of workers, offering an exhaustive exposé on the impact of high rents, reflective of the historic use of land under the feudal system and the dominance of agriculture, even in Smith's time. Next, he turns his attention to the accumulation and use of capital.

The title of this section of *Wealth of Nations* is "Of the Nature, Accumulation, and Employment of Stock." Smith uses the term *stock* to avoid confusing wealth with money. What Smith calls stock we now would simply call capital or assets. Smith himself even uses the term capital in the text, noting there are essentially two forms of capital: circulating capital (which we would call working capital today) and fixed capital (which we would call fixed assets).

While some of his examples of fixed capital would not qualify as fixed assets today (from an accounting standpoint), the general point that Smith makes is sound: capital itself has value only when it is properly employed; otherwise, it is essentially fallow.

The maintenance and use of that fixed capital, he notes, allows for the generation and ultimate use of circulating capital, and it is the reinvestment of circulating capital that builds fixed capital, and so on. This never-ending process of wealth-creation is at the heart of capitalism, and we will see later that this process distinguishes capitalism from closed systems, which presume a static amount of wealth. This is true of nations as well, and Smith goes to great lengths to explain that a nation's wealth is *not* determined by the amount of money in circulation but by the purchasing and productive power of that money (that is, in the nation's ability to create more wealth).

Having explained what capital is, Smith goes on to explain how banking works to keep the flow of circulating capital going, thereby providing liquidity to the real economy. He strenuously warns against the damage banks may cause if they become greedy or are irresponsible in either their lending practices or in the maintenance of their cash reserves.

Smith reminds his readers that paper money is issued in the form of promissory notes and that the system rests upon the faith of the market to exchange those notes upon demand. Providing a concrete example, Smith describes what today we would call a run on a Scottish bank, an event that caused severe distress across the entire banking sector. The bank in question had lent so much money and issued so many bank notes to so many debtors that it had become imprudent in its risk assessments. In conditions much like those of the global financial crisis of 2008, the Scottish bank described by Smith failed spectacularly, resulting in a recession throughout Scotland.

Smith believed strongly in a liberal banking system and backed the notion of a central bank (also known as the Bank of England) whose primary purpose is to control and essentially guarantee the supply of money. He also presumed as an article of faith that bankers, as members of a civilized and just society, would operate in a virtuous manner, putting probity, prudence, and temperance above the temptation of ill-gotten gain.

From banking, Smith turns his attention to the general conditions that cause a country to become prosperous, concentrating particularly on the efficient use of land and on the relationship between town and country. Here he establishes a logical hierarchy of importance: first is agriculture, because that provides subsistence to all; next is industry, because that generates most of the actual wealth; and finally, trade. He states:

> As subsistence is, in the nature of things, prior to conveniency and luxury . . . [t]he cultivation and improvement of the country . . . must, necessarily, be prior to the increase of the town. . . . The town, indeed, may not always derive its whole subsistence from the country . . . but from very distant countries; and this, though it forms no exception from the general rule, has occasioned considerable variations in the progress of opulence in different ages and nations. (296)

In what would also be another shock to today's neoliberals, Smith criticizes past policies that have restricted access to land for the purposes of economic development. He dismisses the basic precepts of inheritance and the maintenance of large estates, as "they are founded upon the most absurd of all suppositions, the supposition that every successive generation of men have not an equal right to the earth, and to all that it possesses; but that the property of the present generation should be restrained and regulated according to the fancy of those who died perhaps five hundred years ago" (301).

More scathing is Smith's criticism of slave labor, which he objects to on both moral and economic grounds. Smith argues convincingly that slavery is fundamentally perverse, being the result of both "pride" and "villanage" (310). While slavery may give the appearance of being economical by removing the cost of wages, its negative effect on the morale of workers renders it economically inefficient. Smith believed passionately that, if they were given the opportunity to share in the benefits of their labor, workers would be far more productive, and slave labor is the antithesis of this belief. Even the renowned abolitionist William Wilberforce appealed to Smith when arguing against slavery in the House of Commons.[11]

As he continues through a comprehensive review of eighteenth-century economic life, Smith turns attention to the symbiotic relationship between towns and countryside. His observation is straightforward: farms create produce to be sold in the markets of towns and the wealth created is reinvested in farms and in local communities. As with the relationship between circulating capital and fixed capital, the process of mutual interdependence and mutual benefit is an ongoing one that creates the wealth necessary to promote the general welfare of the entire population.

For Smith, this is a natural phenomenon, the product of a series of individual decisions, driven by a perfectly normal amount of self-interest. It requires no central planning or administration, but it does require a certain degree of law and order. More importantly, it presumes a high degree of integrity and trust, not only among individuals and institutions, but also in the power and efficacy of markets themselves. Smith expands considerably on these themes in the most often read portion of *Wealth of Nations*, Book IV, entitled, "Of Systems of Political Economy." Smith begins,

> Political economy considered as a branch of the science of a statesman or legislator, proposes two distinct objects: first, to provide a plentiful revenue or subsistence for the people, or more properly to enable them to provide such a revenue or subsistence for themselves; and secondly, to supply the state or commonwealth with a revenue sufficient for the public services. It proposes to enrich both the people and the sovereign. (326)

The primary drivers of economic activity, he argues, should be a combination of universal subsistence (that is, ensuring that scarcity never threatens people's existence), and provision for the common good—not the enrichment of the few, including the sovereign, at the expense of the many.

To today's readers this may seem obvious, but that was not the case in Adam Smith's day. In fact, the mercantile system, which dominated the economic landscape in the centuries leading up to Smith's era, was designed to do just that: enrich the crown and entrenched monopolies, while keeping the masses in a state of relative servitude.

Smith argues that the entire mercantile system was predicated upon the false belief that wealth was defined by mineral reserves (primarily gold) and that, barring the discovery of new mines, the only way for a nation to secure or increase its wealth was to protect its domestic markets from outside encroachment. While governments thought they were protecting their own economies, what they were actually doing was limiting the potential of those economies.

Three primary factors created this limitation: first, the belief that wealth is akin to matter, which can neither be created nor destroyed; second, the belief that money is the equivalent of wealth, rather than a mere measurement of wealth; and last, the lack of understanding—and therefore lack of trust—in the power of naturally functioning (and self-correcting) markets. Smith writes:

> Every individual necessarily labours to render the annual revenue of the society as great as he can. He generally, indeed, neither intends to promote the public interest, nor knows how much he is promoting it.... [H]e is in this, as in many other cases, led by an invisible hand to promote an end which was no part of his intention. Nor is it always the worse for the society that it was no part of it. By pursuing his own interest he frequently promotes that of the society more effectually than when he really intends to promote it. (349)

Thus, even with all the best intentions in the world, economies manipulated by governments are ultimately less efficient than market-based economies, because the cumulative effects of individual economic decisions made by reasonable, self-interested parties will naturally produce economic and social benefits for all.

This does not suggest that Smith rejects all government interventions or regulations, nor does it suggest that Smith believes the private sector to be better equipped than governments to provide public services, such as policing, education, and defense, which he discusses at length in Book V. Smith believed in and appreciated the benefits of good government and was particularly fascinated by democracies, such as the one emerging in the American colonies. He argues that personal freedom is the best guarantor of economic innovation and industry, a theme that would captivate the imagination of such neoliberals as Milton Friedman and Friedrich von Hayek, two hundred years later. In Book V, entitled "Of the Revenue of the Sovereign or Commonwealth," Smith considers those things that are properly the function of the state, as well as the responsibility of the governed.

The primary responsibilities of the state, Smith argues, are protection of its citizens from outside agencies, establishment of justice, and provision of public services that are generally beyond individual capabilities. States, in order to provide these, have the right to levy taxes, and individuals have a responsibility to pay them. Within his argument he establishes what have become known as Smith's four maxims of taxation: proportionality, transparency, convenience, and efficiency:

I. The subjects of every state ought to contribute towards the support of the government, as nearly as possible, in proportion to their respective abilities. . . .

II. The tax which each individual is bound to pay ought to be certain, and not arbitrary. . . .

III. Every tax ought to be levied at the time, or in the manner, in which it is most likely to be convenient for the contributor to pay it. . . .

IV. Every tax ought to be so contrived as both to take out and to keep out of the pockets of the people as little as possible over and above what it brings into the public treasury of the state. (639)

Yes, there would be times when a state might have to go into debt, such as times of war, but in every aspect of his theory of government, Smith believes that nations should always act with prudence, courage, justice, and temperance. Otherwise, they set themselves up for catastrophic failure.

Wealth of Nations in Review

While it is a masterpiece of economics and social science, *Wealth of Nations* is not a perfect piece of work, by any means. Even during Smith's own day, many criticized his various observations and conclusions. We can see, for example, that his labor theory of value was wide of the mark, as were his insistence on the primacy of agriculture and his lack of foresight toward and appreciation for the impact of new technologies in the creation of wealth. But what matters most is what Smith got right.

Smith's understanding of the relationship between economics and political ideology is masterful and has influenced political and economic thinking for centuries. His understanding of and belief in the power of free markets, the necessity of both competition and cooperation in a healthy economic system, and the self-correcting nature of markets (the "invisible hand") are equally sublime. Smith's understanding of wealth creation as an open system was revolutionary, and his beliefs about the living wage, inheritance, estates, and slavery were also considerably ahead of their time, as was his belief in limited, transparent—even democratic—government, supported by fair and just tax policies.

Smith's greatest contribution to economics, however, may be his appreciation for the role of human nature and the complex motives behind economic decision-making. Despite the opinion of some of his critics, Smith does not portend John Stuart Mill's *Homo economicus*, but he professes, instead, to fix economic choice within the entire constellation of moral reasoning—something long-forgotten today by both proponents and opponents of economic liberalism.

From this reading of Smith, we may begin to understand the nature of traditional capitalism, its primary economic driver being a postsubsistence effort to use commerce to ensure general subsistence, while providing for the general wellbeing of society.

In this description of traditional capitalism, access to capital was primarily means-based, although a fledgling credit system was emerging. Wealth was created in a rhythmic fashion, in that economic cycles were still closely tied to agrarian calendars, and the general output consisted mostly of common necessities, sprinkled with a few limited comforts. While trade was strong, most economic activity remained quite local and, sociologically speaking, cult and culture were still generally homogenized. Ethics were still largely influenced by the religious authority of each nation, dominated by a religious orthodoxy that taught salvation by good works and a remote, "God-is-watching" admonition to behave morally.

The result was a generally healthy economic system that would create wealth in considerable measure and improve general living conditions across large sectors of the population. But it was not a system that would last for long. Soon socioeconomic conditions would change so dramatically that every aspect of culture would be affected, including the very structures of wealth creation, distribution, and the institutions of government.

Just around the corner was the Industrial Revolution and the titans of industry would soon become drunk with capitalism. Concern for the common good would become a quaint relic of the past, and workers would be treated as nothing more than extensions of the machines they operated. Once cut adrift from its ethical moorings, the economic success of capitalism would not only demonstrate its economic potential, but it would reveal its inherent dangers. In doing so, it would spawn a movement of resistance that exists to this day. Enter Karl Marx.

4

Karl Marx—
A Critique of Capitalism

The philosophers have only interpreted the world, in various ways. The point, however, is to change it.

KARL MARX

Few people have had a greater impact on political economy, in both theory and praxis, than Karl Marx, yet he was neither an economist nor a politician. Like Adam Smith before him, he was first and foremost a philosopher, although not a moral philosopher per se. Yet instead of being celebrated during his lifetime, his fame would come well after his death. In fact, it is hard to describe the life of Karl Marx as anything other than tragic. Before exploring both his life and his theory of political economy, we need to consider the economic tsunami that had flooded over the capitalist economies of Europe and North America, making the capitalism of Adam Smith's day virtually unrecognizable. That period of upheaval, of course, is better known as the Industrial Revolution.

Industrial Revolution

As with most historic epochs, it is nearly impossible to say exactly when the Industrial Revolution began. The term *Industrial Evolution* is preferred by experts in the field like Joyce Appleby, describing it as a process that flowed somewhat seamlessly from the end of the seventeenth century to the middle of the twentieth. But that definition may be misleading, because of the unprecedented impact of one technological innovation that was influential above all others—the conversion of the steam engine from sophisticated water pump into multihorsepower rotary engine. This development in particular renders the traditional designation *revolution* apropos.

The timeline of the steam engine's evolution is fascinating and serendipitous. In 1698, a fellow by the name of Thomas Savery patented a device that used the power of steam to lift water from a mine, or any other low-lying area, to prevent flooding. It was a simple design and had plenty of flaws, but it was a breakthrough, nonetheless. It had no pumps or moving parts. The engine moved water by creating a vacuum that effectively sucked it from point A to point B. Then, in 1712, Thomas Newcomen improved the design by adding a piston that pumped the water mechanically. This basic design became the platform for fire extinguishers and was well known in the era of Adam Smith, who describes the use of one in *Wealth of Nations*,[1] but neither he nor anyone else could have imagined what the subsequent innovations of James Watt would mean to the use of steam in manufacturing.

In 1769, Watt received a patent for the development of a separate condenser that dramatically improved the heat efficiency of Newcomen's basic design; however, it was the addition of a so-called sun-and-planet rotation device, patented in 1781, that changed everything. Now, instead of simply using steam to move water vertically or to blast air into furnaces, the rotation device allowed steam actually to power machinery of nearly any kind, including looms, mills, presses, spinning wheels—and locomotives.

Because this innovation increased the efficiency of labor by something in the region of two hundred times,[2] the division of labor was multiplied beyond recognition. This, along with many other innovations, such as advances in iron production, coal mining, free trade, the exploitation of colonial resources, and a more efficient banking system, created wealth on an unprecedented scale. That of course, was the good news. Unfortunately, along with wealth came unimaginably devastating changes to nearly every level of society, barring the very rich.

For the first time in history, more jobs were available in towns than in the country. People flocked to towns and cities. When they arrived, though, they experienced conditions that were nothing short of appalling. Factories and living quarters were virtually on top of each other, creating dangerously unhealthy situations. People, including children, worked for exceedingly long hours, seven days per week, often in cramped, uncomfortable, and dangerous environments. Homes were little better: entire families sometimes lived eight to a room, with no central heating or plumbing, open sewers, no electricity, no access to healthcare, no schools, and barely enough wages to live on. The Combination Act in Great Britain made it illegal for workers to organize and form trade unions, while factory owners exploited both domestic and migrant labor in equal measure.

These changes impacted every aspect of society. Wealth inequality soared as the industrialists, ignoring the warnings of Adam Smith, made excessive profits while denying their workers sufficient income to flourish. Family life was ravaged by diseases such as cholera and typhus, as well as by infant and maternal mortality, malnourishment, alcoholism, a decline in recreational opportunities, and spiritual deprivation.

Some so-called do-gooders sought to correct the situation through various associations and charities. The temperance movement was born of these conditions, as were early attempts at social welfare. Philanthropic industrialists like Robert Owen sought to create employee-owned cooperatives in the United Kingdom and in America. A generation later, Titus Salt even created a model town, Saltaire, near Bradford, UK, where better housing and green spaces for workers and their families were complimented by free schools and other community amenities.

It would be at least another generation or two before government legislation began in earnest. Examples of such legislation include the Factory Acts, which regulated working hours for children and addressed other exploitative conditions, and the Reform Acts, which extended voting rights to working-class people. These reforms, while they were steps in the right direction, were seen as too little, too late for the likes of Karl Marx and others who believed the only solution to society's problems was an all-out social and economic revolution. Understanding the conditions of Marx's own life provides a perspective for understanding his call for dramatic and systemic change.

Karl Marx and His Economic Theory

On May 5, 1818, Karl Marx[3] was born into a Jewish family living in Trier, Germany. So that his father could practice law, the entire family converted to Christianity. During his early life Marx showed considerable devotion to Christian thought, especially the idea of sacrificial love, although no evidence suggests he was ever a practicing follower of Christ. He attended the University of Berlin, read law and philosophy, and was greatly influenced by Georg Wilhelm Friedrich Hegel and Ludwig Feuerbach. While he was critical of both Hegel and Feuerbach, he shared the latter's atheist beliefs and many of his materialist presuppositions. Eventually Marx earned a PhD from the University of Jena, *in abstentia,* for a thesis in which he contrasted the natural philosophies of Democritis and Epicurus. Despite his education, he soon grew frustrated in his inability to find employment anywhere as an academic.

In 1843, after a seven-year engagement, and despite having no visible means of support, Marx married his long-suffering fiancée Jenny von Westphalen, the daughter of a Prussian aristocrat, and the pair moved to Paris, where his politics are said to have become more radical even as his philosophy became more practical.

By this point, Marx had rejected not only Hegel and religion entirely, famously labelling religion "the opium of the people," but he now also rejected Feuerbach's lack of appreciation for the *realpolitik* of his more radical associates. It was in Paris that Marx became actively involved in an early communist movement and befriended the man who became his life-long friend and colleague, Friedrich Engels.

When word began to circulate of Marx's intention to publish a book on political economy, he was expelled from France at the behest of the Prussian government, who feared the book's content might be too politically charged. Reluctantly, the Marxes resettled in Brussels, where Marx went into a deep depression. But while there, he and Engels wrote the largest portion of the *Communist Manifesto*, which would be published in London in 1848, in support of their formation of the Communist League.

During the German Revolution of 1848, Marx and Engels became disillusioned with the inability of antigovernment factions to form effective alliances across class lines, which led them, ultimately, to reject philosophies apart from their own radical materialism. They concluded that all of history constituted one long class struggle, with simply no room for political compromise or socialist experiments. Only a total revolution by the proletariat could change that class struggle, they believed, and this became a cause to which they committed themselves wholeheartedly.

For the next ten years—generally unemployed and unemployable and living in the very slums he hoped one day to liberate—Marx formulated his thoughts and committed them to paper. During this time, he accumulated large personal debts and watched as three of his young children died from various diseases not uncommon in poor, working-class homes. His marriage also suffered during this period as he fathered an illegitimate child and Jenny lamented in letters home that theirs was a difficult existence.

Over the ensuing years, things would improve slightly for Marx. He was able to eke out a living by writing for various international magazines and journals, including the *New York Tribune*, and in 1859 he wrote a major political polemic entitled *Contribution to the Critique of Political Economy*. In 1864, he joined the International Working Men's Association (also known as the First International), and in 1867 he published the first volume of his magnum opus, *Das Kapital*.

The latter development notwithstanding, Marx's star would never rise during his own lifetime. In 1871, he joined the ill-fated Paris Commune, supporting the defeated French proletariat against the victorious German establishment. As his political influence waned, he fought ideological battles with both the more militant, Russian elements of the communist movement and the anarchist Left, who opposed his authoritarian personality and his intellectual elitism.

In 1883, having lost his beloved wife Jenny a year earlier, Karl Marx died alone in his study, only to be discovered there by none other than his friend and comrade, Engels. It was left to Engels to complete and publish the final two volumes of that great work begun by Marx, *Das Kapital*.

Das Kapital

First published in 1867, with later editions edited by Engels appearing in 1885 and 1894, *Das Kapital* has been referred to by some as the Bible of the working classes. While it follows the basic form of similar works by such thinkers as political economist David Ricardo and Adam Smith, one might argue that its difference lay in its being more a platform for Marx's polemic than a purely academic tome. *Das Kapital* is built on Marx's foundational presupposition that all of human history is defined by class struggle, so in some ways his method of observation is more eisegetical than exegetical, meaning that he imposed his own interpretation on events; however, for those who agree with his basic assumptions about class and economics, his polemic will resonate logically. The question then becomes, are his definitions and subsequent observations correct?

Unlike Smith, Marx does not start with wealth; he starts with worth. In other words, he presumes that everything has an intrinsic value apart from either its utility or the vagaries of the market. He states that commodities are defined by their properties and their diverse natures, and it is the utility of things that gives them a use-value, rendering the value of commodities themselves "the substance of all wealth."[4]

Marx argues against the notion of exchange being a factor in determining the value of things, because to his thinking, despite market fluctuations in the price of things, their intrinsic value must ultimately be maintained in a zero-sum formulation. Or, as he puts it:

> Exchange value, at first sight, presents itself as a quantitative relation, as the proportion in which values in use of one sort are exchanged for those of another sort, a relation constantly changing. . . . Hence exchange value appears to be . . . purely relative. Let us consider the matter a little more closely. A given commodity is exchanged for other commodities . . . in the most different proportions . . . each . . . must, as exchange values, be replaceable by or equal to each other. . . . Therefore . . . the exchange value [of] . . . two things must be . . . reducible to a third. (27)

Marx ultimately determines that "third thing" to be gold, but in theory it could be anything, as long as the totality of the value of all things remains constant.

Marx's understanding of how labor affects use-value is the cornerstone of his system:

> A use-value . . . has value only because human labour in the abstract has been embodied or materialised in it. How, then, is the magnitude of this value to be measured? Plainly by the quantity of the value-creating substance, the labour, contained in the article. . . . [T]he labour how-

ever, that forms the substance of value, is homogenous human labour, expenditure of one uniform labour power. The total labour power of society, which is embodied in the sum total of the values of all commodities produced by that society, counts here as one homogenous mass of human labour power, composed, though it may be of innumerable individual units. (29)

Such thinking is a complete departure from the thinking of Smith and others and is predicated on the notion that all human labor is created equally. In Marx's mind, it is not the specific effect of human agency on the value of specific commodities that renders them useful or valuable, but the cumulative effect of all human agency on all commodities that give them their general value form. Or, as he explains it:

The general value form is the reduction of all kinds of actual labour to their common character of being human labour generally, of being the expenditure of human labour power. The general value form, which represents all products of labour as merely congelations of undifferentiated human labour, shows by its very structure that it is the social résumé of the world of commodities. That form consequently makes it indisputably evident that in the world of commodities the character possessed by all labour of being human labour constitutes its specific social character. (32)

The general value form, according to Marx, is the starting point of a continual metamorphosis of forms that ultimately results in the perpetual subordination of workers to their masters. He describes how commodities are turned into money, a change of form, in order for money to be turned into commodities again (C-M-C). This closed system, according to Marx, is predicated on the existence of a "universal equivalent form" (63), or money, and produces no "surplus value" (113). But if the formula is reversed and money is converted into a commodity in order for the commodity to be sold at a profit (M-C-M), the resulting surplus value becomes a significant problem for Marx. It is a problem because, first, he believes the creation of wealth, in and of itself, is an illusion, and second, he sees the conversion of surplus value into capital to be inherently unfair to those who actually added value to the commodity in the first place, that is, the universal mass of laborers. Or as Marx himself puts it:

> We have seen how money is changed into capital; how through capital surplus-value is made, and from surplus-value more capital. But the accumulation of capital presupposes surplus-value; surplus-value presupposes capitalist production; capitalist production presupposes the pre-existence of considerable masses of capital and of labour power in the hands of producers of commodities. The whole movement, therefore, seems to turn in a vicious circle. . . . (507)

> Thus the law of supply and demand of labour is kept in the right rut, the oscillation of wages is penned within limits satisfactory to capitalist exploitation, and lastly, the social dependence of the labourer on the capitalist, that indispensable requisite, is secured. (545)

Later we will explore Marx's economic definitions and whether his observations and conclusions about wealth creation and capitalism can be considered accurate, but it is indisputable that the entire underlying thesis of *Das Kapital* was already well expressed in his earlier *Communist Manifesto*. That document, written nearly twenty years earlier, asserts Marx's understanding of human nature and his belief in an inherent struggle between the classes as an article of faith. This not only informed but also molded his entire theory of political economy. Therefore, it is important to understand exactly what the *Communist Manifesto* was and what it proposed in terms of political solutions to what Marx and Engels saw as capitalism's shortfalls.

The Communist Manifesto

Written and published by Karl Marx and Friedrich Engels in 1848, the *Communist Manifesto* was based largely on Engels's previously unpublished catechism known as *The Communist Confession of Faith*. That work was intended to be used in exactly the same way a religious catechism is used, as both a training tool for youth and a systematic expression of fundamental beliefs.

This is not an accident of history. Marx and Engels saw their struggle as an existential one and elevated their beliefs to doctrinal status. If one were to amend the *Manifesto* and replace the word *State* with the word *God*, it would constitute an acceptable example of systematic theology. Since they did not believe in God, their allegiance was instead to the cause of Global Communism, a state of social and economic harmony that would "wrest, by degree, all capital from the bourgeoisie, to centralise all instruments of production in the hands of the State."[5]

The demands of Marx, Engels, and their followers differed according to each country's political situation, but the goals of the *Manifesto* were to end all private ownership of land and collection of rents, impose a heavily progressive tax system; abolish inheritance, confiscate property from émigrés and rebels, set up a state monopoly on the means of production and capital, apply equal liability of all to labor, develop agricultural and industrial armies, abolish the town/country divide, and end child labor, while providing free education for all.[6] It was a very comprehensive and uncompromising list.

A Review of Marx's Theory

Marx and Engels desired to create a government that enforced economic utopia, an endeavor rife with problems. The first problem is that any utopia enforced by armies is, by definition, a dystopia, as the history of both the Soviet Union and the Chinese Cultural Revolution demonstrate. A second problem is that Marx and Engels's fundamental proposition about human nature and the history of humankind as one long class struggle creates a singular lens through which to view a complex system, and it is more of an *a priori* assumption than a self-evident fact. Marx's other presumptions and economic definitions have proven false as well. Furthermore, there is simply no such thing as intrinsic economic value, economics is not a zero-sum game, and wealth is not the sum total of the use-value of commodities. Additionally, Marx's notion of an abstract labor value and the general value form, based on the cumulative effects of all labor, as opposed to either particular labor or the demands of the market, are both fallacies. And finally, he clearly misunderstood the relationship between commodities, money, and capital.

Beginning with the presupposition that wealth cannot actually be created and that all economic systems must therefore be closed systems, Marx sees the M-C-M model as a cyclical aberration of the C-M-C model. Yet wealth can, in fact, be created (or destroyed, for that matter), and the functional beauty of capitalism is that it is an open system, which, using Marx's model, would actually look something like: C-M-C-M-C-M . . . *ad infinitum*, but without fear of surplus value or the need for a universal equivalent form.

That is not to suggest that Marx and Engels got it *all* wrong. They certainly did not, and they addressed many of the economic and social injustices of the day, including a devolving capitalist system that few others dared to challenge with such intensity and veracity. The social conditions they witnessed and experienced were both unacceptable and unnecessary, as were the gross economic inequalities that defined their era. Their belief in the importance of equal access to education, capital, and infrastructure has positively influenced generations. And their condemnation of the evils of child labor and the scandals of abuse and of indifference on the part of those who had the means to correct a myriad of society's ills was at the forefront of subsequent human rights advances; however, their radical solutions were no less odious to reason and ethical constraint than the system they sought to replace.

What remains striking about Marx is that, despite his knowledge of moral philosophy, morality never really enters his vocabulary. Because his political economy is defined in such narrow terms, that is, as class struggle, he approaches societal problems from the standpoint of inefficiency instead of indignation. Consequently, Marx never fully arrives at the root causes of the problems he seeks to address.

More ironically, the *Communist Manifesto* confirms an indelible relationship between faith and economics, and it would not be far-fetched to describe Marxism as a kind of secular religion. While many of its followers today continue to believe in its salvation message, the recent failures of totalitarian Marxist regimes would suggest the god of Marxism is dead. As a system, it has fallen under the weight of its own inefficiencies, something Marxists predicted would befall capitalism. But by the beginning of the twentieth century, capitalism was thriving, at least in those countries where, according to sociologist Max Weber, there was more than just an economic impetus at work: there was a religious motive, the now infamous Protestant work ethic.

5

Max Weber—*The Protestant Ethic and the Spirit of Capitalism*

*And whatever you do, whether in word or deed, do it all in the name of
the Lord Jesus, giving thanks to God the Father through him.*

COLOSSIANS 3:17

Max Weber was born in Erfurt, Prussia, in 1864, nearly fifty years after the
birth of Karl Marx. His father, with whom he had a difficult relationship,
was a politician who served under the premiership of Otto von Bismarck.
The senior Weber tended toward liberal economics and free trade, which at
times saw him at odds with Bismarck. It is probable the young Max was regularly exposed to the highly charged political rhetoric of Berlin in the newly
unified German Empire. He was also, no doubt, greatly influenced by the
strict Calvinist instincts of his mother. And the convergence of these two
worldviews would play an important part in the development of his socioeconomic thinking.

   While Weber himself did not follow his father into politics, he is known
to have had Leftist political leanings, which probably further strained his relationship with his father. Although he rejected the more radical elements of
Marxism in Germany, he certainly sympathized with many of its social concerns. Weber's primary interest in economics was not political; it was intellectual. He pursued his academic career with vigor, obtaining a full professorship
at Freiburg at the age of 30, and a chair in economics at Heidelberg just two
years later. Sadly, in 1897, Weber's father died after the two had been in a serious
and unresolved domestic dispute, which sent Weber into a deep psychological
depression. Ultimately, he resigned his position at the university in 1903.[1]

In 1904, Weber would make a fateful trip to the United States, and it was his account of that trip that would become the inspiration for *The Protestant Ethic and the Spirit of Capitalism* (1930). Originally written as two separate articles for a journal that he himself edited, *PE*, as it is sometimes abbreviated, has become one of the most important works of sociology and economics ever written, and it is critical to our understanding of the evolution of capitalism.

Highlights of *The Protestant Ethic*

The primary subject of *PE* is the distinction between what Weber describes as the traditional capitalism of eighteenth- and nineteenth-century Europe and the so-called modern capitalism he observed in America.

Doubtless, during the nineteenth century capitalism generally, and capitalism in America specifically, morphed into an exceptional engine of wealth-creation. Expansion of the railroads, creation of new banks, exploitation of natural resources, discovery of gold, introduction of new manufacturing technologies, availability of labor (both domestic and immigrant), and an overall optimism in the efficacy of markets led not only to a long and sustained period of economic growth but also to an exponential increase in national wealth.

Of course, several downturns hit the economy during that time as well. The effects of the American Civil War, which cost over six hundred thousand lives and brought nonmilitary economic activity to a virtual stand-still, were devastating, as was the global currency crisis that led to the Depression of 1873. But once the war and the subsequent period of reconstruction ended, the American South began to recover its economic equilibrium, and soon the entire country was once again producing more wealth than seemed imaginable even a generation earlier. This prompted many interested observers to ask the simple question: why?

Why was capitalism working so spectacularly in America? Was it merely an economic inevitability? Most scholars seemed to think so, with the general consensus being that modern capitalism was merely a socioeconomic phenomenon, rooted in technological and political advances, and no more. America's penchant for individual liberty and limited government meant that adventurous entrepreneurs could take risks and start businesses with the hope of seeing exceptional gains in return. This intensification of avarice was not a new theory, though, and plenty of daring entrepreneurs outside America were also willing to risk their capital to reap great rewards in the end.

Others simply suggested that it was a natural evolution from economic romanticism to economic rationalism, while others believed it to be nothing more than a terribly efficient manifestation of Marx's theory of materialism and class exploitation. Still others thought that it was merely the effect of an increase in interest-based lending combined with soft-touch financial regulations, resulting in easy access to capital for investment purposes.

While each of these explanations had some merit, none was terribly unique. The conditions described could be found in most capitalist economies, yet none of those countries seemed to be experiencing growth on a scale equal to America's.

Weber had a different theory. He believed that modern capitalism was rooted in something much deeper than just socioeconomic conditions; he believed that it sprang from a particular ethos that sought to align religious belief with economic activity, resulting in a kind of devotional zeal that powered the engine of wealth-creation in America.

Weber based his theory, not merely on his observations of American capitalism, but on what he witnessed in other countries as well. In the very opening of his book he observes that "for any country in which several religions coexist . . . people who own capital . . . tend to be, with striking frequency, overwhelmingly Protestant."[2]

While that revelation was already circulating in the public domain, most people argued that it was more an effect than a cause. The most economically independent parts of Europe embraced the Protestant Reformation and so they were already wealthier than their predominantly Catholic neighbors. Weber disagreed. He argued that the phenomenon was accelerated in the centuries following the Reformation and that modern capitalism was so distinct from anything that had gone before that there must be something endemic to the belief system itself, both in theory and praxis, that brought about its transformation.

Weber's theory was quite simple. Having rejected the totalitarian authority of the Roman See, Protestants replaced the tyranny of the Roman Catholic Church with an even more encompassing despotism: the voluntary, yet comprehensive "organization of the believer's life" (4), especially as exhibited by adherents to a sect with which he had personal experience, Calvinism.

Interestingly, in defense of his position, Weber does not initially quote from either John Calvin or Calvinist sources. Instead, he refers to the writings of the American polymath and folk hero Benjamin Franklin. Weber admits that Franklin himself was not a Calvinist, but Weber suggests instead that he embodied a particular ethos that was firmly rooted in America's Puritan heritage. This remnant of Calvinist influence was, for Weber, the essential "spirit of capitalism."

Quoting from a work of Franklin's aptly entitled *Necessary Hints for Those That Would Be Rich* (1736), Weber shares several of the author's better-known aphorisms, such as "time is money," "credit is money," "money begets money," and "a good paymaster is lord of another man's purse." He observes that, at first glance, they appear to be virtuous merely because Franklin deems them to be useful (17); yet, despite Franklin's predilection for utilitarianism, Weber notes that because Franklin combined the application of these aphorisms with a puritanical rejection of hedonistic delight, there must have been something about the accumulation of wealth itself that Franklin and others found morally compelling. Weber found the answer to his quest in Franklin's own autobiography, noting:

> In his autobiography, Franklin answers (although he is himself a bald Deist) with a maxim from the Bible that, as he says, his strict Calvinist father again and again drilled into him in his youth: "Seest thou a man vigorous in his vocational calling? He shall stand before kings" (Prov. 22:29). As long as it is carried out in a legal manner, the acquisition of money in the modern economic order is the result and manifestation of competence and proficiency in a vocational calling. This competence and proficiency is the actual alpha and omega of Franklin's morality. (18)

While Franklin was a contemporary of Adam Smith, his influence on American culture lasts to this very day, and while Smith was equally familiar with Calvinist doctrine, there was far more religious enthusiasm in the American colonies at that time than there was in Great Britain. This was especially true after the Great Awakenings of the late eighteenth and early nineteenth centuries, when Calvinism in America enjoyed a momentous revival. Even when strict religious observance began to wane in the second half of the nineteenth century, the ethos of Calvinism had become so indelibly linked with both economic thinking and social custom that the only thing necessary for their perpetuation was the establishment of "groups" (19) who would unwittingly "carry" (19) this thinking from generation to generation. Thus, Weber concludes, it became the moral duty of all people to ensure that their lives were well and properly organized around their economic activities, thereby maximizing their utility, not for the sake of pleasure, but for the sake of virtue. Before examining these groups, however, it is essential to take a closer look at the Protestant notion of calling.

Weber asserts that calling, or vocation, was central to Luther's theology, but his theology of calling did not develop in a vacuum. It evolved from a wider concern for clerical elitism and corruption. Luther's main thesis was an attack on the church's presumptive authority in all matters spiritual, including the interpretation of Scripture and the dispensation of sins. He particularly railed against the sale of indulgences and challenged the church hierarchy to prove its claims to priestly exceptionalism, as well as its defense of a sacred/secular divide. In defense of his position, Luther referred to the writings of the apostle Paul in Colossians 3, as well as to the apostle Peter's first epistle (1 Pet. 2–3). Luther famously stated in a treatise known as *The Babylonian Captivity of the Church* (1520) that

> the works of monks and priests, however holy and arduous they may be, do not differ one whit in the sight of God from the works of the rustic laborer in the field or the woman going about her household tasks. . . . All works are measured before God by faith alone.[3]

Such a high view of work was unique to Protestantism. And Luther went on to suggest that all work, if performed in obedience to one's divine calling, was no less than an act of worship, citing again the testimony of the apostle Paul in his defense: "Therefore, I urge you, brothers and sisters, in view of God's mercy, to offer your bodies as a living sacrifice, holy and pleasing to God—this is your true and proper worship" (Rom. 12:1).

Luther also suggested that the way people conduct themselves in their ordinary vocations could be as effective in winning people to Christ as anything spoken from a pulpit. This theology is sometimes known as the priesthood of all believers, although Luther never actually used that term, and was supported by the following passage from Scripture:

[Y]ou also, like living stones, are being built into a spiritual house to be a holy priesthood, offering spiritual sacrifices acceptable to God through Jesus Christ. . . . [Y]ou are a chosen people, a royal priesthood, a holy nation. . . . Live such good lives among the pagans that . . . they may see your good deeds and glorify God. . . . [I]f any of them do not believe the word, they may be won over without words by [your] behavior . . . when they see the purity and reverence of your lives. . . . (1 Pet. 2:5–3:1)

According to Weber, this radically new concept of calling challenged the Roman Catholic notion of ascetic withdrawal, or what Weber calls "estrangement from the world" (8) and replaced it with a newly sanctified and highly pragmatic work ethic. Nevertheless, according to Weber, Luther's teachings were still not sufficient enough to have had that significant an impact on the nature of modern capitalism. In fact, he notes that despite a high view of work, Luther did not elevate work to the level of "duty" and suggests that Luther himself was far more traditional in his economic thinking than modern.

It would take the writings of John Calvin to breathe life into "this-worldly asceticism" (53) and to produce the religious denominations (that is, groups) necessary to perpetuate its ethos and dramatically influence economic activity.

In the chapter entitled "The Religious Foundations of This-Worldly Asceticism," Weber notes that the four religious groups most responsible for the transmission of Puritanism are Calvinism, Pietism, Methodism, and what he calls the "baptizing sects" (that is, Mennonites, Quakers, and so on) (53). Weber admits that there are significant differences in faith and praxis between and within these groups; however, he patches over those differences by finding common themes, what he calls "ideal types" (55). Chief among those types, according to Weber, is the doctrine of predestination, which he sees as the primary "psychological motivator" (55) for followers to both order their lives according to strict moral principles and to seek evidence of their place among the elect. Weber calls this evidence of election the "*character indelebilis*" (74), which believers in the doctrine of predestination would have logically expected to experience themselves and witness in the lives of other true believers.

Weber bases his theory largely on the theology of seventeenth-century English Puritan Richard Baxter, whose famous work *Christian Directory* (1673) extolled the very virtues at the heart of modern capitalism. According to Baxter and others, idleness was a greater threat to the soul than the accumulation of wealth, and hard work is naturally the best antidote to idleness. Work and productivity are expected of the righteous, regardless of wealth or standing, and while every person may be called by God to a specific function, what matters most is the effectiveness and faithful diligence with which each person carries out that function, elevating work from the realm of utility to that of "duty" (106).

Wealth in this construct is no longer a sign of avarice but is the natural outcome of a well-ordered and productive life. Enjoyment of wealth must still be avoided, and while believers are duty-bound to be as productive as possible, within the constraints of God's law, they are warned against the dangers of accumulating excess riches and the obvious temptations therein. Or as Weber himself explains it:

> Hence, wealth is only suspect when it tempts the devout in the direction of lazy restfulness and a sinful enjoyment of life. The striving for riches becomes suspect only if carried out with the end in mind of leading a carefree and merry life once wealth is acquired. If, however, riches are attained within the dutiful performance of one's vocational calling, striving for them is not only morally permitted but expected. (109)

One result of this ethic is the emergence of groups subscribing to this belief system that produce sets of highly motivated, highly skilled workers. If they are, in turn, supported by a financial system that encourages investment and makes capital more readily available, society will produce highly motivated, well-financed entrepreneurs. All that remains then for such societies to flourish are the "sects, clubs, or fraternal societies" (136) necessary for the perpetuation of the virtues and values at the core of the system. Weber notes this is precisely what happened in America:

> The sects . . . united men through the selection and the breeding of ethically qualified fellow believers. . . . The sect controlled and regulated members' conduct exclusively in the sense of formal righteousness and methodical asceticism. . . . [C]apitalist success . . . if legally attained, testified to [one's] worth and [one's] state of grace . . . and put a halo around the economic "individualist" impulses of the modern capitalist ethos. (147)

The Protestant Ethic and the Spirit of Capitalism in Review

Weber's fascinating observations and conclusions continue to be debated among scholars, and while he landed on an explanation that offered insights that few others discovered, it is also clear that he got some important things very wrong. From the beginning, Weber misunderstands the theological essence of Calvinism and Reformed[4] thinking, grossly overstating the impact of predestination as a psychological motive and providing a jaundiced view of Calvinism, which seemingly had more to do with his own childhood religious experiences than a deep reading of Calvin's work. Weber also undervalues the effects of thrift and stewardship on the preservation of capital and the positive impact of Calvin's liberal views on usury and interest, while at the same time overstating the case for membership in civic organizations.

Weber does articulate many ideas accurately. He understands, for instance, that Reformed theology and the Calvinist sects took an all-encompassing approach to life. He rightly notes that in Reformed thinking there is no room for a sacred/secular divide and that such beliefs deeply impacted economic activity in America. He also understands and thoughtfully describes Reformed theology's emphasis on holiness and the requirement for believers to reflect the characteristics of the divine in their daily lives. Weber also ably articulates the difference between Calvin's theology of work and Luther's, even as he fails to appreciate Calvin's ontology of work (a topic we will explore in a later chapter).

In considerable and accurate detail, Weber explores the deep-seated tension between the Puritan compulsion toward economic efficiency and its aversion to riches and pleasure, and he emphasizes with great effect the endemic relationship between culture, including religious belief, and economic systems. Furthermore, he demonstrates clearly and logically how well-ordered societies that create economic systems built on thrift, stewardship, and an expectation of honesty and fair dealing are likely to create sects for the purpose of perpetuating them. Weber also exposes the tenuous nature of those carrier-groups: over time they drift further and further away from both their original religious foundations and the ethical principles they were created to protect.

Moving from Traditional to Modern Capitalism

A desire to ensure general subsistence and enhance the welfare of society was the primary driver of traditional capitalism, and access to capital was mainly means-based. Traditional capitalism followed a rhythmic, agrarian cycle that supplied common necessities, sprinkled with a few limited comforts. Religious orthodoxy that taught salvation by good works and a remote, "God is watching" admonition to behave morally comprised the ethics of traditional capitalism.

Modern capitalism, as we have seen through our consideration of Marx and Weber, was driven by a desire to create and accumulate wealth for fundamentally individualistic reasons. Access to capital was largely based on the availability of a new concept, credit. The all-encompassing regimentation of modern industrial life produced products and services on an unprecedented scale but at a significant cost to humanity. International trade expanded exponentially in the modern era, and the homogenization of cult was set against the marginalization of culture. The ethics of modern capitalism consisted of a this-worldly asceticism that served as both a self-governing code of conduct and as evidence that a God who is active in the affairs of humans has predestined the elect to salvation.

Modern capitalism was an exceptionally efficient economic system that would create unimaginable wealth, but as the ethical constraints and moral codes it depended upon eroded, the moral impetus behind wealth-creation was soon replaced by greed. The societal norms that self-regulated markets and business conduct were rendered obsolete by the moral relativism of postmodernity. Just as traditional capitalism gave way to modern capitalism, so modern capitalism would soon give way to postmodern capitalism.

6

Postmodern Capitalism

Above all, you must understand that in the last days scoffers will come,
scoffing and following their own evil desires.
                                                            2 PETER 3:3

In chapter 1, I defined postmodern capitalism as "capitalism that is devoid
of a moral compass and resistant, if not impervious to ethical constraint." So
what is meant here by postmodern? Definitions of *postmodern* vary widely,
with sociologists, philosophers, historians, and theologians offering different
descriptions according to preconceptions in their own disciplines. For our
purposes, I will concentrate my definition on what Paul Fiddes calls the mood
of postmodernity:

> While postmodern thinking emerges at the somewhat rarified heights
> of academic debate, it does reflect a more popular "mood" to which it
> is responding and to some extent affecting. . . . [F]our sets of ideas have
> flowed into the world-view that we can call "postmodern": immersion
> in the world, a hermeneutic of suspicion, openness of meaning, and
> the impact of the sublime.[1]

Fiddes is neither a critic nor a fan of postmodernism, and he actually
prefers the term *late modern* to describe the epoch in question. That said, he
is an astute observer of the phenomenon we commonly call postmodernism,
and his observation of its mood is particularly insightful. Postmodernism does
indeed reflect an "immersion in the world" ethos, and it provides a philosoph-

ical basis for deep inquiry into complex issues, from social to existential. What he calls "openness of meaning," whereby the deconstruction of texts may lead to insights and meaning heretofore unknown to casual observers, opens up a host of possibilities for dialogue, and he even goes so far as to compare the multivalent reading of texts to Augustine's polysemic interpretation of the Bible and the medieval practice of fourfold exegesis.[2] And Fiddes rightly observes that postmodernism's reinterpretation of the sublime "offers common ground for theology and thinkers of the late-modern world to explore a sense of transcendence."[3]

For those who seek the redemption of our economic system, the postmodern mood would suggest an endless array of possible antidotes to the current crisis, but a particular obstacle presents itself in the form of what Fiddes calls a "hermeneutic of suspicion," which in common parlance may be referred to as an inclination to question authority and to dismantle *a priori* truth claims, including moral absolutes, that emanate from those in positions of authority.

Based largely upon the works of Jean-François Lyotard, Jacques Derrida, Michel Foucault, and others, postmodernity takes the premise that knowledge is subjective and that the limits of language itself make it virtually impossible to articulate, and therefore to know, objective realities. According to this worldview, truth is an epistemological impossibility. Logically then, religious metanarratives, revelation, and religious truth claims, including the ethical codes of conduct that often accompany them, are not merely questioned but, in a rather Nietzschean manner, rejected outright.[4]

This particular aspect of the postmodern mood affects not only *how* people think (namely, skeptically) but also *what* people think about an array of issues relating to human behavior and ethical conduct. When it comes to issues of right and wrong, commandments for instance, have little value, unless the source of those commands has been rigorously scrutinized and empirically verified. *Prima facie* observations are preferred to theological or philosophical constructs, and short-term, temporal utility usually outweighs any consideration of long-term utility. As one might expect, this lack of moral authority has led to the proliferation of moral relativism, and it is this particular aspect of postmodernity that is pertinent to our study. Moral relativism has found its way into every sphere of life, including business ethics, resulting in the evolution of an economic system that, while capable of producing great wealth, may also do great harm.

This is a relatively recent phenomenon. For instance, the capitalism of Adam Smith was rooted in the Enlightenment presumption that certain truths were self-evident. These include the existence of God and a moral ordering of the universe. This and the capitalism observed by Max Weber, with its unwavering belief in the active participation of God in human affairs and humankind's duty to obey God's precepts, are both long gone. The capitalism of Smith and Weber has been replaced by another form of capitalism that produces the good, the bad, and the ugly: postmodern capitalism.

Capitalism—The Good

Despite its many and varied critics, capitalism has been an exceptional vehicle in the creation of global wealth. Since 1800, the world's population has grown six times larger, but per capita gross domestic product (GDP) has grown eleven times greater.[5] Since 1990, global poverty has more than halved from 43 percent to 21 percent, and average GDP growth in developing countries has increased by an average of 6 percent (three times that of developed countries).[6] As average incomes have grown, so has longevity, with the average person living twenty years longer than recorded in the middle of the last century, and infant mortality has fallen by an astonishing 65 percent.[7] Overall living standards, health care, education, infrastructure, and information technology have all improved dramatically, and human beings have experienced a degree of flourishing never before known to humankind. In short, capitalism works, but it does not necessarily work for everyone, and it certainly works better for some than others.

Capitalism—The Bad

Despite these gains, over one billion people still live on less than $1.25 per day, wealth continues to be unevenly distributed between the global north (rich) and the global south (poor), and the gap between rich and poor is growing exponentially. According to a recent report by the charity Oxfam, 99 percent of the world's combined wealth is in the hands of 1 percent of the population and as few as eight individuals are as wealthy as half the population of the entire world, combined (3.6 billion people).[8] This singular, staggering statistic must not be ignored, especially by proponents of capitalism. Wealth disparity of this magnitude is unprecedented and unsustainable, and if it is not addressed it will result in social upheaval on an equal scale. This has been obvious to social commentators and philosophers since the first millennium BCE when Plato warned against both the evils and the dangers of great wealth disparity and the Buddha, the Tao Te Ching, and the Old Testament prophets all railed against the greed and conceit of the rich and called for justice for the poor.

But there are other problems inherent in the current system as well that pose existential threats to capitalism itself. One such problem is the ticking time bomb of sovereign, or national, debt.

Nearly all governments, whether local, state, or national, raise taxes to provide services to their citizens. Traditionally, the expenditures of those governments roughly equal their tax revenues. At times, though, usually during recessions or wars, governments must spend more than they collect in taxes. To raise the extra funds, they issue interest-bearing bonds, thereby incurring sovereign debt. When this happens, it is called "deficit spending," the accumulation of which constitutes a government's debt burden.

According to economic orthodoxy, during peacetime, governments should lower taxes and increase deficits, thereby increasing government debt, only when the economy is in severe recession. The combined effects of increased liquidity and additional government spending are justified as vehicles for increasing economic activity and "priming the pump" for the general economy. But when the economy recovers, governments are supposed to raise taxes and reduce deficits in order to control inflation, keep their economies from over-heating, stabilize their currencies, and reduce their debt burdens.

This is exactly what happened in the United States between 1981 and 2000, when Reagan-era tax cuts produced their desired results and triggered economic growth while increasing the national debt. Between 1989 and 2000, Presidents George H. W. Bush and Bill Clinton raised taxes during their terms, and while the increases were politically unpopular at the time, the result was as expected: continued economic growth, reduced budget deficits, and even several budget surpluses. Beginning with the George W. Bush tax cuts in 2001 and 2003, however, successive governments have abandoned that formula, and the resulting increase in peacetime national debt has been astronomical.

When a company publishes its balance sheet, one of the first things an investor looks at is the company's debt ratio—the amount of debt as a percentage of the company's assets. If a company is carrying too much debt, it may not be able to pay its creditors and could go bankrupt. Therefore, prudence requires companies to maintain a debt ratio that is not too burdensome. The percentages vary according to industry standards and according to other factors, such as a company's cash position, but generally speaking creditors start to get nervous once debt ratios climb above 60 percent. The same is true of sovereign debt. Instead of comparing the percentage of debt to assets, the metric commonly used is the percentage of debt to a country's GDP.

Since 1940, America's average debt-to-GDP ratio has been approximately 61 percent, but that includes the period during and just after World War Two, when the national debt soared to just over 120 percent. During the postwar era between 1960 and 2000, its national debt-to-GDP ratio averaged around 48 percent. But since that time, things have changed dramatically, and in the last ten years alone the national debt has doubled from $10 trillion to $20 trillion, bringing the debt-to-GDP ratio to approximately 104 percent,[9] making America's one of the most heavily leveraged advanced economies in the world—all of which happened during peacetime.

This trend is worrying for several reasons. As we saw in chapter 1, the cause of the global financial crisis and the recession that followed was corporate greed and mismanagement, not a normal cyclical downturn. Nevertheless, the government responded with unprecedented levels of deficit spending. Combined with that additional deficit spending was an unprecedented increase in artificial liquidity, known as quantitative easing (QE), whereby the Federal Reserve Bank purchased over $4.5 trillion in treasury- and mortgage-backed securities, which is tantamount to "printing money." What no one knows is how much additional debt the economy can bear before the markets get nervous and decide that the recent economic recovery was more the result of QE than the strength of the economy itself. If that happens, America's ability to service its massive debt burden could become suspect, and the largest economy in the world could be faced with a sovereign debt crisis, the results of which would be catastrophic.

The debt problem is not merely a government issue; it is endemic to the entire economy. According to recent figures, personal indebtedness in the United States stands at $12.35 trillion[10] and is nearly back to where it was just before the global financial crisis of 2008. The average American household owes more than $36 thousand dollars in non-mortgage debt and approximately $130 thousand dollars in total debt, including mortgages, against an average annual income of only $60 thousand dollars. Still more worrying is the recent decision of Fannie Mae (the Federal National Mortgage Association) to reintroduce its 97 percent loan-to-value (LTV) ratio mortgage product.[11] While LTV mortgages are not as egregious as the NINJA mortgages discussed in chapter 1, the trend is slowly but surely heading toward the same conditions that led to the wide-scale defaults that in turn triggered the global financial crisis.

There are other considerations. Global demographics are putting demands on public services, especially in developed countries such as the US and UK, where the social costs of state pensions and medical care could require governments to dramatically increase taxes or take on more national debt. In addition, the environmental impact of industrial growth is genuinely staggering. In the last one hundred years, sea levels have risen nearly seven inches; global temperatures have risen one degree Celsius; global ice sheets have been in retreat; and the number of extreme weather events has nearly doubled. Most of these changes have occurred in the last fifty years, as carbon dioxide levels in the atmosphere have climbed to unprecedented levels. While there may be meteorological explanations for some of the increase, the overwhelming consensus among climatologists is that increased economic activity has been the primary cause of the spike in carbon dioxide.[12]

Nearly all of these phenomena can be addressed through various government policies and require no more than the political will of the people aligning with the political foresight of their leaders. Of greater concern to our study are the gross abuses of capitalism that cannot easily be dealt with through legislative means; they are the moral failures that have wreaked great havoc on individuals, investors, communities, and nations, and if these are not addressed, they threaten to undermine the future of a functional economy and capitalism itself.

Capitalism—The Ugly

In the opening chapter, I recounted in some detail the events and decisions that led to the collapse of New York investment bank Lehman Brothers, but that was only one in a series of corporate scandals that could fill volumes. All of the details are different, and while some of them involved criminal activity, all of them involved moral turpitude on a wide scale. The misdeeds often highlighted in the tragedies of failed banks, stock swindles, misappropriation of funds, and insider trading deals are almost always committed by people whose actions reflected the perverse cultures of the companies for whom they worked. Two of those stories are worth retelling.

Before its demise in 1995, Barings Bank was one of the oldest and most respected merchant banks in the world. It was started in 1762 by Sir Francis Baring; it counted the Queen as one of its most illustrious customers; and it helped the fledgling United States government make the famed Louisiana Purchase. It was not a particularly large bank with just under $1 billion in capital, but it was very prestigious, and its demise sent shock waves around the world. Its troubles began in 1993 when the bank sent a young trader named Nick Leeson from London to run the Barings Futures division in Singapore. The Singapore operation dealt with both the Singapore International Monetary Exchange (Simex) and the Osaka (Japan) stock exchange. Leeson controlled both the trading desk and the back-office operation.

Leeson's original assignment was to exploit arbitrage opportunities across the region. Arbitrage is normally a low-risk/low-profit operation whereby a stock is purchased on one market and simultaneously sold on another foreign market, with the profit being nothing more than the currency differential between the two markets; but Leeson decided to do something quite different. Under the guise of phantom investors, Leeson was actually trading derivative contracts on the company's behalf on both markets, using a hedge device known as a straddle. A straddle places both a put (buy) and a call (sell) option on the same derivative with the same strike price on the same expiration date. This allows the investor to make money whether the stock goes up or down, providing the stock's movement is dramatic enough to cover the cost of the option premium itself. If the stock does not move significantly, though, the investor loses whether the stock goes up, down, or does not move at all. It is an investment with limited risk (the cost of the option premiums) but high upside potential, as long as there is volatility in the market.

Compared to arbitrage, straddles are much riskier transactions, and when Leeson had a good run and started making much larger profits than were expected, instead of questioning his activities, the bank rewarded him with large bonuses. Note, however, that trades of this nature can also produce significant losses over time. When his losses began to mount, instead of coming clean with his bosses back in London, Leeson took advantage of his back-office position and hid them in an error account, in the hopes that his luck would turn around and he could recover them before anyone noticed the discrepancy in the books.

As his losses grew worryingly high, he placed a huge bet on the Japanese Nikkei 225 index, hoping that its mid-1990s run of poor performance would recover and he would ride the recovery. Unfortunately for Leeson and for Barings, that didn't happen. In fact, when an earthquake hit Japan and the Nikkei 225 lost one thousand points in a single day, the additional losses were more than Leeson could hide in his error account, and his reckless actions literally broke the bank.[13]

While some like to relate this episode as the actions of a single "rogue trader," Leeson got away with the large-scale gambles only because the bank had a culture of asking no questions when people were making a lot of money for its shareholders. This case also highlights the problems inherent in remuneration schemes that not only reward reckless behavior but also encourage it. It was not only Leeson who benefitted from his unrealistic profits; it was his entire department, including his boss—the person who should have been asking hard questions of him instead of turning a blind eye to his behavior. This is also a lesson in what can happen when companies do not exercise good governance.

Another example of endemic corruption that extended beyond one company and affected the entire financial sector was the previously mentioned LIBOR scandal. LIBOR—London Interbank Offered Rate—is the interest rate that banks charge each other for unsecured short-term loans. As the UK Council of Foreign Relations explains:

> To calculate the Libor rate, a representative panel of global banks sub-
> mit an estimate of their borrowing costs to the Thomson Reuters data
> collection service each morning at 11:00 a.m. The calculation agent
> throws out the highest and lowest 25 percent of submissions and then
> averages the remaining rates to determine Libor. Calculated for five
> different currencies—the US dollar, the Euro, the British pound ster-
> ling, the Japanese yen, and the Swiss franc—at seven different matu-

rity lengths from overnight to one year, Libor is the most relied upon global benchmark for short-term interest rates. The rate for each currency is set by panels of between eleven and eighteen banks.[14]

While it is generated in London, the LIBOR is the benchmark rate used to determine the interest charges on $300 trillion worth of loans worldwide, such as variable rate mortgages, government securities, and countless other debt instruments. It is one of the pillars of the entire global financial system, and it was assumed for generations to be a thoroughly reliable and trusted arbiter of actual market conditions.

In 2012, it was revealed that five of the banks that contribute to the LIBOR calculation (Deutsche Bank, Barclays, UBS, Rabobank, and the Royal Bank of Scotland) were colluding with each other to manipulate the rate in order to help their traders fix derivatives contracts, or in the case of Barclays Bank, to shore up the bank's financial position during the global financial crisis.

As the investigation unfolded, other banks turned out to be involved as well, including US banks JPMorgan Chase and Citigroup, as well as France's Société Générale. It was a scandal of unequaled proportions. The involved banks paid $9 billion in fines, a number that may well triple before all is said and done.

While some of the traders themselves have been convicted of crimes, no one at the top executive level of the banks involved has been prosecuted, some of the accomplices have been acquitted, and others are appealing their sentences. Considering the scale of the fraud and the number of casualties involved, the penalties imposed seem laughable and only add to the consensus that the financial services sector is rigged and that corruption and collusion between banks, central banks, regulators, and politicians is rampant.

These two examples of corporate scandals in the financial sector both show a clear trail of corruption. There are countless others: the insider trading scandal of 1986, the savings and loan scandal of 1989, the Madoff Ponzi Scheme of 2008, the Vatican Bank scandal of 2013, the Wells Fargo scandal of 2016, and the list goes on. More shockingly, despite legislative reforms such as the Dodd-Frank Wall Street Reform and Consumer Protection Act of 2010 that attempted to regulate certain aspects of the sector, very little has actually changed.

It is back to business as usual, with a very small number of financial executives making huge sums of money, despite the fact that they do not actually create any wealth per se. They create the opportunity for wealth to be created by providing the investment vehicles necessary for capital to be put to use in the general economy (so-called intermediation), but most of their revenue is generated by effectively "churning money," not by creating wealth. To put it into perspective, traditionally the financial sector represented approximately 3 to 4 percent of GDP; now it represents twice that,[15] and as we have discussed already, too much liquidity is not a good thing. When too much cash chases too few assets, bubbles are inevitably created, and bubbles always burst. Easy access to credit can also encourage excessive consumption, which in turn can lead to excessive debt and eventual wide-scale defaults.[16] We need a sound financial sector, but we need it to be a prudent one, too.

Corporate wrongdoing in sectors other than the financial also involve wide-scale deception, including the Enron scandal, which at the time was the largest corporate failure in US history; the Rolls Royce bribery case that involved several projects in several countries and resulted in a $1 billion fine being imposed on the company by US authorities; the Volkswagen emissions deception; the Tesco and Toshiba accounting scandals; and even bribery at the heart of global football (FIFA).

Exploitation and inequality within companies themselves are also problems, as demonstrated by the growing wage gap between corporate CEOs and the people who work for them. At one time, a CEO was expected to cap his or her salary at about twenty times the annual pay of the lowest-paid full-time employee. Now, the average CEO is paid somewhere in the region of three hundred times that of a full-time minimum wage employee. While some shareholders have tried to question this practice, the compensation committees of large companies have largely turned a deaf ear to their complaints.

Ever since the so-called Nixon Shock of 1971, when US President Richard Nixon suspended the dollar's convertibility into gold, the relationship between wealth and money has become suspect, with money no longer assumed to be an accurate representation of genuine wealth. People at top positions are making vast amounts of money, but real wealth is not being created in the economy at the levels we might expect, and the ones who suffer the most are those being squeezed in the middle and those completely left out at the bottom. Such is the state of postmodern capitalism.

Modern Capitalism and Postmodern Capitalism Compared

So how is postmodern capitalism different from the modern capitalism observed by Max Weber? For one thing, the ethos of capitalism has changed. The primary driver of capitalism is no longer wealth accumulation but conspicuous consumption. The economy is no longer built on a stable credit system; it is built on unsustainable amounts of individual, corporate, and sovereign debt. As a general principle, work itself is no longer seen as a calling but as a profession, with all aspects of life, including our economic activities, compartmentalized rather than integrative. The industrial economy that once made *products* for use locally and abroad has been replaced by an information economy that focuses instead on the development of global *brands*.

Sociologically, culture has become homogenized, while the cults of religion and other values-based associations have become marginalized. Work is no longer viewed as sanctified but as intentionally secular (that is, "of the world"), temporal, utilitarian, and, generally speaking, without a moral compass rooted in a higher moral authority. Consequently, moral accountability driven by a belief in God has become unmoored. "God is dead" is increasingly society's, and therefore capitalism's, guiding principle. It resembles a dystopian reality that needs either fixing, replacing, or reforming. And considering the large-scale economic impact of capitalism's evolution, all options *must* be on the table.

7

Utopia or Redemption?

Be careful what you wish for, lest it come true.

ANONYMOUS PROVERB

In the wake of the September 2008 crash, people began to sense a change of mood in the body politic. After years of uncritical acceptance of the status quo, people living in free-market, liberal democracies such as America and Britain began to question the economic legitimacy and social impact of unbridled capitalism. They began to ask hard questions about wealth inequality, executive pay, taxation, corporate governance, and monetary policy. They even challenged some of capitalism's most basic assumptions about competition, private ownership, and the efficacy of self-correcting markets.

Before long, movements emerged that captured the public's imagination. Fueled by a combination of traditional media hype and the impact of social media, a whiff of revolution filled the air, as least for a while. People were not content with the prospect of merely fixing the current system; they wanted to replace it with something new and better; they wanted an economic utopia.

Even a cursory review of all the proposals put forth by various proponents of radical change cannot be covered here. However, so we can understand the general tone of the socioeconomic debates, I will explore several representative movements and ask whether they offer viable alternatives to the current system or whether they are well-intentioned constructs whose risks outweigh their potential rewards.

The Occupy Movement

On September 11, 2011, New Yorkers marked the tenth anniversary of al-Qaeda's attack on the World Trade Center. Like previous memorials, the event was a somber one as people from every walk of life and social stratum gathered to pay their respects to those who died on that dreadful day when America and everything it stood for came under attack by a foreign entity. Less than a week later, only a few yards away in nearby Zuccotti Park, America appeared deeply divided along economic lines, and one of the pillars of American life, free-market capitalism, was subjected to a peaceful, yet impassioned, attack from within.

Self-appointed representatives of the so-called 99 percent stood in utter defiance of the so-called 1 percent who, according to some analysts, benefit disproportionately from America's economic success, own too much of its wealth, and contribute too little to the overall well-being of society. Chanting the slogan "we are the 99 percent," the group calling itself "Occupy Wall Street," marched throughout lower Manhattan and took up residence in tents. Their relative success in bringing attention to the problem of wealth disparity in America spurred similar protests in other cities. The Occupy Movement became a global phenomenon.

That said, the long-term impact of the Occupy Movement remains questionable. In New York, the protests lasted just over a month before Zuccotti Park was forcibly cleared for "sanitation reasons." In other places, such as London, the protests lasted for several months. While similar protest camps were established in hundreds of cities around the world, the movement did little more than change the popular narrative from one of rote acceptance to one of protest, without offering real alternatives to the current system.

One among many problems with the Occupy Movement was the demographic makeup of the groups of protesters themselves. In New York and London particularly, the movement, dominated by highly educated, white, middle-class males from the world's wealthiest economies, lacked support from a broad demographic. Some commentators have suggested it was less a case of the 99 percent criticizing the 1 percent than the second-wealthiest percentile criticizing the wealthiest percentile.

Nevertheless, the Occupy Movement has increased awareness of wealth disparity, even if it offered no real solutions to the problem, though the voice of one French economist has surfaced from the movement, and in his book, *Capital in the Twenty-First Century,* he presented possible solutions.

Capital by Thomas Piketty

Books on economics written by academics rarely make the *New York Times* Best-Sellers list, much less seven-hundred-page tomes written by relatively unknown French authors. That changed in April 2014 when the English publication of Thomas Piketty's 2013 book entitled *Capital in the Twenty-First Century* made the list, reaching the number one spot in only four weeks. By his own admission, no one was more surprised than the author himself. Thrust into the international limelight, the forty-something, self-confessed homebody (Piketty admits to being less than well-traveled) was suddenly forced to defend his methods, observations, conclusion, and policy recommendations to nonacademic audiences around the world. His efforts produced mixed results.

Examining nearly two centuries' worth of data, Piketty observed that capitalism will often, if not inevitably, lead to a distorted concentration of wealth simply because the rate of return on capital (r) regularly outpaces economic growth (g). His $r > g$ formula is both accurate and elegant. But the numbers do not speak for themselves. For instance, Piketty admits that the post-war era between 1946 and 1979 does not fit his model but suggests it was merely an anomaly caused by post-war reconstruction efforts and advances in technological innovation.

He also presumes that correlation equates to causation when it comes to rates of return on invested capital. Capital growth may indeed traditionally outpace overall economic growth, but there is nothing inevitable about that phenomenon. Piketty also works on the assumption that past performance is an automatic indicator of future results. Capital returns are not automatic, however, and reflect the cumulative effects of positive risk/reward calculations and strategic investment decisions, as much as any bias in the system. In fact, the $r > g$ formula may have more to do with stagnant wages than it does with return on invested capital (ROIC).

Among the misses in Piketty's analysis is the fact that, while the rich may be getting richer, especially in mature economies such as those of the US and European Union, economic liberalization on a global scale has effectively brought over one billion people out of poverty and raised living standards to heights unimaginable only a generation ago.

Despite the flaws in some of his arguments, Piketty's book captured the zeitgeist of the Occupy Movement and a general dissatisfaction with economic elites benefiting disproportionately from capitalism without paying a price for their failures. Unfortunately, the solutions he recommends are both unimaginative and unworkable—and, by his own admission—hopelessly utopian.

For instance, Piketty recommends the introduction of a global wealth tax. The rates he suggests range from 0.1 percent for those with net assets over €200 thousand ($220 thousand) to 2 percent for those with assets over €5 million ($5.5 million). Although a popular concept in some quarters, wealth taxes ultimately prove to be impractical, unenforceable, and unfair to those with relatively modest assets and little liquidity. Furthermore, no evidence suggests that wealth taxes actually work. They rarely, if ever, achieve their revenue goals and are extremely costly to impose, as demonstrated by such diverse experiments as the seventeenth-century window tax—a tax on the number of windows in a house—or the recently abandoned tax schemes in countries such as Austria, Denmark, Germany, Finland, and Italy, all of which failed miserably. Nonetheless, the concept still resonates with large sections of the population, as does the aptly named "Robin Hood Tax," a proposed tax on all financial transactions, that appeals more to romantic images of economic chivalry than sound economic reasoning.

Piketty also recommends an increase in the top rate of income tax to something in the region of 75 percent. He argues that this figure will produce a significant increase in tax revenues without inflicting sufficient pain on top-rate taxpayers to encourage capital flight. Unfortunately, as demonstrated by the experience of the French socialist president François Hollande, who introduced just such a tax in his first year in office, it was a sore failure. Hollande went on to rescind it shortly thereafter. Not only were the revenues meager, but it also hurt France's reputation in the business community, reduced its appearance of economic competitiveness, and encouraged both capital flight and tax avoidance.

Conversely, in the United Kingdom, when the government reduced its top tax rate to 45 percent, it removed incentives for capital flight and tax avoidance, increasing revenues by £9 billion ($14 billion) in the process. Similarly Norway, which prides itself as a bastion of social democracy, since lowering its overall tax burden by some 17 percent in 2004 (from 47 percent to 39 percent), has seen its GDP nearly double from $260 billion to $500 billion, while France's economy over the same time period has grown by a modest 33 percent from $2.1 trillion to $2.8 trillion.

The inefficiencies of closed economic systems and punitive taxes are well attested, yet they still remain popular for those seeking an economic utopia. But for some, a utopian dream leaves little room for economic pragmatism, which may begin to explain the phenomenon of UK Labour leader Jeremy Corbyn.

·

Jeremy Corbyn and the Rise of "Old Labour"

When Tony Blair convinced the British Labour Party in 1995 to rebrand itself "New Labour" and to abandon its long-held commitment to "common ownership of the means of production, distribution, and exchange" (Clause 4 of the party's 1918 socialist manifesto), many thought the Labour Party had permanently jettisoned its utopian ideals and settled for a more pragmatic form of social democracy. Yet, while the changes to Clause 4 certainly made Labour seem less anachronistic in an age of globalization and much more electable in an era of political centrality, the old guard never really let go of the dream. When the party suffered defeats in both the 2010 and 2015 general elections, its response was to go back to its roots and, through a combination of old-guard grandees, hardline trade unionists, and a new wave of young registered supporters (that is, anyone willing to pay £3 for the right to vote in the leadership election), they elected Jeremy Corbyn, the sixty-six-year-old MP for Islington North, its new leader. The era of New Labour was over. To say that Jeremy Corbyn's election was a surprise would be an understatement; his assent sent shock waves through the halls of Westminster and caused considerable consternation within the ranks of the political establishment, including among a majority of the Parliamentary Labour Party, who saw his leadership as electoral suicide.

So what exactly is Jeremy Corbyn proposing? In economic terms, the answer appears to be a resounding return to traditional socialism. He is radically opposed to austerity, believing the government should both borrow more money and tax the rich more aggressively. He supports the renationalization of industries privatized over the last thirty years, such as utilities and transport, and he hopes to abolish the Private Finance Initiative. He supports a reduction in corporate tax relief and the introduction of People's Quantitative Easing, a scheme to inject liquidity directly into the economy while sidestepping the financial sector completely. He opposes private involvement in the provision of national health services and supports tuition-free higher education. He champions the notion of a radical economic strategy and a return to the pre-Thatcherism economic policies of the 1960s and 1970s.

Corbyn's policies, those of a tried-and-true activist, bear little resemblance to the political pragmatism of recent Labour Prime Ministers Tony Blair or Gordon Brown. He reflects a mood of discontent and disenfranchisement, especially regarding economics and public policy. As with Piketty, Corbyn captured the imagination of a generation confused by recent calamities and dissatisfied with the status quo. In this he is not alone, as shown by the emergence of an unlikely US presidential candidate, the previously little-known and remarkably resilient senator Bernie Sanders of Vermont.

Bernie Sanders—An American Socialist

Since the end of World War Two and the beginning of the Cold War, one word above all others has been anathema to US politicians: *socialism*. Among the many reasons for this, perhaps the two most obvious are a general confusion about what socialism actually is and a widely held conviction that socialist experiments in Europe and elsewhere have not been successful.

Confusion over what socialism actually is may be traced to deliberate and, some might say, cynical attempts by its opponents to convolute democratic socialism with totalitarian Marxism. In an era when American men and women were giving their lives to fight the "red menace" of communism in places such as Korea and Vietnam, few people were interested in the subtleties of socioeconomic theory. The world was seen as black and white; the bad guys were "commies," the good guys were Americans, and the notion of a third way was virtually nonexistent. Nothing demonstrated the intellectual vacuity of this thinking more than the actions of the US House of Representatives's Un-American Activities Committee (HUAC), which operated from 1938 to 1969, and the US Senate Government Operations Committee, chaired by Senator Joseph R. McCarthy between 1950 and 1954.

In what can be characterized only as modern-day witch-hunts, members of Congress sought to root out communism with a zeal normally seen in religious fanaticism. Left-leaning figures were fair game, and the list of people accused of being members of communist organizations, past or present, or communist sympathizers grew with each public hearing. Soon both panic and paranoia crept into the political landscape; no one wanted to be painted with a red brush. Clear-headed thinking ultimately won out. Former President Harry S. Truman famously quipped that the House committee was "the most un-American thing in the country," but the damage was done and, until very recently, anything hinting of socialism was simply beyond the pale of American political discourse.

The other negative influence on American perceptions of socialism was the anemic performance of socialist-leaning economies in Western Europe during the second half of the twentieth century, along with the near-total economic failure of Marxist economies in Eastern Europe and Asia. The failure of the *dirigisme* project in France, which imposed state economic planning and management; the staggering national debt of Italy and Greece; and the UK's sobriquet "sick man of Europe" caused many commentators to conclude that socialism simply does not work.

This perception seemed to be validated by the 1979 election of UK Prime Minister Margaret Thatcher and the subsequent swing to the right of many other European governments. When the Berlin Wall fell a decade later and the economic decay of Eastern Europe was exposed for all to see, and when China, the largest communist country in the world, began embracing free-market capitalism, it was as though the argument was well and truly over: free-market capitalism works and socialism does not—end of story. Or so many thought.

The global financial crisis radically changed these perceptions and, to the surprise of political pundits everywhere and the chagrin of Hillary Clinton and the Democratic Party establishment, a spokesman for America's hard left emerged as a legitimate presidential candidate.

Prior to announcing his intention to run for president in April 2015, Bernie Sanders was not well known outside the Beltway. Having never belonged to either major political party, an anomaly that changed when he officially joined the Democratic Party in November 2015, he often chided both sides of the aisle for being pawns of special-interest groups. Rarely, if ever, was he viewed as a viable candidate for president. That changed, however, when he began polling as a strong contender to the presumptive nominee, former US Senator and Secretary of State Hillary Clinton. At first, he may have been seen as a political curiosity, but when he won eight of the first seventeen primaries, it became evident he was not only a serious contender for the nomination, but that he was a candidate whose message resonated with a large and previously under-represented portion of the population.

Sanders's platform was not dissimilar to Jeremy Corbyn's. He proposed higher taxes on everyone making more than $250 thousand per year (including a 52 percent top-rate of personal income tax), higher corporation taxes, a tax on financial transactions (the famous Robin Hood Tax), in increase in inheritance tax, a doubling of the minimum wage, a $1 trillion national works project, an end to various free-trade agreements, free higher education for everyone, additional labor unions, a break-up of the big banks, and a single-payer healthcare system which he calls Medicare for All.[1] His is the most socialist agenda in recent US memory.

While their proposals are rooted in traditional socialism, neither Sanders, nor Corbyn, nor Piketty goes as far as British academic Dr. Eve Poole, who has attacked free-market economics generally, and proposed a utopian ideal delivered from the effects of capitalism's "seven deadly sins."[2]

Eve Poole and Capitalism's Seven Deadly Sins

Less well known than other economic and political figures, Eve Poole has nevertheless struck a nerve with the publication of her book *Capitalism's Toxic Assumptions: Redefining Next Generation Economics* (2015). Building on her work as a commissioner for the Church of England and later as a management consultant for Deloitte, Poole set out to explore the fundamentals of capitalism as a doctoral student at Cambridge University. Combining her knowledge of theology (she holds an undergraduate degree from the University of Durham) with her knowledge of business (MBA, Edinburgh University) and her personal convictions as an evangelical Christian, she has concluded that the problems associated with capitalism's excesses are not caused by failures of the regulatory system or tax policies, but they are, in fact, due to the very DNA of capitalism itself.

Poole argues that the West's entire economic system is flawed because it is built upon seven basic assumptions, namely competition, the "invisible hand," utility, agency theory, market pricing, the supremacy of the shareholder, and the legitimacy of the limited liability model. She argues that unless or until we destroy these basic assumptions, we cannot hope to build a better economic system or a fairer society.

Competition, she notes is the "linchpin of the entire system"[3]; pricing, she believes is manipulated by the "invisible hand"[4] and ultimately determines supply and demand. Furthermore, she contends that because modern pricing theory is based upon "demand and not supply," relies on the "wisdom of the crowd," and produces "tragedies of the commons," it is inherently "unjust." She also suggests that it has led to the "commoditization of money."[5]

Capitalism's assumption of utility, she states, is also problematic, because it encourages a consequentialist ethic that may be logical on an individual basis (that is, *Homo economicus*) but that is insufficient on a macro scale. This presumption, she contends, is also responsible for economic modeling that is often skewed and that, most importantly, leads to agency theory.

According to Poole, agency theory, which deals with the relationship between principals and their agents or representatives, is based upon a primitive and flawed understanding of human nature and leads to human resource policies that favor employers over workers, create tension between management and shareholders, foster inefficient business practices, and ultimately enshrine the maximization of shareholder value over all other metrics.

The maximization of shareholder value, according to Poole, is part and parcel of shareholder supremacy. Shareholder supremacy, she believes, leads to an overemphasis on share price, which in turn leads to "short-termism," the "manipulation of reporting data," a shift in emphasis from "retain and invest to downsize and redistribute," and "high-frequency trading."[6] But it is the limited liability model of which she is particularly critical, noting that shareholders in limited liability companies risk only their invested capital and have no more "skin in the game." This, Poole suggests, creates an upside bias that "drives reckless behavior," reinforces both shareholder supremacy and agency theory, and ultimately "blanks out the wider stakeholder community."[7]

Poole envisions replacing the current, fundamentally flawed model with a new economic utopia where the "seven deadly sins" of capitalism have been destroyed forever and replaced by a new construct built on a new set of assumptions. Basing her theory upon research into such diverse fields as theology, economics, psychology, game theory, and gender studies, she believes that competition should be replaced by cooperation, the "invisible hand" by increased state regulation, utility by an ethic of mutuality, market pricing by so-called just pricing, agency theory by a presumption of human benevolence, and the limited liability model, predominantly led by men, by more democratic models led by female executives.

Many aspects of Poole's writing resonate as clear and well conceived, especially for those who care for a theological and moral framework, but her work is not without its flaws. Poole's implication that Adam Smith's "invisible hand" possesses some form of agency misreads Smith. For him, the so-called invisible hand "coordinates" (Poole's term) nothing and is no more than an anthropomorphic description of the phenomenon of self-correcting markets.

Competition and cooperation, Poole suggests, are somehow mutually exclusive, but evidence from evolutionary biology would suggest otherwise. In the natural world, the two are known to work in tandem.[8] Competition keeps a market honest and benefits those involved, including the consumer, without precluding competitors working together when and where it is appropriate. "Coopetition," as it is sometimes called, is common in business, provided it does not lead to collusion or other unethical practices.

With regard to the relationship between pricing, supply, and demand, contrary to Poole's suggestion, pricing does not determine supply and demand; it reflects supply and demand. It also has no bearing on the so-called commoditization of money. The medieval notion of just pricing is flawed, as well, for a variety of reasons, including problems associated with the so-called intrinsic theory of value. No commodity has an intrinsic economic value, which was a flaw in Marx's thinking as well.

As for agency theory, Poole asserts that it reflects a primitive view of humankind, yet it still is an accurate view of human nature, and despite agency theory's obvious shortcomings, it continues to be our best defense against moral hazard and other inherent conflicts of interest.

Underestimating the genius of the limited liability model also seems to limit Poole's criticism and strategy. Without the limited liability model, it would be difficult to raise the capital necessary to generate economic growth. Also underappreciated is the relationship between investment risk and reward, as well as the risks and responsibilities that company directors bear.

While promoting genuinely savvy insights into capitalism's shortcomings, many of Poole's ideas run the risk inherent in all utopian models: the unintended consequences of wholesale change may prove more problematic than beneficial, in the long run.

The Trouble with Utopia

Whether driven by political will or economic theory, well-meaning people creating an economic utopia are destined for disappointment from the first, beginning with the obvious hurdle of the mere size and complexity of the global economy. When Karl Marx and Friedrich Engels penned the *Communist Manifesto* in 1848, the world was a very different place. With the exception of industrialized Britain, most of the world's economies were still agrarian. While increased urbanization had clearly begun and consumption of non-food goods and services had added to overall GDP, the greatest economic shock of the times, the European subsistence crisis, was triggered by the Irish potato famine, not by factors related to industrialization or capital flow. Also, the world was much smaller when Marx and Engels wrote; its population stood at just over one billion people and the entire global economy, which was dominated by the British Empire, was estimated to be worth around $1 trillion.

Today, you will find a very different picture. With over seven billion people living on the planet, the global economy is worth nearly $80 trillion. Twenty countries produce approximately 80 percent of the world's wealth, and the economic landscape ranges from agrarian to industrial to post-industrial. While all of the major economies are interconnected through a vast array of trade agreements, political alliances, and, perhaps most significantly, electronic interactions, they are also separated by significant political, cultural, religious, legal, technical, and economic differences. While homogeny is fundamental to utopia, economic homogeny is a virtual impossibility in a system as large and complex as today's global economy.

Besides the size and complexity of the global economy, many who seek an economic utopia fail to discern different kinds of inequalities, some resulting from nature, rather than the failure of systems. Resources are not evenly distributed around the world, nor are people's skills and abilities.

Large demographic, population, and climate differences also contribute to economic inequality. Added to those differences are the problems of unexpected influences and unintended consequences. Sometimes events, whether positive or catastrophic, natural or human-made, radically alter the economic landscape. History has shown that many well-intentioned attempts to solve one problem have resulted in the creation of even more serious hazards down the road. This persistent problem of utopian failure may be acutely seen in the economic degradation of closed economic systems, where the desire to equitably redistribute wealth ultimately destroys mechanisms for the creation of wealth.

Finally, there is the problem of what theologians call the Fall—that is, the corruption of the created order and human sinfulness. Since the time of the Enlightenment, philosophers have tried desperately to suggest that societies' problems may be permanently solved through nothing more than the application of human reason and natural benevolence. History has proven this to be folly. While human ingenuity and our propensity for right behavior has solved many of the world's ills, our predilections for power, pleasure, and personal aggrandizement have also created the opposite effect.

The twentieth century saw a rise in proponents of utopian ideals maintaining that the use of revolutionary terror was a necessary evil. As Mao Zedong famously stated, "Political power grows out of the barrel of a gun," and, whether through military force or other coercive tactics, including punitive taxation, it does not take much for a well-intentioned utopia to become a feared and despised dystopia.

If utopia fails to provide an answer, what are people of goodwill to do when they encounter an economic system completely out of control, as we have with postmodern capitalism? As I suggested at the beginning of this book, when it comes to our current socioeconomic predicament, the greatest challenges we face are not structural in nature; they are moral. So we must look to moral constructs, including those rooted in our religious traditions, for guidance. Redemption is one such construct that warrants our further consideration.

A Model of Redemption

The Oxford Online Dictionary defines *redemption* as "the action of saving or being saved from sin, error, or evil." While the term is often used in reference to an individual's eternal state of grace (that is, salvation), it may also apply to any attempt at correcting errors of the past. One of the most important things to understand about redemption is that it is a process of healing, not a ready-made cure. It involves an acknowledgment of the past and the errors inherent therein, and it requires honest and probing assessments of past actions, their causes, and their effects. The objective here is not to replace capitalism with an alternative economic system, but to overcome the sins of the past by addressing the moral issues that produced the current crisis. Rather than formulating a quick fix to a problem that took generations to create, this approach seeks to transform our economic system by reclaiming the moral values that once undergirded it.

In the following chapters, we will explore various tools that we can use to redeem our economic system. Among these tools is a cache of wisdom from across various cultures and traditions. Such wisdom includes not only the cardinal virtues mentioned in chapter 1 but other universal virtues, as well, such as faith, hope, and love. Tragically, this wisdom has been expunged from the lexicon of business and economics.

As we mine the depths of religious wisdom, note that space does not permit us to consider all faith traditions. We will concentrate on the Judeo-Christian tradition, because it holds a unique position of influence in the West. That is not to suggest that other traditions, both religious and secular, do not have much to say as well about ethical business conduct or economics—they do. What I hope to demonstrate is the universality of biblical and theological principles relating to business and economics that are applicable despite the complexity and the diversity of our global economic landscape.

8

God and Mammon—
A Biblical Perspective

In regard to this Great Book, I have but to say, it is the best gift God has given to man. . . . But for it we could not know right from wrong.
ABRAHAM LINCOLN

One may reasonably ask what religious belief has to do with economics. At first glance, the two would appear to be completely different areas of concern, yet an examination of religious texts would suggest otherwise. From the Hebrew Scriptures to the Gospels, from the Qu'ran to the Sunnah, from the traditions of Hinduism to the teachings of the Buddha, Tao, and Confucius, all global religions actually have much to say about work, worth, wealth, and ethics.

The Hebrew Scriptures (or the Old Testament)

While the Scriptures contain teachings that span millennia and deal with every imaginable aspect of life, many are surprised to discover that the Bible has more to say about work and economic activity than the topics of heaven, hell, and sexual ethics combined. As the Bible is the bedrock upon which the Judeo-Christian tradition is built, it makes sense for us to take a closer look at what it actually has to say about such things.

The Bible begins not merely with the story of God, but with the story of God at work in the creation narratives (Gen. 1 and 2). By divine fiat, God creates everything from nothing and establishes a process for the continuation of that work through the participation of creation itself. This of course, includes the creation of humankind, who is uniquely made "in the image" of God and to whom the cultural mandate of stewardship and dominion is given (Gen. 1:1–28). While the introduction of sin and its consequences, the Fall, distorts the natural order of things and work becomes "toilsome" (Gen. 3:1–24), the mandate continues unabated.

Note what the writer of Ecclesiastes says about the centrality of work to the human experience:

> What do workers gain from their toil? I have seen the burden God has laid on the human race. He has made everything beautiful in its time. He has also set eternity in the human heart; yet no one can fathom what God has done from beginning to end. I know that there is nothing better for people than to be happy and to do good while they live. That each of them may eat and drink, and find satisfaction in all their toil—this is the gift of God. (Eccles. 3:9–13)

While demonstrating a clear understanding of the toilsome nature of work, the writer also appreciates its intrinsic value. The value of work is not defined by its creative merit, its difficulty, or its utility (in order to "eat and drink"), but in the recognition of work as being a "gift of God."

In all human labor, the writer sees the participation of humankind in the creative process begun by God "from [the] beginning" and made "beautiful in its time" as fundamental to our very being. In theological terms, it means that work is ontological, reflecting what it means to be human. We work, not merely because we must, but because it is part of our nature as creatures uniquely created in the image of a God always at work.[1]

For evidence of this, one only has to ask a person one has just met what he or she "does" for a living, and one will likely get an "I am" response (that is, "I am a teacher," "I am a lawyer," and so on). Naturally, people associate who they are with what they do, not just because so much of our precious time, energy, and resources are invested in our work, but also because human beings were actually created by God to work. In fact, Scripture often describes people by both their names and their occupations (for example, Abel is described as a shepherd, Cain as a farmer, Noah as a vintner, Bezalel as a builder, and so on), even when those designations have no bearing on the narrative at hand.

As James Francis puts it:

> [T]he modeling of the transcendent in religious discourse . . . reflect[s] the idea of God as . . . the Worker par excellence. . . . [While] work may be hard and toilsome, it is productive and creative, [it] is a uniquely human activity express[ing] who we are and aspire to be, . . . using creatively all the materials of our life which are to hand.[2]

This is not to say that work is not also "deontological"—it is. Human beings have a duty to fulfill God's mandates,[3] and numerous passages throughout the Bible warn against the dangers of idleness and slothfulness. After the Fall, plenty was replaced by scarcity, requiring the full participation of people in the economic activity of their communities, a theme revisited by the apostle Paul in his admonishment of the Thessalonians who refused to work (2 Thess. 3:10).

Finally, work is rightly described as teleological, or necessary for survival and human flourishing. All work is celebrated in the Bible, including that for which one receives no remuneration, such as housework and charitable work. What one does is just as important as how one does it, because both motive and conduct matter to God. Work is both an individual exercise and a communal exercise, the ultimate purpose of which is to bring glory to God.

In addition to establishing the critical nature of work, the creation narratives also anticipate the creation of wealth and the development of economic systems, including the use of money as a means of exchange. The second creation narrative, for example, refers to the existence of gold (Gen. 2:12), which would logically be used either as currency or for personal adornment, both of which suggest the presence of surplus goods and the creation of wealth. Later in Genesis we read that Abraham had indeed become "very rich in livestock, in silver, and in gold" (Gen. 13:2), and throughout the Old Testament there are references to traders and merchants.

In the Hebrew Scriptures, however, there is also a constant tension between the rights of individuals to benefit from their economic activities and their broader obligations to seek the common good, with special concern for those who are less fortunate, both within the community and outside of it. So, while a person may have the right to own private property, that person is also required to treat those under his or her care with dignity and respect (Exod.

21–22). The accumulation of wealth is not to be at the expense of others, nor is it to be the result of dishonest behavior (Exod. 23:1–10; Prov. 11:1); and the long-term benefits to individuals, communities, and even nature itself are to be placed above the short-term benefits of any given person. Consequently, we read of prohibitions of unfair treatment of strangers, widows, and orphans (Exod. 22:21–24), restrictions on usury (Exod. 22:25–27), and establishment of the sabbatical year (Exod. 23:10–12) and the Jubilee (Lev. 25:1–54).

While trade and exchange abounded, direct comparisons between ancient Israel's economic landscape and today's political economy are virtually impossible. That said, throughout the Old Testament we can see certain ethical principles emerge and carry on throughout the rest of Scripture that are applicable today and therefore warrant closer attention.

Consider, for instance, the lessons that may be taken from Proverbs 31:10–31 and its description of a "wife of noble character." This is a remarkable passage for several reasons. First, despite Israel's engrained patriarchy, it claims to be the wisdom of a woman (the mother of King Lemuel), and second, it holds up the business conduct of a woman as the ideal. Whether Lemuel was in fact a veiled reference to King Solomon or, as some recent scholars have suggested, an Assyrian ruler whose wisdom was appropriated by the Israelites, the message is unmistakably clear, universally applicable, and timeless.

The woman described in Proverbs 31 is a woman of substance whose conduct and ethics are a model for everyone involved in economic activity.[4] Here is how the text begins: "A wife of noble character who can find? She is worth far more than rubies" (v. 10). Implicit in this opening statement is the importance of character in the cultivation of ethical mores. The book of Proverbs is predicated on the belief that wisdom is to be sought above all things, and throughout this passage, as well as the entire book, we see the proposition that material gain is nothing compared to the attainment of wisdom. Everything that follows in this narrative, from the woman's work ethic to her honest yet savvy business dealings, to the treatment of her workers and her care for the poor, reinforces a simple hierarchy of values: God's primacy, followed by wisdom, then virtue, then everything else.

As we continue to read the passage, we see that, first and foremost, she seeks to do that which is "good" (vv. 11–12); she works hard (v. 13), provides for those under her care (vv. 14–15), invests in the future (v. 16), and makes a profit (vv. 17–19). But then her concern turns immediately to the poor and the needy (v. 20), and her family takes its proper place in the governance and welfare of the city (v. 23), setting an example for future generations to follow (vv. 24–29).

An ideal is clearly established here: hard work, the economic use of material goods, the ability to face the future with courage and confidence in both methods and results will inevitably lead to flourishing. The one who is praised is the one who has worked diligently, lived a temperate lifestyle, and been prudent in business dealings; this is the one who has demonstrated justice by caring for the poor and needy. For these things the woman of virtue receives praise from her family, but her greatest reward has been the gaining of wisdom, and her "faithful instruction" (v. 26) is gladly shared with others.

Just as the guilds of medieval Europe were responsible for the welfare of their cities, so too is the family of this woman responsible for their city. As Jesus himself taught, "From everyone who has been given much, much will be demanded; and from the one who has been entrusted with much, much more will be asked" (Luke 12:48b). With economic success comes civic responsibility, whether in the form of fair taxation, or personal involvement, or both. The biblical principles are clearly established here and throughout Scripture, including in the words of the prophet Jeremiah to the Jews in exile when he admonishes them to "seek the peace and prosperity of the city . . . because if it prospers, you too will prosper" (Jer. 28:7). The biblical model of prosperity is clearly one of both personal and communal responsibility—both personal and communal wealth.

At the end of the story, a moral code underlies the model we have been given:

> Charm is deceptive, and beauty is fleeting; but a woman who fears the LORD is to be praised. Honor her for all that her hands have done, and let her works bring her praise at the city gate. (Prov. 31:30–31)

We see this model throughout the Old Testament, and it builds upon the basic premise that all economic activity is designed to glorify God, who has given his people all good things. In return, the fruits of labor should be dedicated to the common good, and, in the process of creating and using wealth, we are commanded to act virtuously and avoid the pitfalls of temptation and sin, which if left unchecked will inevitably lead to vice and eternal punishment.

The virtue of prudence is best expressed in the Decalogue of Exodus 20. The Ten Commandments are not just proscriptions; they constitute a prescription for virtuous conduct. Beginning with an acknowledgment of God's sovereignty and exclusive right to human fealty and respect, the commands clearly define the rights and privileges of the entire community. Parents are to be honored, human life defended, marriage respected, private property protected, truth-telling and honesty upheld, greed and envy despised—establishing without doubt the principles of moral behavior.

Similarly, the rules of justice and fairness are established in Deuteronomy 23:15-25, where the right to refuge is granted to runaway slaves (v. 15), and their protection from oppression is guaranteed (v. 16). The proceeds of prostitution, both male and female, are condemned, and charging interest within the community is strictly prohibited (vv. 17-19). Promises must be kept and vows honored, and while it is prohibited to steal from someone's vineyard or grain field, the gleanings are viewed as community property and may be used for immediate sustenance but may not be hoarded or harvested (vv. 21-25).

Earlier we looked at Thomas Aquinas's definition of courage: opposing that which opposes virtue itself. Leviticus 19 highlights spiritual courage where, once again, the needs of the poor are specifically mentioned (vv. 9-10), honesty, including the payment of workers' wages, is addressed (v. 13), the rights and dignity of the differently abled are upheld (v. 14), justice is championed (v. 15), slander is condemned (v. 16), and hatred and vengeance are forbidden (vv. 17-18).

Last of all, temperance—particularly the avoidance of greed, pride, and other forms of wickedness—is dealt with forcefully in Psalm 10. Portrayed as the lament of one who has been oppressed, the words here speak for themselves:

> Why, LORD, do you stand far off?
>   Why do you hide yourself in times of trouble?
> In his arrogance the wicked man hunts down the weak,
>   who are caught in the schemes he devises.
> He boasts about the cravings of his heart;
>   he blesses the greedy and reviles the Lord.
> In his pride the wicked man does not seek him;
>   in all his thoughts there is no room for God.

His ways are always prosperous;
>   your laws are rejected by him;
>   he sneers at all his enemies.
He says to himself, "Nothing will ever shake me."
>   He swears, "No one will ever do me harm."
His mouth is full of lies and threats;
>   trouble and evil are under his tongue.
He lies in wait near the villages;
>   from ambush he murders the innocent.
His eyes watch in secret for his victims;
>   like a lion in cover he lies in wait.
He lies in wait to catch the helpless;
>   he catches the helpless and drags them off in his net.
His victims are crushed, they collapse;
>   they fall under his strength.
He says to himself, "God will never notice;
>   he covers his face and never sees."
Arise, LORD! Lift up your hand, O God.
>   Do not forget the helpless.
Why does the wicked man revile God?
>   Why does he say to himself,
>   "He won't call me to account"?
But you, God, see the trouble of the afflicted;
>   you consider their grief and take it in hand.
The victims commit themselves to you;
>   you are the helper of the fatherless.
Break the arm of the wicked man;
>   call the evildoer to account for his wickedness
>   that would not otherwise be found out.
The LORD is King for ever and ever;
>   the nations will perish from his land.
You, LORD, hear the desire of the afflicted;
>   you encourage them, and you listen to their cry,
defending the fatherless and the oppressed,
>   so that mere earthly mortals
>   will never again strike terror. (Ps. 10:1–18)

The proverbial wicked man here might easily fit the type that returns without faith in our picture of postmodern capitalism: the one who continually "hunts down the weak" and "blesses the greedy."

The New Testament

The New Testament offers a wide array of commentary about work and economics as well, but the settings for the two Testaments are quite different. New Testament writers were generally familiar with the Hebrew Scriptures and were versed in their traditions and ethical principles, the Torah (Law) and its later interpretations. The New Testament epoch, however, began and ended within a period of about one hundred years and was informed by the customs, traditions, and laws of the Roman Empire under whose authority the Jewish people and early Christians functioned.

As we saw in an earlier chapter, the Roman mandate included times of considerable economic activity and international trade. Roman rule provided a well-attested legal system, common languages (both Latin and Greek), a common currency, a moderate road network, a system for taxation and other administrative activities, and a time of general peace and prosperity.

The Roman system also inflicted gross inequalities, built primarily on class stratification, citizenship, and religious persecution. Corruption was rampant, as was the exploitation of workers, primarily in the form of slave labor. Elites saw menial work as beneath their station, and the only profession involving physical labor that had any standing was that of a soldier. In this system, being rich meant being an oppressor. Collaborators often sought social advancement by working as tax collectors for the Romans, which allowed them to use their positions to extort others.

Operating parallel to the Roman system were local, traditional economies, especially among occupied groups of people. These smaller economies normally involved religion-based programs of reciprocity and redistribution, sometimes administered through religious centers such as synagogues, or in the case of Jerusalem, the temple itself. Against this backdrop, Jesus and his followers preached the gospel, "speaking truth to power."

Our biographical knowledge of Jesus is limited mainly to the Gospel accounts. Those "memoirs of the apostles," as second-century theologian Justin

Martyr would later call them, were concerned more with the mission, ministry, and teachings of Jesus than with details of his personal life. Nonetheless, we are able to glean from the Gospels an indication of who Jesus was, and judging by the uniqueness of his background, his complicated family life, and his strong religious upbringing, we may assume these influences had a significant impact on his approach to ethics.

The Gospels paint a picture of a man born into a poor (Luke 2:7, 24) yet pious family (Matt. 1:18–25), steeped in the religious traditions of his Jewish ancestors. He was also familiar with the life of the ascetic, as shown by his relationship with his cousin, John the Baptist (Matt. 3:1–17; John 1:19–34; John 5:31–35), and his own time of preparation in the wilderness (Matt. 4:1–11). The absence of any mention of his earthly father in the passages relating to Jesus's adulthood, despite several references to his mother and brothers, suggests his mother was a widow. It also appears he followed his earthly father into the profession of carpentry (Mark 6:3; Matt. 13:55) as was expected of a firstborn son. In other words, while he was fairly typical for his time and place, Jesus would have possessed a working knowledge of the marketplace and a heightened sensitivity toward the poor, the widowed, the orphaned, and the religiously persecuted.

Judging by his teachings, we see that Jesus clearly understood the nature and the centrality of work and often used work settings in his parables, knowing they would ring true to his audiences. In Matthew 20, he tells the parable of the landowner who hires men to work in the vineyard. When those who worked the least number of hours were paid the same as those who had worked all day, he knew his listeners would grasp the gratitude of those who benefitted most from the graciousness of the owner. Similarly, in the parable of the talents (Matt. 25:14–30), Jesus tells the story of a man who entrusts his wealth to various servants and rewards the ones who make the most of what they are given and punishes those who do nothing. Jesus used these stories to demonstrate God's grace and judgment, yet they hit their mark as listeners related them to their real-life settings. Jesus also understood the practicalities of work. This is demonstrated by a wonderful story in the Gospel of Matthew (17:24–27) when Jesus sends the apostle Peter out to fish so they can pay the temple tax. Jesus tells Peter that he will catch a fish and find in its mouth coins sufficient to pay both their duties. While some may interpret this as a miraculous event, I prefer to think that Jesus was being both practical and a little bit "cheeky." Peter was, of course, a fisherman by trade, and both men would have known exactly what Jesus was suggesting. Work produces money—and they needed money to pay the tax!

When it came to work, wealth, and ethics, though, Jesus did not speak only in parables. At times, he spoke very directly and graciously about God's treatment of those who are oppressed—and very harshly about those who are the oppressors.

> Looking at his disciples, he said: "Blessed are you who are poor, for yours is the kingdom of God. Blessed are you who hunger now, for you will be satisfied. Blessed are you who weep now, for you will laugh.... But woe to you who are rich, for you have already received your comfort. Woe to you who are well fed now, for you will go hungry. Woe to you who laugh now, for you will mourn and weep." (Luke 6:20–21, 24–25)

Jesus also spoke clearly about the dangers of wealth becoming an idol. We see this in his encounter with a rich young man who came to Jesus seeking the way to eternal life. Jesus told him to "sell [his] possessions and give [them] to the poor," which proved to be more than the man was willing to do (Matt. 19:16, 21–24). The man's problem was not that he was wealthy, per se. As we see from other stories in the Gospels, Jesus did not demand that every wealthy person he encountered sell of all his or her riches before becoming one of his disciples (recall the cases of Zacchaeus and Joseph of Arimathea, for example). Yet in this particular case, the man's wealth had clearly become an idol. Before he could follow Jesus, he would be called upon to give up that idol. Jesus also made clear that this was a common problem for those who are wealthy.

Jesus also warned that "worrying" about money, riches, and pleasure could become a distraction from what was truly important in life (see Luke 8:1–15; Luke 12:1–34). But perhaps he delivered his greatest warning to those who were wealthy but failed to share their wealth with the poor, as told in the parable of the rich man and the beggar named Lazarus:

> There was a rich man who was dressed in purple and fine linen and lived in luxury every day. At his gate was laid a beggar named Lazarus, covered with sores and longing to eat what fell from the rich man's table. Even the dogs came and licked his sores.

The time came when the beggar died and the angels carried him to Abraham's side. The rich man also died and was buried. In Hades, where he was in torment, he looked up and saw Abraham far away, with Lazarus by his side. So he called to him, "Father Abraham, have pity on me and send Lazarus to dip the tip of his finger in water and cool my tongue, because I am in agony in this fire."

But Abraham replied, "Son, remember that in your lifetime you received your good things, while Lazarus received bad things, but now he is comforted here and you are in agony." (Luke 16:19–25)

We see in these and other stories Jesus's view of wealth, poverty, and justice. They comprise a clear indictment of those who hoard wealth and refuse to share it with those who are less fortunate. They also clearly indicate that God takes the side of the poor.

In addition to the Gospels, the New Testament contains additional teachings and admonishments about work, wealth, poverty, and justice. In the book of Acts we meet the apostle Paul, who would go on to write nearly a third of the New Testament. A Hebrew scholar, Paul was also an artisan and a tentmaker, a trade he continued to practice while on his various missionary journeys (see Acts 18:1–4; 1 Thess. 2:9–12). He not only shared the gospel in the synagogue but he also shared it in the public square, including the "marketplace" (see Acts 17:16–34). Like Jesus, he also used occasional work analogies to make a theological point. When describing his work among the Gentiles, for instance, he likens it to that of a farmer or a builder, and explains that he and another disciple each contributed to their common mission, one sowing and the other reaping, one laying a foundation and the other building upon it (1 Cor. 3:6–15).

Paul recognized and taught that every individual possesses certain gifts and that each is called by God to perform whatever tasks are necessary to serve the common good and build God's kingdom on earth. He likened this to the different parts of the body, noting that each part functions separately from the others, yet together they are one body (1 Cor. 12:1–31). Paul viewed all "honest work" as part of Christian discipleship and, like Jesus and the Old Testament writers, warned against greed and idolatry (Eph. 4:17–18, 27–28). At one point, he even equates greed with idolatry (Col. 3:5), which his Jewish listeners would have considered the most grievous of sins.

Paul's admonitions and the sentiments they express are appropriate today. Many people across the economic spectrum have hardened their hearts and have sold their souls, as it were, to greed and mammon, which is material wealth. And note that Paul's concern is not just for his listeners but also for the poor with whom he expects the faithful to share their bounty.

The apostle Peter also had a very high view of work, which he saw as an opportunity for believers to stand out from the crowd as witnesses to the grace of the God in the gospel. Speaking to those in the most difficult conditions imaginable, he encouraged them to remain steadfast and faithful and to use their difficult circumstances and their privileged position as disciples of Christ to be a witness:

> [Y]ou also, like living stones, are being built into a spiritual house to be a holy priesthood, offering spiritual sacrifices acceptable to God through Jesus Christ. . . . [Y]ou are a chosen people, a royal priesthood, a holy nation. . . . Live such good lives among the pagans that . . . they may see your good deeds and glorify God. . . . [I]f any of them do not believe the word, they may be won over without words by [your] behavior . . . when they see the purity and reverence of your lives. (1 Pet. 1 and 2, sel.)

James, the brother of Jesus, also wrote in the New Testament about money and its attendant responsibility. His teaching is, in fact, similar to that of Jesus himself. Writing to ethnically Jewish Christians, who would have been familiar with both the Torah and the nascent Gospels, he encourages the poor while warning the rich:

> Believers in humble circumstances ought to take pride in their high position. But the rich should take pride in their humiliation—since they will pass away like a wild flower. For the sun rises with scorching heat and withers the plant; its blossom falls and its beauty is destroyed. In the same way, the rich will fade away even while they go about their business. (James 1:9–11)

He goes on to warn against the church showing favoritism to the rich at the expense of the poor and underscores the fact that his condemnation is based upon the predatory nature of the rich, their ungodly ways, and the corruption endemic in the socioeconomic system of the day (see James 2:6b–7).

But James does not allow his listeners to sit back and wallow in their economic or social degradation. He insists everyone, in spite of their station, do all that they can for the common good and the welfare of others:

> Suppose a brother or a sister is without clothes and daily food. If one of you says to them, "Go in peace; keep warm and well fed," but does nothing about their physical needs, what good is it? In the same way, faith by itself, if it is not accompanied by action, is dead. (James 2:15–17)

He then supports his assertion by pointing out that even Rahab, a prostitute mentioned in the Old Testament and one of his own ancestors, found a way to use her situation to the glory of God; after that, he praises the wisdom that comes from God and leads to virtue, as opposed to the false "demonic" wisdom of the world that leads instead to destruction (see James 3:13–18).

The admonitions, teachings, warnings, and lamentations of Jesus and the apostles would not be out of place in today's world of business and economics, where greed, oppression, corruption, dishonesty, and moral turpitude are widespread; but neither would their words of encouragement to the faithful and the good-hearted be out of place. They acknowledge the brute fact of their socioeconomic circumstances, yet they also offered their listeners a choice. Either they could resign themselves to the realities around them and conform to them, at great personal and societal cost, or they could resist them and reform them, and in the process, perhaps redeem them.

The World That Was, Is, and Is Yet to Come

The Bible is a metanarrative that tells the story of God's divine plan for humankind, the past, the present, and the future. Despite our estrangement from God caused by human sinfulness, by God's grace we are promised a better future. The book of Revelation gives us a glimpse of the glory that is yet to come and with it an example of what we should strive for in our current context (see Rev. 25:1–5). The Old Testament book of the prophet Isaiah offers an additional description of the same future vision. Here the prophet describes the "new creation" this way:

> "See, I will create new heavens and a new earth. . . . They will build houses and dwell in them; they will plant vineyards and eat their fruit. No longer will they build houses and others live in them, or plant and others eat. . . . [M]y chosen ones will long enjoy the work of their hands. They will not labor in vain, nor will they bear children doomed to misfortune; for they will be a people blessed by the Lord, they and their descendants with them. . . . The wolf and the lamb will feed together, and the lion will eat straw like the ox, and dust will be the serpent's food. They will neither harm nor destroy on all my holy mountain," says the Lord. (Isa. 65:17–25, sel.)

The return to Eden that this passage envisions is a promise for the future, but it reflects God's intention for humankind from the beginning, and much of it can be realized even today. Our desire to create an environment as close to that ideal as possible is met not by substituting it with an inferior human-made version, but by living lives today that reflect the beauty, the goodness, and the bounty that God has provided for us. We can achieve this only if we reject and refute the forces that corrupt and pervert the divine plan and choose the common good over selfishness, peace over conflict, stewardship over exploitation, faith over fear, hope over despair, virtue over vice, and love over hatred.

The entire biblical story leads us to these ends, and we have a treasure trove of theology, ethics, history, and wisdom available to us from the across the ages to help us explore these principles in both theory and praxis. These principles have been explored by three theological giants whose work has stood the test of time and whose teachings have shaped the West's views on work, wealth, and virtue for centuries: St. Augustine, St. Thomas Aquinas, and the Swiss reformer John Calvin.

9

Theology and Economics

When the particular virtue opposed to a particular vice is spoken of, all that is usually meant is abstinence from that vice. We maintain that it goes farther, and means opposite duties and positive acts.

JOHN CALVIN

Of all the church fathers, perhaps none is more revered or important to the development of Christian orthodoxy than the fifth-century bishop of Hippo, St. Augustine. Born into a mixed family (his father was pagan and his mother Christian), Augustine was a man consumed by questions of faith, religion, virtue, and philosophy. In his early years he became especially enamored of Manichaean Gnosticism, and the radically dualistic nature of the prophet Mani's teaching allowed Augustine to live a lascivious lifestyle devoid of moral guidance or personal accountability, something that no doubt appealed to his youthful passions. But the more he studied the primary sources of this belief system, the more disturbed he became by its fundamental fantasies, and he turned instead to more classic neo-Platonism. But this, too, seemed to lack a narrative consistent with his own experience of the world, leading him to consider anew the faith of his mother.

As he immersed himself in the Scriptures and in the doctrines of Christianity, Augustine found that only in the Gospels could he find truth sufficient to satisfy both mind and soul. While he continued to find much common ground between Plato and Christianity, the uniqueness of the incarnation, the sufficiency of the cross, and the overarching ethic of love convinced him to fully embrace Christianity and be baptized at the age of thirty-two.

From that point on, Augustine embarked on a truly remarkable career of both churchmanship and intellectual vigor, being ordained within four years of his baptism and elevated to bishop five years after that. He was instrumental in the development of Christian orthodoxy as he fended off the heresies of, among others, the Donatists and the Pelagians, whose beliefs about human nature offended Augustine's commitment to the doctrine of divine grace. He wrote well over one hundred apologetic, theological, and exegetical treatises, plus an estimated eight thousand sermons (several hundred of which have survived). Some of his more important works, and those that pertain to this study, include *Confessions* (ca. 397 CE), *The City of God* (ca. 410 CE), *On the Works of Monks* (ca. 401 CE), *On the Morals of the Catholic Church* (ca. 388 CE), and his sermon on Luke 16:9 (ca. 383–430 CE).

Augustine: Theologies of Work and Wealth

As with the biblical writers, in order to understand Augustine's view of what we would call political economy today, the place to begin is with his theology of work. This was honed in the trenches as bishop when it came to his attention that some monks in his North African diocese refused to submit to the will of their superiors and perform acts of manual labor. Their argument was based on the belief that physical work was beneath their station, and having given up all of their worldly possessions to join the order, they believed prayer and devotion were their only responsibilities. When confronted with the fact that even the apostle Paul continued to work with his hands while devoting himself to the gospel, they responded that this was merely an aberration brought on by material necessity and that physical labor had no spiritual value. In disagreement, Augustine penned a response:

> [T]he blessed Apostle Paul willed the servants of God to work corporal works which should have as their end a great spiritual reward, for this purpose that they should need food and clothing of no man, but with their own hands should procure these for themselves.[1]

As to their claim that their sacrifice of worldy riches should excuse them from their corporeal duties, Augustine noted that while their offerings were indeed generous, they none the less had a moral duty to set an example for other monks, who could not rely on such an excuse and who were merely lazy. Noting that their first considerations should be the spiritual needs of their brothers and not their own rights, he states:

> Wherefore even they which having relinquished or distributed their former . . . means, have chosen with pious and wholesome humility to be numbered among the poor of Christ. . . . [Y]et if they too work with their hands, that they may take away all excuse from lazy brethren who come from a more humble condition in life, and therefore one more used to toil; therein they act far more mercifully than when they divided all their goods to the needy.[2]

For Augustine, as with the apostle Paul, slothfulness is inimical to virtuous conduct, and the natural antidote to slothfulness is honest work.

As supportive as Augustine was of corporeal work, he was even more concerned about the temptations associated with the accumulation of wealth, even if that wealth was the result of honest efforts. While he was clear to note that wealth itself is not a spiritual impediment, he believed love of wealth was most certainly problematic. In his sermon on Luke 16:9 he states:

> Thou dost possess these riches. I blame it not: an inheritance has come to you, your father was rich, and he left it to you. Or you have honestly acquired them: you have a house full of the fruit of just labour; I blame it not. Yet even thus do not call them riches. For if you call them riches, you will love them: and if you love them, you will perish with them.[3]

In a fashion reminiscent of the apostle James, this stern warning to those who possess much also highlights the contrast between the economic landscape of the New Testament writers and Augustine's situation. While the widespread corruption of the established order in first-century occupied Jerusalem lent itself to a more general condemnation of the rich, the situation in fifth-century Roman North Africa called for making a distinction between wealth itself and the corruptible influence of wealth when it is elevated in the human heart to the status of "riches." It is not money that is the root of all evil; it is the "love of money" (1 Tim. 6:10a) that must be guarded against.

For Augustine, everything, including ethics and virtue, boiled down to love. As the Roman Empire began to crumble around them, some observers wanted to blame Christianity for its demise. They believed that Rome's abandonment of their traditional deities and ancient philosophies in favor of Christianity was the cause of their grief. Augustine pointed out, however, that

> the teachings of the philosophers are not the commandments of the gods, but the discoveries of men, who, at the prompting of their own speculative ability, made efforts to discover the hidden laws of nature, and the right and wrong in ethics, and in dialectic what was consequent according to the rules of logic, and what was inconsequent and erroneous. And some of them, by God's help, made great discoveries; but when left to themselves they were betrayed by human infirmity, and fell into mistakes.[4]

It is true that philosophers such as Plato often got things right, but according to Augustine, they got them right without knowing the source of their wisdom. They did not understand that God was the author of their discoveries, and when they tried to judge for themselves what was right and wrong in ethics, they ultimately failed because their knowledge was incomplete. To Augustine this was a genuine tragedy. While he continued to admire certain aspects of Greek philosophy, he lamented the inability of the Romans to discern the source of their truth, namely the God of love found in the Gospels:

> As to virtue leading us to a happy life, I hold virtue to be nothing else than perfect love of God. For the fourfold division of virtue I regard as taken from four forms of love. For these four virtues (would that all felt their influence in their minds as they have their names in their mouths!), I should have no hesitation in defining them: that temperance is love giving itself entirely to that which is loved; fortitude is love readily bearing all things for the sake of the loved object; justice is love serving only the loved object, and therefore ruling rightly; prudence is love distinguishing with sagacity between what hinders it and what helps it. The object of this love is not anything, but only God, the chief good, the highest wisdom, the perfect harmony. So we may express the definition thus: that temperance is love keeping itself entire and

incorrupt for God; fortitude is love bearing everything readily for the sake of God; justice is love serving God only, and therefore ruling well all else, as subject to man; prudence is love making a right distinction between what helps it towards God and what might hinder it.[5]

Aquinas: A Pragmatic Theology of Wealth

For centuries, Augustine's influence on Christian thought was unmatched, yet within fifty years of his death, Rome fell and the church found itself split between East and West. In the East, the church was threatened by the influence of an emergent Islam, leading to its relative isolation and entrenchment, but in the West the church's influence grew as it filled the administrative void left by the empire's collapse. This resulted in the church's meteoric rise to power, with the pope in particular exercising unparalleled political influence. As the church became one of Europe's wealthiest landowners, its collusion with secular authorities became inevitable, and the result was a long, slow spiritual decline. The centuries proved this out: crusades, the Inquisition, political machinations, moral turpitude, and other abuses fed the flames of corruption that would eventually lead to the abominations of the Borgias and the Medici, whose actions would later ignite the Protestant Reformation.

Yet during these dark times, genuine piety and theological reflection were still alive in the monasteries of Europe. Among the most influential groups was the Dominican order, formed in 1216 by its namesake, St. Dominic, for the express purpose of correcting heresy through the systematic training of its preachers. The Dominicans established priories near, and at times within, all the great universities of Europe, including Paris, Bologna, and Oxford, earning the order an unparalleled reputation for academic excellence.

Surely the order's greatest son was the thirteenth-century theologian St. Thomas Aquinas, whose work and methodology, which combined the church's traditional teaching with the dialectic of Aristotle, would define Roman Catholic Scholasticism for centuries. Having already reviewed his teaching on the cardinal virtues in chapter 1, in this chapter we will consider his contributions to a theology of political economy.

Born into a wealthy Italian family, Aquinas had intended from an early age to join the Dominicans and teach theology. His views on political economy were common for his day. Like Augustine and the biblical authors before him, he was wary of the corrosive effects of wealth accumulation, but he saw no intrinsic harm in ownership of private property. He believed it was natural for humans to acquire and have dominion over "external things" and to use those things profitably, yet he cautioned against haughtiness and reminded his readers that all good things are derived from God and ultimately belong to God, stating that,

> man has a natural dominion over external things, because, by his reason and will, he is able to use them for his own profit, as they were made on his account. . . . The rich man is reproved for deeming external things to belong to him principally, as though he had not received them from another, namely from God.[6]

He had a quite pragmatic understanding of the ethical use of one's material wealth. He noted, for instance, that liberality was a virtue, but he thought it absurd for a person to be so liberal as to fail to provide for his or her own basic needs. He also believed it wise for people to exercise thrift and to save their wealth to ensure its availability when needed in the future:

> It belongs to a virtuous man not only to make good use of his matter or instrument, but also to provide opportunities for that good use. Thus it belongs to a soldier's fortitude not only to wield his sword against the foe, but also to sharpen his sword and keep it in its sheath. Thus, too, it belongs to liberality not only to use money, but also to keep it in preparation and safety in order to make fitting use of it.[7]

Along with Augustine and the apostle Paul, he believed in the material as well as the spiritual benefits of manual labor, writing,

> Manual labor is directed to four things. First and principally to obtain food; wherefore it was said to the first man (Genesis 3:19): "In the sweat of thy face shalt thou eat bread," and it is written (Psalm 127:2): "For thou shalt eat the labors of thy hands." Secondly, it is directed to the removal of idleness whence arise many evils; hence it is written (Sirach 33:28, 29): "Send (thy slave) to work, that he be not idle, for

idleness hath taught much evil." Thirdly, it is directed to the curbing of concupiscence, inasmuch as it is a means of afflicting the body hence it is written (2 Corinthians 6:5–6): "In labors, in watchings, in fastings, in chastity." Fourthly, it is directed to almsgiving.[8]

Aquinas was especially concerned with the dangers associated with greed, warning against certain practices he viewed as wicked, including what we today would call price gouging (that is, artificially increasing the price of something in order to take advantage of a person in dire need) and usury (lending money at interest). In keeping with the long-standing teachings of the Judeo-Christian tradition, and citing Aristotle (the "Philosopher") for good measure, Aquinas argued:

> Now money, according to the Philosopher (Ethic. v, 5; Polit. i, 3) was invented chiefly for the purpose of exchange: and consequently the proper and principal use of money is its consumption or alienation whereby it is sunk in exchange. Hence it is by its very nature unlawful to take payment for the use of money lent, which payment is known as usury: and just as a man is bound to restore other ill-gotten goods, so is he bound to restore the money which he has taken in usury.[9]

Behind these examples, the overarching logic to Aquinas's theology begins with his belief in the fundamental goodness of God's creation that, while tainted, is not totally corrupted by sin. Building on this premise, Aquinas sees the potential for human goodness through the sheer exercise of free will and reason. He believes that every human being has the ability to become good by doing good and that in his or her individual quest for happiness, each person must choose which path to take.

Consequently, Aquinas is less fatalistic than St. Augustine but agrees with his view of evil as the privation of goodness. For Aquinas, the entire human experience is tension between those things that are in harmony with God's grace and those that are in dissonance, including vice and virtue. For him, goodness is natural and sinfulness unnatural, and the moral conduct of one's affairs will be determined by the habits one develops. Therefore, all that is required for an economy to be virtuous is for people to develop virtuous habits and to exercise those habits in the regular course of business.

While it remains a popular understanding of human nature, Aquinas's theology differs slightly from the theology of John Calvin, whose teachings, as we have explored in chapter 5, had a far greater impact on the development of Western political economy than either Augustine or Aquinas. It warrants further consideration.

Calvin: Theologies of Wealth Creation, Stewardship, and Interest

One of Christianity's most important theologians, John Calvin was a prodigious thinker and an exceptionally prolific writer, but what sets him apart from other theologians before or since was his devotion to the unique authority of the Bible. While he was thoroughly versed in Catholic doctrine and Greek philosophy, Calvin's knowledge of the Scriptures led him to produce a work of systematic theology so complete that it remains a foundation of Christian thought. Published in Basel, Switzerland, in 1536, *The Institutes of the Christian Religion* inspired Christians to be not merely hearers of the Word, but doers or, as Max Weber would later conclude, to order their lives according to a this-worldly asceticism. Calvin's attempt to apply this principle to his adopted city of Geneva, Switzerland, met with mixed results, but his efforts continued to inspire later generations of Calvinists, including those who developed and nurtured the fledgling traditional capitalism observed by Adam Smith and the later modern capitalism observed by Max Weber.

Calvin rejected any compartmentalization of a believer's life. All of life, including economic activity, is to be lived according to God's precepts and in response to God's grace. For instance, Calvin had this to say about work as worship:

> [I]t is the duty of believers to present their "bodies as a living sacrifice, holy and acceptable unto God, which is their reasonable service" (Rom. 12:1). Hence [the apostle Paul] draws the exhortation "Be not conformed to this world: but be ye transformed by the renewing of your mind, that ye may prove what is that good, and acceptable, and perfect will of God." The great point, then, is, that we are consecrated and dedicated to God, and, therefore, should not henceforth think, speak, design, or act, without a view to his glory.[10]

If the result of that belief is economic excellence, so be it, but it was not the motivating factor for Calvin or his followers—their desire was simply to obey God and bring him glory through their "reasonable service."

Calvin also had no theological objections to private property or wealth accumulation, provided the wealth was accumulated ethically. He notes, though, that everyone has a moral duty to look after their neighbor's property as well as their own, and that they should help those in need, as well as pay their debts. Regarding the eighth commandment ("thou shalt not steal"), he commented,

> This commandment, therefore, we shall duly obey, if, contented with our own lot, we study to acquire nothing but honest and lawful gain; if we long not to grow rich by injustice, nor to plunder our neighbor of his goods, that our own may thereby be increased; if we hasten not to heap up wealth cruelly wrung from the blood of others; if we do not, by means lawful and unlawful, with excessive eagerness scrape together whatever may glut our avarice or meet our prodigality. On the other hand, let it be our constant aim faithfully to lend our counsel and aid to all so as to assist them in retaining their property.... And not only so, but let us contribute to the relief of those whom we see under the pressure of difficulties, assisting their want out of our abundance. Lastly, let each of us consider how far he is bound in duty to others, and in good faith pay what we owe.[11]

Both Augustine and Aquinas held similar views, and it was certainly the belief of the English and American Puritans who gave birth to capitalism. But as history has proved, later generations strayed from this austere reading of wealth creation and stewardship, despite its alignment with centuries of Christian tradition.

One important area in which Calvin differs significantly from either the Scholastics or the church fathers is the question of usury and the legitimate charging of interest. In a letter on the subject written to a friend in 1545, Calvin argues that the Bible is ambiguous when it comes to the charging of interest, stating, "I am certain that by no testimony of Scripture is usury wholly condemned."[12] Instead, he argues that, while it was forbidden in most cases (and thoroughly prohibited among Jews themselves), there were cases where it was permitted and that usury is "not wholly forbidden among [Christians] unless it be repugnant both to Justice and to Charity."[13]

With that, Calvin sets out the following principles, which governed the charging of interest in Geneva and other Protestant communities for centuries. First, no interest was to be charged on loans to the poor or the needy. Calvin thought that to be an abomination as it preyed on those to whom charity should be shown. Second, interest in financial gain should not preclude charity (that is, charity was the higher road for Christians to take). Third, no loan should contravene natural justice (that is, the Golden Rule) and that a borrower's gain should meet or exceed the lender's gain on any given transaction. Fourth, Calvin believed that interest rates among Christians should not be set by the world's standards, but by God's standards, with charity once again being the first consideration (although obeying the civil law was the minimum standard required). Last, before lending money to anyone, consideration should be given to the impact of any loan on the community as well as on the individual borrower. In short, while Calvin understood the economic necessity of allowing interest to be charged, he set its use within a biblical framework of virtue.

Calvin, in fact, had much to say about virtue, seeing it as a remnant of the *imago dei*. This allowed it to fit neatly within his theological system that, unlike Aquinas's, began not with the inherent goodness of humanity but with its depravity. In describing the effects of original sin, Calvin says:

> When viewing our miserable condition since Adam's fall, all confidence and boasting are overthrown, we blush for shame, and feel truly humble. For as God at first formed us in his own image, that he might elevate our minds to the pursuit of virtue, and the contemplation of eternal life, so to prevent us from heartlessly burying those noble qualities which distinguish us from the lower animals, it is of importance to know that we were endued with reason and intelligence, in order that we might cultivate a holy and honorable life, and regard a blessed immortality as our destined aim.[14]

Calvin held a similar view of ethics:

> For conscience, instead of allowing us to stifle our perceptions, and sleep on without interruption, acts as an inward witness and monitor,

reminds us of what we owe to God, [and] points out the distinction between good and evil.[15]

And when it comes to his understanding of each individual's moral responsibility to care for others and society as a whole, Calvin goes farther than previous theologians and philosophers. In considering the purpose of the moral law, he states unequivocally:

> When the particular virtue opposed to a particular vice is spoken of, all that is usually meant is abstinence from that vice. We maintain that it goes farther, and means opposite duties and positive acts. Hence the commandment, "Thou shalt not kill," the generality of men will merely consider as an injunction to abstain from all injury. . . . I hold that it moreover means, that we are to aid our neighbor's life by every means in our power. And not to assert without giving my reasons I prove it thus: God forbids us to injure or hurt a brother, because he would have his life to be dear and precious to us; and, therefore, when he so forbids, he, at the same time, demands all the offices of charity which can contribute to his preservation.[16]

Calvin viewed political economy as part of the natural order of things, ordained by God from the beginning, and despite human depravity, intended by God to be conducted in ways that reflect God's grace, God's glory, and God's character of love. This is not merely the preserve of God's elect, but by God's common grace is available to and expected of all people of good will.

The teachings of Augustine, Aquinas, and Calvin, rooted as they are in biblical theology, when taken together, give us a motif that is remarkably universal in its application and particularly useful in our efforts to redeem our current economic system. Their teachings suggest a quiver comprised of three arrows: common grace, wisdom, and virtue.

IO

Common Grace, Wisdom, and Virtue

Out in the open wisdom calls aloud, she raises her voice in the public square; on top of the wall she cries out, at the city gate she makes her speech.

PROVERBS 1:20–21

As I stated at the very outset of this book, capitalism is a subject, not an object. The capitalism we have is the capitalism we have created, and the moral code by which it operates is merely a reflection of society's values. For those who wish to see postmodern capitalism redeemed it is important to keep in mind the highly complex, highly diverse, pluralistic society in which we live. While there may have been a certain degree of religious hegemony in the past, no such unanimity of belief exists today. The challenge becomes even more acute when we consider the landscape of global capitalism, where the complexities of cult and culture make it even more difficult to find common moral ground from which to operate.

Common Grace

While no consensus exists on the particulars of right conduct, areas of common ground across all religious traditions, and even among those with no religious faith, make it possible to construct a business ethic that is universally applicable. All human beings, whether they acknowledge it or not, possess both the image of God (*imago dei*) and a deep-seated sense of the divine (*sensus divinitatis*) that are the very building blocks of what theologians call common grace.

While John Calvin never used the term *common grace* himself, the concept is a natural extension of his theological system. Even as Calvin clearly professed what he termed the total depravity of humankind, he acknowledged the ability of humans to discern the difference between right and wrong without the benefit of law or revelation. In order to square the circle, Calvin argued that while humankind is indeed depraved from a *soteriological* perspective, we are not totally depraved from a strictly *anthropological* perspective. That is to say, because all human beings are created in the image of God, we all still possess certain attributes of the divine imprimatur. This is the first pillar of common grace.

Additionally, by allowing the human experiment to continue after the fall, God provided for certain undeserved benefits to be bestowed upon humankind in order for God's ultimate purpose of redemption to be fulfilled. These include a limited degree of providential care across the entire created order, as well as the limited restraint of sin, thereby allowing life to continue in an imperfect, yet functional, even civilized, manner.

The next pillar of common grace is another legacy of our creation pedigree: a universal sense of the divine, or "some sense of the Deity," as Calvin put it.[1] Religious belief exists everywhere in the world, and while Calvin wrote some five hundred years ago, his words anticipate the objections of Enlightenment, modern, and even postmodern skeptics when he says:

> It is most absurd, therefore, to maintain, as some do, that religion was devised by the cunning and craft of a few individuals, as a means of keeping the body of the people in due subjugation. . . . [T]hey never could have succeeded in this . . . had the minds of men not been previously imbued with that uniform belief in God, from which, as from its seed, the religious propensity springs.[2]

Know it or not, acknowledge it or not, there lies in the breast of every human being a shrouded yet indelible knowledge of God and both an ability and a desire to reflect the goodness of God, which explains the fact that the overwhelming majority of people in the world (84 percent) still profess faith in God[3] and most still associate religious belief with moral guidance.[4]

One need only consider the ethical foundations of various religious systems to quickly discern the commonality between them. Islam possesses many of the same beliefs about the ontology of ethics that Judaism and Christianity share, and all three Abrahamic faiths put a high premium on right conduct and moral discipline. Similarly, Hinduism and Buddhism, while not as proscriptive as the monotheistic faiths, highly value the development of virtue and the avoidance of vice. Likewise, Taoism and Confucianism place great emphasis on the development of good character and the desire to seek harmony and the common good. Even those who subscribe to moralistic atheism ground their beliefs in a kind of natural law based largely on human empathy and an evolutionary desire to protect the species. The net result is that people of faith need not fear the need to compromise their religious convictions in order to achieve common moral ground, and people without faith need not conclude that invocations of the divine necessarily constitute a hidden agenda of proselytization.

Still, some would prefer to see religion expunged from the philosophical landscape in favor of a totally secular approach to ethics. But this approach is flawed for several reasons. First, secularism is itself a belief system and a worldview, and to suggest otherwise would be nonsensical. Second, as long as religion remains an important source of cultural identity and moral guidance, it will continue to influence business and business cultures. Finally, secularism presumes that economic pluralization and religious belief are somehow incompatible, but that is more an *a priori* assumption than a self-evident or established fact. Religious traditions have a place at the table in relation to ethics, and if allowed, they have great potential to positively inform the debate.

The global economy is a vast and complex constellation of powerful and influential businesses, capital, governments, organizations, and institutions, but it is also a vast network of individual people with minds, wills, and consciences. It is ultimately the morality of the decisions individual people make, and the virtuousness of the business cultures they form, that will determine what kind of capitalism evolves. As the traditional guardians of virtue, ethics, and morality, religious faiths are uniquely placed to influence the future of the global economy, not merely because faith communities have political strength in numbers, but because their traditional values still have currency in the marketplace of ideas. Among those ideas is a belief in the universal benefit of wisdom.

Wisdom—Seven Biblical Pillars

As Paul Fiddes notes in his masterful book on wisdom entitled *Seeing the World and Knowing God: Hebrew Wisdom and Christian Doctrine in a Late-Modern Context* (2013), much of our current thinking about wisdom is derived from the Greek words *technē, phronēsis,* and *sophia. Technē* is associated with craftsmanship, *phronēsis* with practical reason, and *sophia* with higher-order knowledge of the truth. While all these terms are useful in their particular spheres of influence, they fall short of the Hebrew notion of *hokmah*, which is used throughout the wisdom literature of the Old Testament. This kind of wisdom, Fiddes notes, is not exclusively theoretical or practical but is both observational and participatory, secular and religious simultaneously. It is exceedingly practical in that it applies to everyday life, yet it is mysterious in the sense that it reveals the mind of God. It is secular in the sense that it belongs to everyone but religious in its holiness. This wisdom is a prism through which we may interpret the world around us and vice versa, and it is a tool that may be employed in the redemption of fallen things, including political economies such as postmodern capitalism.

Wisdom is described in the Bible as follows:

Wisdom has built her house; she has set up its seven pillars. She has prepared her meat and mixed her wine; she has also set her table. She has sent out her servants, and she calls from the highest point of the city, "Let all who are simple come to my house!" To those who have no sense she says, "Come, eat my food and drink the wine I have mixed. Leave your simple ways and you will live; walk in the way of insight." ... The fear of the Lord is the beginning of wisdom, and knowledge of the Holy One is understanding. (Prov. 9:1–6, 10)

All that one needs for sustenance and pleasure is in wisdom's "house." She calls from the "highest point in the city" because her offer is to everyone, especially those who do not yet know her (that is, the "simple"), and the rewards are life, enlightenment, and knowledge of God. Conversely, in the following verses (13–18), Folly makes her invitation to a similar banquet, but her house is full of "stolen water" and forbidden foods, that while "sweet" and "delicious" for a while, ultimately result in a banquet of death and destruction. The choice could not be clearer.

The New Testament epistle of James, the brother of Jesus, makes a similar contrast between two kinds of wisdom, worldly wisdom and Godly wisdom.

> Who is wise and understanding among you? Let them show it by their good life, by deeds done in the humility that comes from wisdom. But if you harbor bitter envy and selfish ambition in your hearts, do not boast about it or deny the truth. Such "wisdom" does not come down from heaven but is earthly, unspiritual, demonic. For where you have envy and selfish ambition, there you find disorder and every evil practice. But the wisdom that comes from heaven is first of all pure; then peace loving, considerate, submissive, full of mercy and good fruit, impartial and sincere. Peacemakers who sow in peace reap a harvest of righteousness. (James 3:13–18)

This latter listing is presumably the seven pillars mentioned in Proverbs 9:1. The choice, again, could not be starker. "Selfish ambition" is seen as "demonic" because it violates the most basic precepts of charity and is on a par with greed in its wickedness.

In the context of economic activity and business specifically, biblical wisdom would seem to be at odds with conventional wisdom about how one should conduct one's affairs. The dog-eat-dog world of business seems out of touch with peaceable behavior, yet as we discovered earlier, Adam Smith would not have thought so. He would have agreed with the basic premise that good business requires moral behavior and would have been scandalized to see how far contemporary business practices have drifted from ethical moorings.

At first consideration, we might conclude that invoking biblical wisdom in the world of business is a fantasy, yet like so many other assumptions about capitalism, it is an assumption with no basis in fact. Historically the opposite is true, as shown by the biblically informed ethical codes of medieval guilds, Calvin's Geneva, the merchant advice manuals of the mercantile era, and the numerous codes of business conduct and corporate credos that permeated the business landscape of America in the early part of the twentieth century. While the question still needs to be proven in today's economy, it is likely more viable than not, given that certain values are equally rooted in both secular and religious thought. Clearly, though, an older model of this virtue-based economy cannot be religiously legislated, but it must be the result of cultural changes, an understanding of common agreement regarding the value of ethics, and a shared view toward the renewal of hearts and minds. Before embarking on such a mission, however, we might find it worthwhile to consider the nature of these seven pillars in light of their application to contemporary business and economics.

Purity, the first pillar described by the apostle James, comes from the Greek root word *hágios,* often used to describe things that are pure from within, even holy. The connotation is that divine wisdom is different from the world's wisdom. It is not cleverness, and it does not rely on utility for its benefits to be self-evident. It is fundamentally good, and it is driven by a desire to *be* good and *do* good, regardless of personal cost. In the context of business and economics, purity applies to both motive and action, intention and consequence.

Consider for a moment a company's decision to lay off employees. Such a decision is not in and of itself an immoral act. At times, companies must restructure businesses for a variety of reasons, often beyond their control. If the motive for such a decision is the long-term viability of the company, and if it is done in a way that treats the laid-off workers as people, not redundant resources, and ensures that their well-being is taken into full consideration before they are let go, restructuring may, in fact, be a wise and ethical thing to do.

Imagine a very different motive for restructuring a business. Imagine a publicly traded company that is doing well but whose top executives have millions of shares in outstanding stock options. Imagine one of those executives insisting on the restructuring of a subsidiary for the express purpose of informing stock analysts on an upcoming conference call that the division in question would increase its short-term profitability, thereby garnering a buy recommendation from those analysts. Imagine this recommendation driving up the stock price and the executive in question exercising his options, pocketing millions of dollars in the process.

Decisions such as this are perfectly legal and happen all of the time, but often at great expense to the people who lose their jobs, as well as to their families and their communities. Ironically, the long-term interests of the companies' other stakeholders are also lost. The wisdom of such a decision is not determined by a short-term economic result but by the purity of the executive's motives. Individual or corporate motives and the actions they produce must be morally pure in order for them to be considered genuinely wise.

Peacefulness, the second pillar of wisdom, comes from the Greek root word *eiréné,* implying a desire to seek the common good. This is the same word normally translated *welfare* in the Septuagint translation of Jeremiah 29:7, and it is the Greek equivalent of the Hebrew word *shalom.* In Jeremiah 29, the people of Israel who have been taken into exile are encouraged to get on with economic activity—to "build houses, plant vineyards," and so on—and to "seek the peace and prosperity of the city . . . because if the city prospers [they] too will prosper" (Jer. 29:7).

The implication here is that economic activity exists first and foremost for the purpose of promoting the general welfare of the people, not merely for the accumulation of personal wealth for a few enterprising individuals. This is not a uniquely Hebraic concept. Belief in a constellation of peace, harmony, welfare, and liberty as fundamental to a well-ordered society are at the heart of the American experiment. Consider the words of the preamble to the US Constitution:

> We the People of the United States, in Order to form a more perfect Union, establish Justice, insure domestic Tranquility, provide for the common defense, promote the general Welfare, and secure the Blessings of Liberty to ourselves and our Posterity, do ordain and establish this Constitution for the United States of America.

The American founders believed in a society where the poor were provided for, and where the opportunity for extrication from poverty was paramount. Thomas Jefferson, who was himself a large landowner, agreed with Adam Smith that inheritances and primogeniture enshrined economic inequality that was unjustifiable and immoral. Even Benjamin Franklin, whose teachings, according to Max Weber, gave impetus to America's ethic of economics, believed that the best way to alleviate poverty was to create an economic environment conducive to economic opportunity for all. Today's economic reality is quite the opposite of the one envisioned by America's founders. One percent of Americans today have an annual income thirty-eight times greater than 90 percent of their fellow Americans,[5] and the overall concentration of wealth among America's richest households is the worst among eighteen Organization for Economic Cooperation and Development (OECD) countries.[6]

Of greater concern is the difficulty people at the bottom of the economic ladder, especially people of color, have in accessing investment capital for their small businesses. According to a recent report by the Congressional Black Caucus Foundation, minority-owned businesses are three times more likely to be turned down for business loans than white-owned businesses, and when they are given business loans, they pay much higher interest rates.[7] Even within corporate America itself, there are staggering inequalities. According to a recent report in the *New York Times*, while executive pay fell slightly between 2014 and 2015, the average CEO of a company with revenue in excess of $1 billion still has an annual salary that is five hundred twenty-three times the average American's full-time salary.[8] Additionally, the top rates of individual income and capital gains taxes went from approximately 40 percent (39.6%) and 21 percent respectively in the 1990s, when the United States enjoyed a budget surplus, to 35 percent and approximately 16 percent (16.1%) in the 2000s when America's national debt began to soar.[9]

Inequalities of this magnitude are unsustainable and dangerous, and they lead to a plethora of other social ills such as crime, drug addiction, suicide, teen pregnancy, and the very economic enslavement that Franklin, Jefferson, and others scorned in their desire to "promote the general welfare."

The third biblical pillar of wisdom is *consideration of others*, or *gentleness*, from the Greek *epieikés,* which relates specifically to how people treat each other.

When I was in the corporate world, I worked with many CEOs who had Type A personalities. They were often outgoing, but they were also demanding and did not suffer fools. Some were bullies. They were rude and dismissive of other people's needs and emotions, and in some cases they were borderline narcissistic. They seemed to thrive on demeaning others and insisted on lock-step allegiance to them and their agendas. Especially unbecoming was their treatment of people in the service professions or those at the bottom of the corporate ladder. They invariably created toxic work environments and rarely retained top talent because of it.

Others—those who embodied the seven pillars, especially that of consideration—learned to control their egos in ways that their peers and subordinates respected, and they were generally successful; but they were not the best-known CEOs by a long shot. Despite popular opinion, the best chief executives are not the tyrants one reads about; they are the gentle giants who are happy not to have their names in the business press and who prefer to run healthy organizations full of happy and productive employees.

Consider the example of Lars Rebien Sørensen, former CEO of Danish drug maker Novo Nordisk, who, according to the 2015 Harvard Business Review rankings, was first among senior executives worldwide. Despite the company's exceptional performance, Sørensen was paid a fraction of what a similarly ranked executive would make in the United States. His rationale was the fact that while he did not make as much money as a US executive, he still made more money in a year than most of his employees would make over the course of their entire careers. He also believed in creating a cohesive work environment, and huge wage disparities can cause resentment that is not conducive to collaborative working and decision by consensus.

Furthermore, despite being a publicly traded company, Novo Nordisk uses triple bottom-line accounting (that is, combining financial results with environmental and social concerns) to assess its annual performance. Most publicly traded companies manage to a series of short-term economic metrics; Novo Nordisk measures its economic performance with a twenty- to twenty-five-year view in mind and with social and environmental horizons that are both immediate and forward-looking. Perhaps Mr. Sørensen summed it up best when, at the close of an interview with Harvard Business Review relating to his position at the top of their rankings, he stated,

> I should have said at the beginning that I don't like this notion of the "best-performing CEO in the world." That's an American perspective—you lionize individuals. I would say I'm leading a team that is collectively creating one of the world's best-performing companies. That's different from being the world's best-performing CEO—it's a very big difference, especially in a business in which the timelines are 20 or 25 years.[10]

It is a very big difference indeed, and one that reflects Mr. Sørensen's wisdom.

The next pillar of wisdom is *submissiveness* or *reasonableness*, from the Greek word *eupeithēs*. The Greek word itself is a rather unusual compound that literally means "well persuaded" and suggests someone who is willing to listen to the counsel of others, not someone obstinate or headstrong. One of the most common mistakes we make as a society is confusing reasonableness with indecision. Many politicians have paid the price for flip-flopping on issues, when in fact they may have simply been acting on better information or the advice of someone whose opinions are trustworthy.

Obstinacy and hubris in business are often the result of leaders possessing an over-inflated confidence in their own cognitive abilities. The corporate world is full of people whose inflated sense of self caused them to act recklessly and without proper counsel, eventually leading to spectacular, even catastrophic, downfalls. One film about the rise and fall of the Enron Corporation, an energy-trading and utilities company, was aptly entitled *The Smartest Guys in the Room*, a self-assessment that some of the executives maintained to the end. But they were not as smart as they supposed, and when the markets and the authorities finally caught up with them, they caused a collapse of unequaled proportions costing several fortunes and ruining countless lives.

Obstinacy, of course, is not reserved for the boardroom; it is also a common problem among policy makers and their advisors. Many people in high office have shipwrecked their administrations because they refused to listen to sound advice, or worse, created environments where dissent was either ignored or censured.

That said, as with all virtuous acts, exercising reasonableness can come at great personal cost. In 1988, then Vice President George H. W. Bush famously ran for president on the slogan "read my lips, no new taxes." Sadly for him, two years later as president, he was faced with both a ballooning national deficit and a hostile Congress, and instead of bringing the country to a standstill over the budget, or perpetuating a tax regime that was no longer fit for purpose, he made a courageous decision to raise taxes. Within two years of that decision, the deficit had peaked and a few years later, the economy was accelerating and the country was running a budget surplus. He paid a big price for doing the right thing, losing the next presidential election, but history has shown the wisdom and reasonableness of that decision.

Mercy and *good fruits* comprise the next pillar of wisdom, and they are in fact, two sides of the same coin. *Mercy*, from the Greek word *eleos*, relates specifically to love that is expressed within the context of a covenantal relationship. That is to say, it stems more from a sense of mutual interdependence and frailty than a sense of executive pardon for particular transgressions. It is a state of mind that exhibits compassion and a duty of care. Similarly, *good fruits* would seem to be a veiled reference to the "fruits of the Spirit" from Galatians 5:22–23, which are "love, joy, peace, forbearance, kindness, goodness, faithfulness, gentleness, and self-control." Mercy of this kind seeks reconciliation instead of retribution; it seeks opportunities for learning instead of demerit, remedial assistance instead of dismissal, and a cool hand instead of a hot head.

Once, when I was appointed to a senior role in a multi-national business, I was faced with a difficult decision concerning one of my direct reports. He had been with the company for many years and I was an outsider. He had applied for my job and then had to watch me assume the role that he had aspired to. It could have been a very difficult situation for us both. The first day on the job, my boss told me that I had his blessing if I chose to fire the fellow, and I confess it went through my mind as a quick and easy solution to a potentially serious problem. I decided, however, that it was neither the right thing to do nor was it the wise thing to do. Why should he lose his job when he hadn't actually done anything to deserve it? Any concern about his future behavior would have been an unfair assumption on my part, at best; besides, he was clearly a very loyal and capable person.

Instead, I made him my most trusted advisor. I created a new role for him so he would not feel passed over and humiliated by having hit a glass ceiling. And I gave him more responsibility for the parts of the business he enjoyed most and took the things that frustrated him off his plate. The result was not only a highly functioning team but also the formation of a close personal friendship that lasts to this day. I relate this, not because I was a particularly capable executive, but because it taught me that I could overcome many of my own deficiencies by doing the wise thing instead of the expedient thing; it is a lesson I have never forgotten.

The next pillar of wisdom is *impartiality*, from another somewhat obscure Greek word *adiakritos,* which might just as easily be translated "without prejudice," and there are few principles more important to a just society than freedom from prejudice, especially in economic affairs. Older Americans remember well the story of the very brave woman Rosa Parks who in December 1955 refused to accept the discriminatory policies of the Montgomery City [Bus] Lines and forfeit her seat because of the color of her skin. It was an outrageous policy, supported by local segregation ordinances that produced similar policies across a wide range of businesses, from restaurants to movie theaters.

While blatant expressions of prejudice such as these may no longer exist in the United States, countless less obvious examples of economic prejudice still plague our culture, our economy, and our society. Otherwise capable people are regularly passed over for employment because of their age, or their ethnicity, or their sex, even though there are laws prohibiting such practices.

Then there are the banks that continue to redline certain neighborhoods for economic exclusion, and unscrupulous lenders that target those very same communities with offers of usurious loans.

The most rampant discrimination is not against a minority population but against the majority of our fellow citizens: women in the workforce. Despite study after study demonstrating the detrimental effects of gender inequality in the workplace, on average, women are paid about 20 percent less than men across the entire spectrum of the economy, and less than 5 percent of the companies listed on the Fortune 500 are run by women. While there may be some external factors that contribute to these statistics having to do with life choices that some women make, such as temporarily stepping away from a career to raise children, the numbers are simply too extreme not be attributable, at least in part, to gender discrimination.

It is not merely unfair for large swathes of the population to be locked out of the economy; it is also unwise for them to be discriminated against, given the gifts, skills, and contributions they are both willing and able to make. Consider the story of Katherine Johnson, Mary Jackson, and Dorothy Vaughan, three African American women who rose to senior positions in America's space program in the 1950s and 1960s. They are subjects of a recent Hollywood film entitled *Hidden Figures,* and it is not an exaggeration to say that, without them and their brilliant minds, the space program as we know it may not have been nearly as successful as it was. Their success was made possible only by a combination of their own determination not to be discriminated against and NASA's determination to employ the greatest minds available, despite the skin color of the people who possessed them. There are, no doubt, countless women and people of color who want to participate fully in our economic system, but they are held back by a combination of ignorance and prejudice that must be overcome. Goodness and wisdom require it.

Sincerity, the last pillar of wisdom, is derived from another compound word in the Greek—*anupokritos,* which technically means "without hypocrisy." In the Bible, Jesus disdained few things more than hypocrisy. He berated the religious leaders of his day for not practicing what they preached, saying,

> Woe to you, teachers of the law and Pharisees, you hypocrites! You give
> a tenth of your spices—mint, dill and cumin. But you have neglected
> the more important matters of the law—justice, mercy and faithful-

ness. You should have practiced the latter, without neglecting the former . . . on the outside you appear to people as righteous but on the
inside you are full of hypocrisy and wickedness. (Matt. 23:23–28, sel.)

One wonders what Jesus would have to say to religious leaders today who
preach justice and mercy on Sunday but turn a blind eye to economic injustice
from Monday to Saturday, or who publicly support political positions that
entrench gross economic inequalities.

Americans have always been distrustful of government and tend to resent
the tax system; this is a throwback to our days as political revolutionaries in the
eighteenth century. Yet we have always been a people of great liberality, especially in the private sector. In fact, private donors in America do more to support
worthy causes around the world than many governments do, but in recent years
we seem to have lost our passion for generosity. After World War Two, the
United States contributed nearly five percent of its GDP to help rebuild Europe
in what became known as the Marshall Plan, an act of national generosity that
was unprecedented in its day and remains unequaled to this day. It was more
than just a financial recovery plan; it was an expression of American ideals. The
people of Europe were suffering and the US government believed that it had a
moral obligation to help alleviate that suffering. In a spirit reminiscent of the
founders before them, America's leaders saw direct investment in infrastructure
and other means of production as the best way to ensure Europe's long-term
economic success. Of course, this was not only a generous thing to do; it was a
wise thing to do, as it created future markets for American goods, supported the
free enterprise system, and created a bulwark against Soviet aggression.

In contrast, consider how the US government and Federal Reserve Bank
responded to the recent global financial crisis. While they did much to stem
the looming economic meltdown, they did even more to improve the balance
sheets of the very investment banks that caused the crisis. One wonders how
much of the money given over to Wall Street ever made it to Main Street.
With income and wealth inequalities at an all-time high and with many of the
same bad practices that led to the financial crisis reemerging, another crisis is
not unlikely. The question remains whether the government and the Federal
Reserve are willing to take the steps necessary to protect the average American
from the next crisis, or will they hypocritically and unwisely claim to "promote
the general welfare" while further enriching those at the top?

Virtue—Putting Wisdom into Practice

The subject of virtue has been on the minds of philosophers and theologians for millennia, and for good reason: moral reasoning is one of the things that separate us from other species. That is why an understanding of Aquinas's theology of virtue requires an understanding of his theology of the soul, which he believes to be as much a part of human nature as our bodies. According to Aquinas, human beings are created in the image of God and possess both reason and intellect, which he calls the power of the soul.[11] Like Calvin, Aquinas sees this as a universal trait and one that corresponds to "natural reason,"[12] although he emphasizes the need for human beings to cultivate virtue through the exercise of good habits.[13] As with the aforementioned definition of *hokmah* (Hebrew wisdom), virtue exists, not as an abstract concept, but only in its application. In order to be virtuous, individuals, groups, companies, and societies must do virtuous things.

As I noted previously, the mother of all virtues is prudence, because prudence gives intellectual agency to the development of the moral virtues of justice, courage, and temperance. Prudence involves the use of our cognitive abilities to discern what is or is not true, good, and right. It requires consideration of both the ends and the means of our choices, both their causes and their effects. Those who exercise prudence, therefore, must always be forward-thinking, which constitutes a considerable challenge for those who operate within the sphere of political economy.

First consider the plight of corporate executives who make countless decisions that have both short-term and long-term effects on their businesses and, by extension, the welfare of their stakeholders. While many of those decisions may appear to be simple economic choices that can be made on a risk/reward or pleasure/pain calculus, they are often much more complicated. Consider something as seemingly benign as the purchase of component parts for the manufacture of jet engines.

Jet engines are extremely complex and comprised of thousands of individual parts sourced from countless suppliers around the world. The jet engine business is also a highly competitive one, with a handful of manufacturers constantly vying for the same commercial and military contracts every day. One of the ways a manufacturer will seek a competitive edge while retaining its profit margins is to strategically source parts at the best possible price and the best possible payment terms. Manufacturers regularly pit one potential supplier against another until they are confident they have secured the best deal for the company. What happens to the suppliers is generally their problem, as long as they meet the technical requirements of the manufacturer and deliver the desired parts on time and in full. The reasoning behind this process is driven by a commonly held belief in the benefits of "ethical egoism" whereby each actor in a process acts according to his or her own self-interest, ultimately culminating in a satisfactory result for everyone in the chain. This is a logical extension of the invisible hand theory and, generally speaking, it works; however, its efficacy can have serious limitations, especially in the long term.

Often the suppliers who bid on contracts are much smaller entities than the companies to whom they sell. They are often so dependent upon their largest customers that if they were to lose one of them, they would go out of business. They also operate on tight profit margins and often suffer unfavorable payment terms. The combination of high customer concentration and extended payment terms makes it difficult for them to obtain credit from mainstream banks, and so they often have to resort to alternative financing arrangements such as invoice financing, which can be very expensive, further increasing the pressure on their own solvency.

In the short term, the jet engine manufacturers do well in this scenario, but in the long term, they may encounter unforeseen problems. For instance, they may unintentionally put a valued supplier out of business and find that their prices actually go up as a result, while the quality of the parts goes down. If the bankrupt supplier operates in the same community as the manufacturer, their demise could incite public outcry or even industrial action against the manufacturer. In the worst case, it could be that the manufacturer actually receives defective parts, either from a new supplier or from an existing supplier that cuts corners in order to survive. This happens often, with potentially catastrophic consequences.

Even the internal decisions of companies to either cut corners or ignore established protocols and safeguards can be extremely dangerous. This was the case with jet engine manufacturer Rolls Royce, who admitted in 2013 that they knowingly used faulty feed pipes in the manufacture of engines used on the Airbus A380. One of these planes suffered serious engine failure in 2010 on route from Singapore to Sydney, Australia, with 464 people on board. Fortunately, no one was injured in this particular case, as the plane was able to make an emergency landing, but it cost Rolls Royce millions of dollars in compensation claims to Qantas Airlines while also seriously damaging the company's reputation.[14]

A prudent executive should have foreseen the potential for catastrophe in using defective parts, yet someone somewhere in the organization decided to take that risk in order to meet the company's own supply obligations to Airbus. The invisible hand had come to the end of its usefulness in this instance and required the application of an ethic other than that of ethical egoism. Forward-thinking requires the application of virtue ethics and, in this case, prudence.

A similar argument for a higher ethic can be made regarding public policy decision-making. Consider the dilemma of local authorities in areas where applications have been made for permission to drill for oil or shale gas using a process known as fracking. Fracking involves the introduction of water, sand, and chemicals at high velocity into shale beds and other rock formations to force out oil and gas that can then be harnessed for domestic energy use. On the surface, this seems like an easy decision to make. Who doesn't want to exploit the use of relatively cheap and easily accessible domestic energy sources when the perceived alternative is the importation of oil from places such as the Middle East, Russia, and Venezuela? From a short-term perspective there are only advantages to be had, especially for those communities where otherwise dormant land will be used to create significant revenue streams. But if one takes a longer-term view, the benefits become less obvious and the risks more pronounced.

Fracking is still a relatively new process and the environmental impact of its wide-scale use is still uncertain. Unnatural seismic activity related to fracking has been reported, and concerns have been expressed about contamination of local groundwater supplies. Fracking also produces fossil fuels that, when compared to renewable energy sources, are less environmentally desirable. Prudence demands that before granting fracking licenses on a wide scale, further research would be in order to ensure that the rewards outweigh the risks and that the risks posed are not existential in nature. In the current climate, however, political decisions that put long-term considerations before immediacy call for courage, prudence, humility, and all the pillars of wisdom.

In each example above, prudence and culture share a clear relationship. The ability or inability of someone to make a prudent decision is directly related to whether that person habitually makes prudent decisions and whether the decision-maker is expected to use forward-thinking or expediency.

Consider again the case of Rolls Royce. While it is certainly possible that the decision to put expediency before safety was an aberration, other recent events would suggest otherwise. In January 2017, the company announced that it had agreed to pay fines totalling £671 million to the UK's Serious Fraud Office, the US Justice Department, and the Brazilian government after admitting to bribery charges against its intermediaries in India, China, Indonesia, and Thailand. It was one of the worst scandals in British corporate history and one that rocked the entire sector. It would be easy to assume that the perpetrators were local business people who simply succumbed to the notorious custom of offering and taking bribes in those markets, but according to the prosecutor, such was not the case. According to an article on the BBC website, "Sir Brian Leveson, President of the Queen's bench division, stated that 'the conduct involved senior (on the face of it, very senior) Rolls-Royce employees.'"[15]

It is common knowledge among international business people that both UK and US corporate law strictly prohibits the giving or taking of bribes, and Rolls Royce's intermediaries would have known this. The amounts of money involved (millions of British pounds) would have required approval from the highest echelons of the company. The protestations of the company's CEO notwithstanding, it appears a culture existed within Rolls Royce that, at the very least, tolerated unethical behavior.

Conversely, fracking in the UK has not yet commenced on anything other than a trial basis, largely because the Balcombe Parish Council in West Sussex, along with other local governments, has refused to allow widespread fracking until all of the facts are in regarding health and environmental concerns. How did the government get away with it? Very simply, through a culture of prudence that expects public officials to show a duty of care to their constituents, their progeny, and the environment and that exceeds their concern for immediate financial gain. This culture did not develop overnight; it took time for this expectation to evolve. In keeping with Aquinas's teaching, virtue must be habitual in order for it to be genuine.

Creating a culture of prudence is a difficult task, but so too is the cultivation of justice. The word *justice* is derived from the Latin *jus,* which indicates an etymological relationship between law and rights. To do justice is to ensure that every individual is granted his or her natural rights as well as legal rights. Unlike the other moral virtues that deal with self-regulation, justice relates specifically to how human beings treat each other. Justice demands that people be treated equally and with dignity and respect. Favoritism based on attributes other than merits is prohibited, and economic dealings must be fair and equitable.

Aquinas was especially critical of what we would call systemic prejudice today. He was explicit in his condemnation of what he called "respect of persons":

> For instance if you promote a man to a professorship on account of . . . the fact that he is this particular man . . . then there is respect of the person, since you give him something not for some cause that renders him worthy of it, but simply because he is this person. And . . . if a man promote someone to a prelacy or a professorship, because he is rich or because he is a relative of his, it is respect of persons.[16]

The "old boy network," blatant nepotism, and similar privileges violate the precepts of justice because they provide preferential treatment for an undeserving few while denying equal access to those without connections or pedigree. The expression "it isn't what you know, but whom you know that matters" is an example of an entrenched belief in the respect of persons, and it is ultimately detrimental to the economic wellbeing of society.

Under the guise of networking, the children of the so-called "great and good" often occupy coveted places at top universities, only to graduate from those universities to assume corporate positions at the country's largest and most influential companies, especially banks. In America the path leads from Andover to Yale to Morgan Stanley, and in the UK it goes from Eton to Cambridge to Goldman Sachs—and the numbers speak for themselves. At Goldman Sachs, ten percent of the work force hold degrees from Oxford or Cambridge, yet those institutions represent only one percent of university graduates. Similarly, nearly eight percent (7.8%) of Morgan Stanley's employees went to Ivy League schools, even though they represent less than one half of one percent (0.4%) of university students.[17] This phenomenon continues on executive boards and compensation committees, where members award each other large salaries and bonuses, exacerbating problems associated with the excessive concentration of wealth in the hands of fewer and fewer people.

Another area of economic injustice rests in tax codes, which have become so complex and so influenced over the years by special interests that they are genuinely unfair to the overwhelming majority of working people, including the middle class. During his campaign for the presidency in 2016, then-candidate Donald J. Trump argued that the system was rigged in favor of the very rich and promised to eliminate the "carried interest provision" of the tax code, which essentially allows investors, particularly hedge fund managers, to treat their profits as capital gains instead of ordinary income, with the latter being taxed more heavily than the former. (The final 2017 bill, however, kept this provision intact.) He also promised to make the tax system simpler by introducing a $30 thousand basic tax exemption (reduced to $24 thousand in the final bill), reducing the number of tax brackets from seven to four (but the final bill increased them to eight), and limiting the number of itemized deductions allowable to $200 thousand per household (a provision dropped from the final bill). In addition, he pledged to cut the corporation tax from 35 percent to 15 percent (21 percent in the final bill) and to allow independent contractors and similar businesses that pay taxes on earned income at personal tax rates to pay the lower rate instead. Finally, he proposed to reduce the top income tax bracket from just below 40 percent (39.6 percent) to 25 percent (35 percent in the final bill) and promised that the net result of these changes would be "revenue neutral" to the treasury.

Whether or not the overall result will, in fact, be revenue neutral is questionable. The Congressional Budget Office has calculated that the new tax law will add something on the order of $1.5 trillion to the annual budget deficit, but what is blatantly obvious is that the highest wage earners will receive the greatest tax break.[18] If, in fact, the highest wage earners have the most to gain from this, and if the national debt is impacted as anticipated, this law will be the epitome of economic injustice, as it not only disproportionately benefits the rich at the expense of others, but it also burdens our progeny, who are already facing debt levels that are nearly unimaginable.

Of equal concern is the general attitude Americans appear to share about the nature of taxes and their usefulness to society. Even Adam Smith understood the benefits of a reasonable and fair tax system that served the common good. But when challenged during the 2016 presidential debates about his own personal income taxes, which candidate Trump refused to release to the public, he did not deny using available tax loopholes to pay no personal income tax on hundreds of millions of dollars of revenue. Instead, he famously stated that doing so made him "smart." The lack of national outcry was deafening. While it is fair to say that no reasonable person wants to pay more than his or her fair share of taxes, it is uncivil and unjust for the wealthy to glory in not paying theirs. As the late New York real estate investor Leona Helmsley famously quipped, "only the little people pay taxes," a comment she no doubt regretted when she was later convicted of income tax evasion.

Aquinas also subscribed to the concept of *epikeia*, which supports the theory that law itself is an imperfect instrument in the provision of justice and that there may be unintended consequences to certain laws that actually frustrate the common good. In those cases, the "letter of the law" should be discarded in favor of *epikeia,* which he also called "equity."[19]

One case in point might be that of the Royal Bank of Scotland (RBS), and its now-infamous "Project Dash for Cash." In the wake of the global financial crisis, RBS, like many other banks, found itself over-leveraged. In an effort to improve its revenues and its cash position, as well as to reduce its exposure to bad debt, it instructed its bank managers to seek out business customers for possible transfer to its Global Restructuring Group (formerly known as the Special Lending Service). Once under the "care" of the bank's restructuring division, customers were hit with a combination of large management fees and newly reconstituted loans at higher interest rates. In many cases, the bank's practices pushed the companies over the edge, resulting in their insolvencies. Particularly disturbing was that the bank purposefully targeted its smallest and most vulnerable corporate customers and put its desire for profits above its primary function, which was to help turn around struggling businesses.

Subjecting small family firms to this kind of treatment while continuing to treat larger customers in a preferential manner may be legal, but it violates a reasonable concept of justice. The UK Financial Conduct Authority has censured the bank accordingly. The bank has already set aside over £400 million in anticipation of settlements to customers filing civil actions against the bank. As one might expect, the bank's CEO insisted that, "the culture, structure and way RBS operates today is fundamentally different from the period under review."[20] Whether that statement is true remains to be seen; however, the bank, the majority of which has been owned by the British taxpayers since being bailed out in 2009, still faces serious difficulties, especially with its balance sheet. If recent history has proven anything, it is that struggling companies, including banks, are tempted to make unethical decisions when faced with possible insolvency.

Another form of economic injustice is predatory lending. Before 1978, each state in the United States had usury laws that capped the level of interest that could be charged on loans, including credit cards. Some states, though, had higher rates than others. In 1978, the Supreme Court of the United States ruled that credit card companies could charge whatever rates of interest they wanted, as long as the rates charged did not exceed the top rate allowed in each credit card company's home state. That meant credit card companies could set up shop in places such as South Dakota, where the top rate is 18 percent, and solicit credit card customers nationwide. This opened up the floodgates, and soon credit card use became a national epidemic with, as noted previously, the average American household now owing $16 thousand in credit card debt, not to mention student loans, car loans, and mortgages. All told, US consumer debt is nearly four times the average family income.[21]

Especially troubling about this phenomenon is the disproportionate amount of debt held by poor people and people of color, who often use high-interest credit cards to manage their monthly finances, sometimes having to take out pay-day loans, another high-interest vehicle, to pay their credit card debt on time. They are targeted because they are the most needy and because they are often unaware of the cycle of debt they are getting themselves into.

As Dennis Hollinger notes in *Choosing the Good*, when it comes to issues of justice and economics, "Christians have no choice.... Scripture is clear in its mandate to pursue justice, love mercy and to respond with care to those in economic need."[22] The challenge to thought-leaders or policy-makers to speak out against economic injustice is great: doing so rocks the boat, but the virtue of courage requires that people of good will do exactly that.

Aquinas describes courage, or fortitude, as "establishing the rectitude of reason in human affairs,"[23] which seems to contradict the commonly held notion of courage as an irrational, impassioned response to injustice. In fact, the opposite is true. For courage to be genuinely virtuous it must be rooted in reason and wisdom, not rage or sentiment. That is why elected governments are ultimately subject to the decisions of courts, which remove the passionate nature of political discourse from the equation and make judicial decisions based upon logical assessments of the facts and the rule of law. It is also why freedom of speech is necessarily protected in civilized societies, as it ensures the uninhibited expression of ideas, especially when those ideas challenge the status quo, or more importantly, challenge entrenched power structures.

While the expression "speak truth to power" may have its origins in the Quaker movement's desire to launch a non-violent civil rights movement in the 1950s, its effective genesis may be found in the prophetic voices of the Bible, both the Old and New Testaments. Speaking on behalf of a good and a righteous God, religious leaders from Moses to Jesus gave comfort to the oppressed while starkly admonishing those who would deny them their rights. It is in the spirit of their example that Roman Catholic pontiffs from Pope Leo XIII (*Rerum Novarum*, 1891) to Pope Paul VI (*Populorum Progressio*, 1967) to Pope John Paul II (*Laborem Exercens*, 1981 and *Centesimus Annus*, 1991) to the current Pope Francis I (*Laudato si'*, 2015) have written encyclicals specifically addressing injustices in the area of political economy. In these documents commonly known as "Catholic Social Teaching," the church has been highly critical of certain economic practices, including excesses in the financial services sector, unfair labor practices, and exploitation of the environment. Raising the church's voice without resorting to political bias or vitriol, Pope Francis says,

> Underlying the principle of the common good is respect for the human person as such, endowed with basic and inalienable rights ordered to his or her integral development. It has also to do with the overall welfare of society and the development of a variety of intermediate groups, applying the principle of subsidiarity. Outstanding among those groups is the family, as the basic cell of society. Finally, the common good calls for social peace, the stability and security provided by a certain order which cannot be achieved without particular concern for distributive justice; whenever this is violated, violence always ensues. Society as a whole, and the state in particular, are obliged to defend and promote the common good.[24]

The pope was roundly criticized at the time for this encyclical by senior politicians on the political Right, including most Republican presidential candidates, but he held his ground nonetheless.

It is not only religious leaders who have taken a brave stance against the excesses of postmodern capitalism. Even multibillionaires such as Bill

Gates and Warren Buffet have lamented at the market's inability to address extreme poverty and the rising inequality brought on by excessive wealth concentration. Gates famously agreed with several of Thomas Piketty's basic assumptions about wealth distribution, and Buffet purportedly confided to President Barack Obama that markets alone are ill-equipped to address issues of inequality. While the number of individuals committed to the Giving Pledge, whereby the wealthiest people in the world dedicate the majority of their resources to philanthropic causes, has grown, any talk of wealth redistribution is bound to upset a great number of people because it simply does not fit into their doctrinaire *laissez faire* narrative.

In fact, it would not be an exaggeration to suggest that doctrinaire positions on both sides of the political spectrum have hijacked political discourse, especially in the United States. Entrenched political views are polarizing people without actually contributing to the discussion in a reasoned and logical manner. Consider for a moment the debate over a living wage.

The living wage, that is, a wage sufficient to cover one's cost of living in a particular area, is an extension of the minimum wage that regulates the minimum salary employers may pay employees for their labor. Those who oppose the concept argue that it interferes with the free market and is therefore a fundamentally bad idea. They also argue that the economic value of some work simply is not worth an increasing minimum wage and suggest that regularly increasing the minimum wage ultimately forces companies to lay off workers, causing harm to everyone, especially those whom the minimum wage is designed to protect. Those who argue in favor of increased minimum wage protection claim that without such legislation, employers will simply exploit their workers in order to maximize their own profits, and a living wage, they argue, is the minimum anyone should be expected to earn, regardless of the economic utility of their work.

Who is right? Well, in some ways, both. It is true that some jobs simply do not add enough value to the economy to support a living wage, and some low-wage earners could be made redundant if employers are required to pay them a living wage. For example, we may all have to bag our own groceries. But no evidence supports the notion that the imposition of a minimum wage is recessionary. In fact, recent research from the National Employment Law Project (NELP) shows no historic correlation between minimum wage increases and overall employment levels.[25]

The question then becomes, by what metric should a minimum wage be determined? The logic behind use of the living wage is simple and is based on both moral and economic reasoning. Simply put, every person possesses a certain degree of dignity, which may be expressed in economic terms. In other words, the fruits of every person's labor should, at the very least, be sufficient for his or her own subsistence. If this is not the case, the economy cannot be seen as properly functioning. As we noted earlier, Adam Smith would go even further. Smith argued that only when all workers make slightly more than required for subsistence can they become genuine participants in the economy, and the entire economy works best when everyone is fully contributing to and benefiting from it. Despite both the moral and economic arguments in its favor, the debate will continue over the relative benefits of instituting a living wage. It seems obvious to some, though, that the only real objection to the establishment of a living wage is the short-term effect it could have on companies' profits, which brings us to the last of the cardinal virtues, temperance.

How much is too much? Or perhaps the better question is how much is enough? As Aquinas himself notes, it is perfectly natural and reasonable for human beings to desire those things that give us pleasure; however, a virtuous person easily discerns that the moderation of all things is to his or her benefit. Pleasure without moderation appeals not to our higher instincts, but to our animal instincts,[26] and if left unchecked, it destroys individuals and societies.

Aquinas notes that temperance is required not only for the moderation of our natural desires, such as sexual pleasure and sustenance, but is also necessary for the moderation of our base emotions, such as anger, pride, and cruelty. Most striking about Aquinas's philosophy is his belief that human beings are equipped with a natural indicator that our appetites are out of control, which he calls "shamefacedness."[27] In other words, when we violate the precepts of temperance and give ourselves over to greed, gluttony, licentiousness, injustice, self-indulgence, and insensibility, we should be ashamed of ourselves and that shame should inspire us to self-correction.

This belief is not unlike Adam Smith's theory of "self-disapproval" and "blameworthiness";[28] however, Smith notes that culture has an important part to play in our self-censure, noting that,

When Nature formed man for society, she endowed him with a basic desire to please his brethren and a basic aversion to offending them.

She taught him to feel pleasure in their favourable regard and pain in their unfavourable regard. She made their approval most flattering and most agreeable to him for its own sake, and their disapproval most humiliating and most offensive.[29]

There was a time, Max Weber notes, when opulence and conspicuous consumption were seen as vulgar and were generally shunned by "polite so-ciety," especially among the Calvinist sects who took temperance to a new level. As capitalist societies have moved further and further away from their religious moorings, behavior once considered indecent is now celebrated by a culture that has lost a sense of shame. The accumulation of wealth has itself become a postmodern virtue, and a hedonistic tendency toward excessive self-indulgence has become the ideal. Of greatest concern, though, is that instead of compassion for the poor, our culture has developed contempt for the poor, which can only be seen as an abomination in the eyes of God.

As useful as common grace, wisdom, and the cardinal virtues are to the redemption of postmodern capitalism, three additional virtues are absolutely paramount to our best efforts, and they are the theological virtues of faith, hope, and love.

II

Faith, Hope, and Love—
Reclaiming the Theological Virtues

And now these three remain: faith, hope, and love. But the greatest of these is love.

1 CORINTHIANS 13:13

Once I was asked to address a civic group on the question of God's existence. I began by asking the audience: "Is there anyone here who doesn't live by faith?" One young man raised his hand. "Are you sure about that?" I asked. "Yes," he replied. I then asked him if he was carrying any money. He rather hesitantly produced a five-pound note. I took it from him and said, "I'll bet you this fiver that you not only live by faith, but that you order the majority of your life around a faith proposition." With that, I went on to explain the concept of fiat currency. "So you see," I explained, "you carry this little piece of paper in your pocket only because you believe that presenting it in a shop will secure five pounds' worth of goods from the shopkeeper. If the world were to lose faith in the pound, as happened to a dozen different currencies in the last century—including the German Deutschmark in the 1930s—this piece of paper would be worth nothing." I then proceeded to put it into my own pocket, much to the amusement of the audience, including the young man in question, to whom I eventually returned it, having made my point.

Reclaiming Faith in the Economy

The simple fact is we all live according to a wide variety of faith propositions, some more certain than others. The question is not whether we live by faith; the question is whether we believe in things *worthy* of our faith.

All of us put our faith in nature, for instance, even though our knowledge of it is relatively limited. Take for instance the experience of the first European sailors to travel south of the equator. They left the Northern Hemisphere assuming they could navigate by the stars, yet the constellations of the Southern Hemisphere are completely different from the night sky they were accustomed to and they had to adapt accordingly. Similarly, when early settlers traveled to the antipodes they were surprised that the seasons were reversed and instead of a spring planting had to rummage whatever they could find in preparation for the unexpected onset of winter. Nonetheless, we logically expect the earth to rotate on its axis and orbit the sun, and we expect gravity, the laws of thermodynamics, and the other laws of science to work as they always have, although technically there are no guarantees they will and no guarantees that their application will be useful in all circumstances.

Many put great faith in medical science, although most of us would likely be shocked to learn how inexact medical science is. We learn more every day about how the human body works. The more we learn, the more we realize that we have only just scratched the surface of medical knowledge. As advances are made in the development of genetically based treatments, for instance, it is not outrageous to think that future generations of physicians will view our current practices involving surgery, chemicals, radiation, and so on with the same combination of horror and amusement that we view leeching. Yet it is perfectly reasonable for people to have faith in medical science, even in its relatively primitive state.

Once we begin to move away from the physical sciences, people's faith begins to wane, as we must rely on other faculties besides our five senses. In order to have faith in something, we must first have some cognitive knowledge of it. Then, as with all virtues, it must become knowledge that is *applied*. Faith therefore has two parts, the object of our faith (that is, what we believe in) and its effect (that is, its application to our lives). This is true not only as it pertains to religious faith but to faith in all things.

Much has been written recently about our post-truth culture. Concepts such as fake news and alternative facts did not exist until very recently. Basically, we live in a post-truth culture because we live in a post-faith culture. We have lost faith in the veracity of our institutions, including the church, the government, the free press, and the markets. The hermeneutic of suspicion discussed in chapter 6 has produced a society in which unbelief is becoming the new norm, but without faith there can be no trust, and all social interactions are ultimately built on trust.

This is of grave concern to sociologists, theologians, and behavioral scientists, as well. As an article in the journal *Nature* notes,

> Trust pervades human societies. Trust is indispensable in friendship, love, families, and organizations and plays a key role in economic exchange and politics. In the absence of trust among trading partners, market transactions break down. In the absence of trust in a country's institutions and leaders, political legitimacy breaks down.[1]

Societies simply cannot function properly without faith properly applied.

Perhaps the most exhaustive exploration in Scripture of both faith as a concept and faith in action may be found in Hebrews 11. First, faith is defined as "confidence in what we hope for and assurance about what we do not see" (Heb. 11:1). In the next section of this chapter, we will take a closer look at the relationship between faith and hope, but it is the second part of the definition that is pertinent here. The notion of assurance, from the Greek *hypostasis*, is related to the substance or the reality of things that we cannot physically see. While such things cannot be seen they may still be perceived, and by their agency they are revealed as trustworthy.

A case in point would be the laws of aerodynamics, for which there is ample evidence, but which we cannot actually see. Someone once explained to me the relationship between thrust and lift and in doing so described how a two-hundred-ton airplane can stay in the sky. I did not actually demonstrate my faith in those laws until I strapped myself into an airplane seat and allowed it take off with me inside. That is faith: the reality and the trustworthiness of that which I cannot see, but that which I may experience as true.

The writer of Hebrews goes on then to describe the logic of believing in a God who cannot be seen but for whom there is more than ample evidence:

"By faith we understand that the universe was formed at God's command . . ." (Heb. 11:3) and " . . . anyone who comes to [God] must believe that he exists and that he rewards those who earnestly seek him" (Heb. 11:6). The author then proceeds to give an account of the faithfulness of God's people throughout history, and more importantly, of God's faithfulness to them. The moral of the story is the same as the apostle James's own admonition to the church that "faith without deeds is dead" (James 2:20). We must have faith in order to survive, and we must have faith in the right things if we are to flourish.

The motto printed on every US dollar is "In God We Trust," to some a curious maxim. Why would the currency of a supposedly secular state bear such a blatantly religious message? Interestingly, the motto was adopted when the United States was facing its greatest existential crisis, namely the Civil War. It is not uncommon for the feckless to seek the assistance of God when faced with the dread of uncertainty. Even President Lincoln himself is reported to have said,

> Nevertheless, amid the greatest difficulties of my Administration, when I could not see any other resort, I would place my whole reliance on God, knowing that all would go well, and that He would decide for the right.[2]

Seeking the redemption of postmodern capitalism, people of faith are called to stand firm in the conviction that faith is, as theologian Paul Tillich put it, our "ultimate concern."[3] The endeavor is not restricted to believers. The faculties necessary for the application of ethics in political economy are common to all, but their commonality does not preclude the requirement that participants have faith in something greater than themselves. Whether that is faith in God or in wonder at the evolutionary benefits of collective action, the proper functioning of an economy that works for everyone requires some form of transcendent faith.

We also need faith in our institutions, including governments, businesses, and media outlets. Our trust in those things has eroded to levels unimaginable less than ten years ago. In the United States, trust in government has been in decline since the assassination of President John F. Kennedy, the Vietnam War, and Watergate. In the UK, it has been in decline since the end of the Second World War. Since the onset of the global financial crisis and the proliferation of social media as sources of "news," the decline has been precipitous, with one commentator referring to it as an "implosion of trust."[4] Recent polls in Britain and the United States indicate that general dissatisfaction with the "establishment" is continuing unabated, and the populist movements filling the void have taken on characteristics reminiscent of more troubled times.

Faith in government is vital, because governments exist to uphold the rule of law. The alternatives to properly functioning governments are anarchy, mob rule, or dictatorships. Faith in business is vital because businesses create the wealth necessary for economic flourishing. Faith in the media is important because the media are our only bulwark against tyranny.

So why have we lost faith in these institutions? The reasons are many, but they gather at one clear point: a general perception that governments, businesses, and media outlets are fundamentally dishonest and self-serving and cannot, therefore, be trusted.

These concerns are not unfounded. Our governments have lied to us and in doing so have cost us dearly in blood and treasure. Our business and financial institutions have been deceptive and, often with the duplicitous cooperation of governments, have perpetrated great schemes against us, with little or no censure for their actions. Media outlets, often owned or controlled by large corporations or quasi-governmental entities, have themselves fallen under suspicion and are perceived as being biased collaborators instead of honest brokers of information. If people do not trust the veracity of mainstream news reports, they will get their news from their own online sources—unfiltered and often unverified. Basing their decisions on that information, they will form political opinions and produce democratically elected governments accordingly.

The problem with this scenario is that people tend to listen to the voices with whom they already identify, so instead of an uninformed electorate, which used to be the greatest threat to democracies, we have ill-informed electorates capable of producing reactionary, populist governments.

Simply put, people are afraid. Research shows that they are afraid about their future and the futures of their children and grandchildren. They are worried about an assortment of things over which they have little or no control. People are worried about globalization, terrorism, corruption, changing social values, and the overall pace of change.[5] As the old expression goes, "nature abhors a vacuum," and as we have seen over the centuries, if leaders are not addressing people's fears, and if institutions cannot be trusted, demagogues will happily fill the void. Demagogues are purveyors of false hope who promise much and deliver little, and before people realize what they have got themselves into, the damage has already been done.

The good news is that trust in individuals and institutions *can* be reestablished through the very habits espoused by Thomas Aquinas. This is not mere conjecture; it is supported by scientific research into how the body generates oxytocin, the chemical that sends "trust messages" to the brain. Paul J. Zak, founding director of the Center for Neuroeconomics Studies at Claremont Graduate University, and his team of researchers, inspired by Adam Smith's view of sympathy, conducted scientific experiments across a wide spectrum of cultures and concluded that human empathy is universal, as Smith suggested, and may be developed through the repeated practice of positive trust experiences.[6]

In other words, if we are going to redeem our current economic system, we will have to begin by changing the popular narrative of distrust and replace it with a narrative of faith. This is vital to our current task, as the only real antidote to fear is faith, and the fruits of faith are hope and love.

It is no coincidence that at the beginning of his book entitled *On the Threshold of Hope*, Pope John Paul II begins with a discussion, not of hope, but of fear. "Be not afraid," he reminds his readers, was the constant refrain of Jesus to his followers. "These are not words said into a void. They are profoundly rooted in the Gospels."[7]

The word *gospel*, of course, means good news, and Jesus's message was radically forward-looking and positive for those who believed and responded to his invitation. He regularly encouraged his followers to look beyond their meager surroundings and to focus on the future. As with the invitation of Lady Wisdom, discussed previously, Jesus offers his followers the opportunity to choose life through faith, instead of death through despair.

Restoring Hope and Confidence in the Economic System

The relationship between faith and hope is evidenced throughout holy writ. The psalms especially speak of faith and hope as being the antidote to fear of want (Ps. 9:18), fear of dishonor (Ps. 25:3), fear of oppression at the hands of the powerful (Ps. 31:23–24), fear of suffering (Ps. 119:48–50), and even the antidote to a downcast heart (Ps. 42:5).

The prophets, as well, spoke of the power of hope over despair:

> Even youths grow tired and weary and young men stumble and fall; but those who hope in the Lord will renew their strength. They will soar on wings like eagles; they will run and not grow weary, they will walk and not be faint. (Isa. 40:30–31)

In order for an economic system to be healthy, and in order for people to flourish, they must have faith in the system and hope for the future. Corruption, injustice, and fraud all breed cynicism and hopelessness, but honesty, justice, and integrity breed hope and confidence.

It starts first with a general belief in the ability of people to act in a virtuous manner, alongside a confidence that the law will protect people and their property without respect of persons. Next, there must be confidence in the ability of markets to operate without unnecessary interference or prejudice. There must be confidence in the value of currencies and the fiscal policies of the governments that back them. Lastly there must be a presumption of honest dealing but also transparency throughout the system.

When we consider the aftermath of the global financial crisis, we usually pay attention to the legislative response, such as the Dodd-Frank Wall Street Reform and Protection Act, which addressed some of the structural issues that caused the crash in the first place. Banks were subsequently required to hold more assets in reserve against their liabilities (so-called stress tests), consumers were afforded more protection against overly aggressive lending practices, the hedge fund industry was more closely regulated, as was the insurance industry, and processes were put in place to ensure the orderly liquidation of insolvent firms without necessitating government bail-outs. As important as those things were, they actually missed the big picture. The truly remarkable response to the global financial crisis was the election of Barack Obama, America's first African American president, who ran on a platform of unabashed hope with an autobiography entitled *The Audacity of Hope* and the campaign slogan, "Yes we can."

When the presidential campaign season began in early 2007, most people had never heard of Barack Obama. He was a young, black, first-term senator from Chicago with virtually no national experience, no political machinery behind him, and very little support from the political establishment. He did, however, have a message that seemed to resonate with people across the country. Even before the collapse of Lehman Brothers, then-Senator Obama sensed that people were frightened about the economic future of America, but instead of exploiting those fears, he dared people to face them with a spirit of optimism and hope.

Using the story of his own unlikely rise from life as the child of a mixed marriage (his father was a black Kenyan diplomat and his mother a white middle-class girl from Kansas) who grew up in racially charged 1960s America to a Harvard-educated United States senator, he convinced people that America was still the land of opportunity. He appealed to people's innate goodness and the ideals that shaped the American experiment. He rejected the bitter divisiveness of the political classes, and he dared people to embrace positive change over pessimism. While he won the Democratic nomination quite handily, he faced a seasoned and well-respected war veteran in Senator John McCain, the Republican candidate. When Lehman Brothers collapsed, the nation decided that it was time for change, and they were willing to risk their economic futures on the idealistic promises of a political novice.

This observation is not an endorsement of either President Obama or his policies but recognition of the power of optimism. His willingness to pursue what he believed to be the right thing to do, and the hopefulness it generated among voters—especially young voters and people of color—created a groundswell of support that resulted in his unlikely election. Hope is a precious commodity, but if the findings of *The Gallup-Hope Index 2015* are any indication, it is both in short supply and on the decline, especially among young people.

The Gallup-Hope Index is part of a project called Project Hope, which seeks to understand the aspirations of young people, especially as they pertain to their economic futures. As the report itself states, "*The Gallup-HOPE Index* is a one-of-a-kind survey that creates an annual benchmark of the economic vitality of the nation's young people."[8] It measures their economic literacy, their economic habits, and their economic ambitions. Students between the ages of ten and eighteen are asked whether they intend to start a business someday, whether they understand how business and economics work (on an age appropriate scale), whether they themselves are involved in economic activity during their student years, and whether they themselves have money in savings accounts.

On the one hand, the report is encouraging: many young people do see themselves as contributors to the future economic landscape. On the other hand, however, it is a tale of caution: those who see themselves as future entrepreneurs are in a minority and the numbers have been in decline for several years. If our young people lose hope in the future, we will be in dire shape indeed—and not just economically.

Many people have lost hope in our economic system because they have lost faith in the markets themselves. They do not see any obvious relationship between their own economic contributions (that is, their labor) and the wealth of those at the top of the pyramid, who appear to be spinning money according to their own devices. It has often been said that two emotions drive Wall Street: greed and fear. Neither are virtues. Those who have money want more of it, so they invest aggressively, driving the market up; however, once things begin to turn, fear of losing their fortunes causes people to sell, driving the market down. The key for investors, of course, is to buy low and sell high, but the swings and roundabouts caused by greed and fear, the hyper-activity of hedge funds, and the prevalence of high frequency trading (HFT) have created a lot of winners and a lot of losers, and the markets themselves have become divorced from the fundamentals of business.

That loss of faith and the accompanying loss of hope drive people to despair, the results of which can be devastating to society. If there is no confidence in the system, there will be no hope for our economic future.

Putting Love at the Center of Economic Activity

Lastly, there is the role of love in the economy, a virtue that has all but disappeared, much to our detriment. A while back I attended a lecture given by the former archbishop of Canterbury, Rowan Williams. He is a brilliant man of letters and a man of great faith, and I hold him in very high esteem. While he was describing his work on a committee of the House of Lords, I asked him why he did not use the word *love* in his description of the motives necessary for a properly functioning society. He had used every imaginable synonym, but not the word *love* itself. He thought for a while and then said, "I suppose it's because we don't want to appear sentimental when talking about these things," and of course, he was absolutely correct. People are often uncomfortable talking about love in the context of societal issues because our culture has reduced love to nothing more than a mawkish emotion. But the biblical definition of love is rooted in self-sacrifice, the greatest example being God's own love for humankind, displayed in a most unsentimental way—the cross of Jesus Christ.

Hear the words of the apostle John:

> Dear friends, let us love one another, for love comes from God. Everyone who loves has been born of God and knows God. Whoever does not love does not know God, because God is love. . . . There is no fear in love. But perfect love drives out fear. (1 John 4:7–8, 18a)

If faith is "ultimate concern," as Tillich suggests, and hope is concern for the future, then love may be defined as concern for the other and must logically be the centerpoint of a properly functioning economy that works for everyone, not just those at the top.

What might putting love at the center of economic activity look like? The apostle Paul paints an interesting picture:

> Love is patient, love is kind. It does not envy, it does not boast, it is not proud. It does not dishonor others, it is not self-seeking, it is not easily angered, it keeps no record of wrongs. Love does not delight in evil but rejoices with the truth. It always protects, always trusts, always hopes, always perseveres. Love never fails. (1 Cor. 13:4–8a)

This passage has been read at countless weddings and is one of the more widely known verses of Scripture, but I dare say that few people understand it as a guidepost for good economics. We will look at it more closely.

Patience, which the apostle Paul equates with love, is a virtue in many things but especially business and economics. This was evident to Ben Franklin, who famously quipped: "Let all your things have their places; let each part of your business have its time." Franklin understood better than most that business is a nurturing activity and long-term success requires patience. He also knew that impatience can be a recipe for disaster and is often the cause of poor business decisions. The same holds true today.

Under the pressure of quarterly (or even monthly) reporting regimens, executives are literally afraid to report anything other than constantly increasing sales and returns on investment, making it difficult for companies to invest in the long-term future of their businesses. When investment demands are made, few if any are approved if their net present value (NPV) is more than a year, and investments in nonrevenue-producing items are especially hard to come by. Consequently, many businesses fail to invest properly in infrastructure, whether physical plant or enterprise systems, until catastrophic failures force them to do so. The results are waste and excessive costs on a grand scale. In business as in healthcare, "an ounce of prevention is worth a pound of cure," but the demand for immediate results makes it hard to justify such investments.

Lack of patience has also caused companies to kill initiatives before they have had the chance to take root, wasting valuable time and resources. In my own experience running a business, I had to make these decisions on a regular basis. It is not easy to do. No one wants to throw good money after bad, but just because the initial uptake of a product is below forecast does not mean it should be withdrawn from the market. I was running a chemical business once that produced products for commercial use. I asked the laboratory to develop a new line of environmentally friendly products that had the same efficacy as our regular products. The sales team was skeptical at first, and the initial sales were not up to expectations, but as people began to use the new products, and they became accepted by the market, both sales and margins soared. Not only had we benefitted from our patience, but the environment benefitted as well. It was worth the wait.

Then, of course, investors who seek immediate returns on their investments often cause difficulties, not only for the management of the companies whose shares they own, but for themselves as well. Consider the now-infamous story of Ron Wayne, one of the three founders of Apple Computers who, during the company's formative days, sold his ten percent stake in the company for eight hundred dollars. Those shares are now worth approximately $35 billion—clearly the worst case of investor impatience in business history!

Of course, while the story of Ron Wayne is unique, the challenge of impatience in the stock market is an area of widespread concern. The term of stock ownership has gone from what used to be months and even years to milliseconds. Highly sophisticated algorithms are now programmed into supercomputers that can buy and sell shares in the blink of an eye, taking human decision-making out of the equation. While this makes a lot of money for Wall Street brokers, who make a fee on every transaction, it contributes to the phenomenon of stock prices being completely divorced from genuine wealth creation. Stocks are traded, not according to business fundamentals, but according to their value within the construct of a given algorithm. One of the most outspoken critics of HFT is Warren Buffet, who has amassed a fortune buying and holding onto undervalued stocks. A buy and hold strategy, though, requires patience.

Worse still is a lack of patience in the development of personnel. The "hire slow, fire fast" mentality pervades boardroom thinking, but research has shown that it is actually far more cost-effective in the long run, and better for overall staff morale and retention, to nurture people into their roles than to simply fire them the first time they make a mistake. Companies that treat people as disposable assets create toxic work environments and cultures that are egocentric and self-serving. Patience is good for business, and love is patient.

The next descriptor of love that we meet in the apostle Paul's letter is related to patience: kindness. The root word in Greek is *chréstos*, which can be translated as benevolence. Benevolence is more than simply an absence of malice; it implies a desire to seek the highest good of others. In the context of business and economics, that means ensuring that others are not harmed by our actions and always seeking mutually beneficial relationships.

The business sections of bookstores have always had many titles that deal with winning at business. The impression is that economics is a zero-sum game, and if you are not winning you must be losing. In fact, one of the most popular business books of the last few decades has been Sun Tzu's *The Art of War*. But business is not war; it is economic intercourse, and while it may be competitive, it does not have to be strictly adversarial. Some of the most important business breakthroughs of the recent past have involved what is sometimes called "coopetition," where previously bitter rivals have found ways to work together, not for the purposes of collusion, but in order to serve the needs of their mutual customers.

One example is Apple and Microsoft. The tension between Apple founder Steve Jobs and Microsoft chairman Bill Gates is the stuff of legend. They were both redefining personal computing at the same time, and many wondered whether there was room for both of them in the market. One particular bone of contention was the proprietary nature of Apple's Mac operating system, which had its own suite of word processing, presentation, and accounting tools. Microsoft, however, dominated the market with its Windows-based Office products. Over time it became clear that people who loved the intuitive nature of the Mac operating system, with its superior graphics and silent hard drive, were not going to switch back to a PC just to use Microsoft Office. It also became clear that most people who used PCs at work preferred Microsoft Office and did not want to use a different business suite with their Macs at home. The result was a standoff, with Microsoft upsetting a large portion of its business users by not offering the Office suite for Mac, and Apple upsetting many of its home and business users by not making Microsoft Office available to them. The two companies eventually worked it out, however, to everyone's benefit in a classic example of "coopetition." Yes, they still compete with each other on a regular basis, but they cooperated with each other in this instance, finding a win-win solution.

Benevolence is also a necessity in the development and marketing of new products. The notion of *caveat emptor* ("buyer beware") may have some usefulness in transactions where sellers may be genuinely unaware, either literally or constructively, of potential faults with a product that is for sale (for instance, in a real estate foreclosure auction), but it is a pernicious concept in most business settings. The widely held belief that warnings of "buyer beware" indemnify sellers, both legally and morally, is simply untrue, and benevolence presumes a genuine desire to "do good" for one's customers.

One example of a lack of benevolence in business is the planned obsolescence of items that cannot be upgraded to new versions of what are essentially identical products. This is rife in the computer industry, where hardware is often physically incompatible between product generations, and software quickly becomes unsupported by its developers, forcing users who are otherwise quite content with their current products to make costly upgrades. All products have life cycles, and there are always going to be times when spare parts, for instance, become scarce. But the pace of product development is intentionally rapid in the computer industry with rates of obsolescence nothing less than predatory, squeezing additional revenue from a customer base rather than adding value to the customer experience.

The principle of benevolence should also apply to personnel issues, which we will consider in greater detail in the next chapter, but suffice to say, businesses need not be places where people merely work; they can and should be places where people have the opportunity to flourish. Kindness is good for business, and love is kind.

This list continues, as the apostle Paul writes that love "does not envy, it does not boast, it is not proud" (1 Cor. 13:4). Much of our current economic system is built on exploiting envy, boasting, and pride. Consider the advertising industry to see how central these qualities are to our economy. People do not just want more; they want more than the next person has, and Madison Avenue takes that impulse to the bank. Another word for that impulse is *covetousness*, a sin so serious it is prohibited by two of the Ten Commandments. Why? Because envy causes both habitual discontent and friction between people. On a personal level, desire for what another person possesses may lead to anything from casual resentment to outright hatred; within societies covetousness causes class divisions and deep-seated resentments, and on an international level it may lead to outright war.

When I lived in England, I was dismayed to see class envy ingrained across the entire fabric of society. Its roots reach as far back as the days of feudalism, and it is palpable even today, especially in politics. A general lack of trust exists between the general population and the establishment, and a general disregard goes in the other direction as well. Sometimes the envy is misplaced anger at endemic injustice, but some of it is genuine ill will toward entire groups of people, based solely on where they were born, their accents, or what schools they went to. It's a tragic blight on an otherwise magnificent culture.

Interestingly, when I lived in Australia I did not witness that kind of classism at all. Perhaps because they never experienced feudalism, and Australians seem to take a certain satisfaction from the fact that they have done very well for themselves on the back of a lot of hard work and a "can-do" attitude. That is probably why they no longer subscribe to things like the British Honors System, a system for rewarding individuals for service to the British Empire by granting them titles. In fact, when a recent Australian prime minister re-instituted the ancient titles of knight and dame to the nation, he was roundly ridiculed for it, and was soon after forced from office.

America, on the other hand, has lost much of its egalitarian ethos, slowly but surely gravitating toward a class system of its own. The poor are seen as victims of their own devices, and the rich and famous have become American royalty. The difference between American royalty and British royalty is that the latter is built on primogeniture, while the former is built solely on the accumulation of material wealth. As the Bruce Springsteen song goes, "Poor man wanna be rich, rich man wanna be king," and the treadmill of envy drives an economic engine that seeks to fulfill the fantasies of every covetous soul.

Even governments exploit our covetous desires: consider the proliferation of lotteries available today, games of chance that feed on people's lack of hope in a properly functioning economy and that turn people, instead, to the false hope of unimaginable riches that cost only a dollar to buy. That seems like a small amount of money to pay for false hope, but many poor people, in a state of desperation, do not discern the absurdity of the mathematics behind the lottery and often spend hundreds of dollars they cannot afford in the mistaken belief that buying multiple tickets miraculously changes the odds of winning. If the odds of winning the lottery are fourteen million to one, those odds do not change, no matter how many tickets one buys. In theory, multiple tickets may slightly improve the probability that a person has a winning ticket, but the possible combinations of numbers involved are so astronomical, the mathematical impact of multiple tickets is infinitesimal. It is truly a case of throwing good money after bad.

A close relative of envy, of course, is boasting, not just because those who boast exalt themselves in an idolatrous manner, but also because their self-aggrandizement implicitly ridicules others.

I once worked for a fabulous company in the office furniture industry called Steelcase, Inc. It was by far the largest in the sector, and it was regularly rated one of the best companies in America to work for, but Steelcase did not spend a lot of time promoting the company's virtues. The company chose instead to focus on the needs of its customers. Soon after I was hired, my wife fell ill and I was not able to make the daily commute into New York City, and I wondered whether I would lose my job because of it. The company was under no legal obligation to keep me on, they were self-insured (which meant they would have to foot the medical bills), and few would have blamed them if they had just cut me loose to fend for myself. Instead, they did the exact opposite. They not only ensured my wife had the best possible care, but they also allowed me to set up an office in my home so that I could be near her and my three young children. A few years later, I asked the CEO why he did not let more people know what a great company Steelcase was, and his answer has remained with me to this day. "The whale who spouts, gets the harpoon," he responded with a wry smile. Blowing one's own horn offers small benefits and great risks. While there was certainly a tinge of utility to his modesty, I knew from my own experience that it was deeply rooted in the company's virtuous business culture and the CEO's belief that boasting is not only unseemly but also unhelpful.

The CEO of Steelcase was a modest man, but he was still very proud of the company he had built. His pride was one of satisfaction in a job well done, not the kind of pride that is a vice in the face of love's virtue. That kind of pride (the Greek word is *phusioó*) is better translated *arrogant*, and love is never arrogant. Arrogance afflicts many successful people and companies alike and is inevitably destructive. Hence the famous idiom "pride goeth before a fall," based on Proverbs 16:18. It hinders people's ability to assess themselves or their businesses critically. In individuals, it causes a distorted view of self that often leads people to treat others with contempt, thereby destroying relationships. It also clouds people's judgment and leads to decisions based upon the visceral estimation of one person ("gut instinct") instead of the reasoned consensus of an informed group or the wisdom that virtues grow. One example is the rise and fall of former Warnaco CEO Linda Wachner.

Linda Wachner's was seemingly an American success story. She had risen up the ranks from retail fashion buyer to CEO of one of the largest clothing companies in the world. She orchestrated a management buy-out (MBO) of the company in 1986 and proceeded to make a string of acquisitions; by 1999, the company had revenues of nearly $2 billion. But she also had a reputation for being an incredibly difficult person to work with who built an organization based on fear and intimidation both internally and externally. She regarded herself highly, as evidenced by her huge pay packages. Over time, her abrasive management style and her string of damaged relationships began to catch up with her, and when profits at the company began to wane and losses started to mount, she found herself isolated and overwhelmed, with no options left but to declare the company bankrupt in 2003. As Steve Forbes put it in an article in 2009:

> Her ego, coupled with a seemingly insatiable appetite for power and Olympian-sized pay packages, placed a fatal strain on her company and brought her down. The CEO who managed others through intimidation ended her career dismissed for nonperformance and without the

customary golden parachute. In summing up her tenure at Warnaco, one of her former subordinates commented to the *New York Times* that "She was the main reason it (the company) fell apart. There is some genius there, but she could not run a $2 billion corporation by herself."[9]

The words "There is some genius there" expresses the real tragedy. Ms. Wachner was a gifted person who worked hard and built what should have been a successful business, but her self-aggrandizement eventually brought down the company. Gifted people and great businesses are the most susceptible to arrogance, which makes their falls always so spectacular. Tragically, their demise hurts many in the process. When businesses fail, many people besides the CEOs feel the pain. Employees, suppliers, customers, and shareholders all suffer the consequences, and in the case of many publically traded companies, the people whose decisions brought down the companies leave with their fortunes, if not their reputations, intact.

Without love at the center—that concern for the other—business leaders fall prey to their own self-aggrandizement in a culture that worships wealth. Love eschews envy, boasting, and pride. So should business.

The apostle's next words tells us that love does not "dishonor others," is not "self-seeking," is not "easily angered," and "keeps no record of wrongs" (1 Cor. 13: 5). There is no place in business for holding grudges or seeking vendettas. In the male-dominated and often cutthroat world of business, grudges and vendettas are all too common, and as with all business decisions, the ones who suffer the most are not the ones who make the decisions, but the ones who have to clean up the mess afterwards.

In various accounts of the collapse of Lehman Brothers, there are stories of bitter rivalries coming back to haunt CEO Dick Fuld. Did then-Secretary of the Treasury Henry Paulson do everything he could to save Lehman Brothers, or was something going on beneath the surface that involved more than Lehman Brothers's balance sheet? Were the bankers summoned by Paulson and then-president of the New York Federal Reserve Bank Timothy Geithner to orchestrate a rescue package really interested in saving Lehman Brothers, or were they happy to let their old nemesis hang out to dry? The Machiavellian intrigue on Wall Street is legendary, and if even a fraction of it is true, it is shameful.

Business is not a game. It involves real people who work tirelessly to make life for themselves and their families a little better than it was for the generation before them. There is simply no place for CEOs who use business as a personal *Game of Thrones*.

The word *company* comes from the Latin words *cum* (together) and *panum* (bread), describing a community of people who work together to meet their mutual needs. Similarly, the word *corporation* is rooted in the Latin *corpus* (body). When thought of in those terms, the notion of a company seeking the destruction of a rival is as morally unjustifiable as burning down a neighbor's house. It is simply absurd to suggest that it is part of the natural order of things or survival of the fittest. It is true that businesses that do not adapt to changing markets or meet their customers' needs may not survive; *that* is the natural order of things. Purposefully seeking the destruction of a competitor, though, is the economic equivalent of cannibalism, which has no place in a healthy society.

Underscoring the point that there is no room for that kind of business cannibalism, the apostle Paul tells us that love "does not delight in evil, but always rejoices in the truth" (1 Cor. 13:6). Libel laws notwithstanding, many companies purposefully distort the truth, either to enhance their own reputations or to hurt the reputation of their rivals.

Imagine, for instance, a person who works for a company who then joins a competitor and bad-mouths her former employer to a mutual customer. Or a person who starts a rumor that his competitor is in financial trouble and about to go out of business, when in fact, he has no idea whether or not that is true. Or imagine a stock trader giving a sell recommendation on a company because she is holding a short position on that company's stock, or a business presenting an embellished view of its finances in order to encourage unsuspecting investors to buy their stock. Each of these examples shows a delighting in evil and perversion of the truth.

A particularly offensive example of this behavior was when the executives of Enron encouraged their own employees to invest heavily in the company's stock as part of their pension plans, when the executives knew they were "cooking the books" and the company was in dire straits. An even more egregious example, though, was the case of Bernie Madoff and the collapse of Bernard L. Madoff Investment Securities, LLC in 2008.

Bernie Madoff was a Wall Street icon. He started out as a penny stockbroker and went on to become chairman of NASDAQ, the second-largest exchange in the world and the first to take advantage of computer technology to execute trades on Wall Street. His own firm was the marvel of Wall Street in the 1980s and 1990s, as he regularly produced double-digit returns for his investors, regardless of the market's volatility. He had a very exclusive clientele, comprised mainly of wealthy Jewish families and charities, which added to the mystique of his firm.

As the firm grew larger, though, and competitors were unable to duplicate his system, people started to wonder whether his returns were, in fact, too good to be true. This triggered several SEC investigations between 1999 and 2006. The combination of his insider knowledge, the complexity of his purported methodology, and the sheer magnitude of his reputation allowed Madoff to convince the SEC that his business was totally legitimate, and he was completely exonerated at the time. Within two years, though, the firm was bankrupt, and it was revealed that he had, in fact, been running the world's largest-ever Ponzi scheme.

A Ponzi scheme, named after Charles Ponzi, a 1920s-era stockbroker who ran such a scheme, is very similar to a pyramid scheme in which new capital invested into a business or a fund is used to pay what are supposed to be dividends to existing investors. As long as new money keeps coming in, and little or no money is going out, a scheme can stay afloat for a very long time. But if existing investors decide to withdraw their capital in large numbers, a scheme will quickly collapse. This was exactly what happened to Bernie Madoff. In 2007 and 2008, as the effects of the subprime mortgage crisis and the global financial crisis became apparent to investors, and the market went into a long decline, people began to get nervous and cash out of their equity investments. This included many of Madoff's investors. When the cash calls became too great and he could not cover them, he confessed to his sons, who were also his business partners, that the entire business was a fraud. It was they who turned their father in to the authorities. Soon after, the company went bankrupt, costing unsuspecting investors a fortune.

While Madoff will spend the rest of his life in jail for his crimes, that is little consolation to the people who saw their life savings vanish or to the charities that had to cut back on their services to their communities. The total losses associated with the Madoff scheme is in the billions of dollars, and it is all because Mr. Madoff delighted in evil and shuns the truth.

In his last word in this section about love, the apostle Paul writes that love always "protects," "trusts," "hopes," and "perseveres," and that it "never fails." Love, like prudence, is always forward-looking; like justice, it seeks the common good; like courage, it strives after righteousness; and like temperance, it is content with godliness and resistant to evil. Love is not a sentimental emotion but a reflection of God's own character. This should be equally daunting and encouraging to us. It is daunting because human love will always be limited in its scope and its efficacy, but it is encouraging because, as we have seen in earlier chapters, every person is created in the image of God and is therefore capable of great love—in personal relationships, in communities, and in our economic activities.

Pursuit of an economic system reflective of wisdom and virtue is not only desirable but also essential. When capitalism emerged from the primordial ooze of feudalism and mercantilism, it was rooted in a religiously inspired ethic. As it has evolved over time, it has drifted further and further from that ethic, morphing into the postmodern capitalism I have described previously as "devoid of a moral compass and resistant if not impervious to ethical constraint." Capitalism itself is not the problem; the corruption of capitalism is. If we are going to redeem capitalism—and to enjoy and share in the fruits of capitalism—we are going to need all the tools of virtue and love at our disposal.

And the tools we have are very powerful indeed. We have the tools of wisdom and Scripture, with its two thousand years of theology and moral teaching. We have common grace and an innate ability to discern right from wrong, regardless of one's religious beliefs or lack thereof. We have a storehouse of wisdom that spans millennia and is as diverse as the communities that have preserved it. We have the cardinal virtues and all of their subsidiary virtues, and most importantly, we have the theological virtues of faith, hope, and love.

Armed with these tools, we can embark on the journey, but it will take a great deal of time and a lot of effort. There are no quick fixes to our current problems. Our journey will involve the evolution of cultures, both macro and micro. It will involve the establishment and reinforcement of common values, the development of an economic *lingua franca* that supports those values, and the repeated experience of an economic system that works for everyone—a journey toward virtuous capitalism.

An old riddle goes something like this: "How does one eat an elephant?" The answer: "One bite at a time." Such is the case with the redemption of postmodern capitalism. In the next chapter we will explore three areas in which we may begin the process: the redemption of work, the redemption of business, and the redemption of money and markets, as they are the building blocks of our economic system.

12

Redeeming Capitalism
from the Bottom Up

Paying good wages is not charity at all—it is the best kind of business.
HENRY FORD

On October 31, 1922, Benito Mussolini became prime minister of Italy. A few months later, a single mother of two named Lena Amodeo Bottini, who barely spoke a word of English, boarded the passenger liner *Conte Rosso* in Genoa, Italy, for the arduous journey to America. After arriving in New York, she lived in typically cramped quarters and worked tirelessly scrubbing floors to make ends meet, determined to eke out a better life for her two young children, Giuseppina and Francesco. When her son reached age fourteen, he became the man of the house and started working odd jobs in a local gentlemen's club, putting in long hours to help support his family and to put himself through school to become a qualified accountant. Before proposing to his Anglo-Irish girlfriend, Mary Dawkins, he laid out his plans for their future. He would work as hard as he could to give her the large traditional family they both desired. He would embody the American Dream, working two, even three jobs at a time if required to ensure they wanted for nothing.

In the end they both held up their ends of the bargain, emerging from the tenements of New York City to the leafy suburbs of Long Island, putting six children through private school, and watching them grow up to be useful, productive citizens. But before they married, the young man changed his name from the operatic-sounding Francesco Giuseppe Mario Bottini to the more American-sounding Frank Barnes. He was my father.

There is nothing particularly unusual about this story; America was built by millions of immigrants with identical aspirations and very similar stories. They shared a dream and they shared a high view of work. It would have been wrong to call my father a workaholic, but he genuinely loved work, and he was the hardest working person I ever met. He was also the most generous person I ever met. In forty-five years of marriage, my parents took only one vacation, a cruise for my mother's fifty-fifth birthday. Like most people of their generation, every other penny they made they spent on others, starting, but not ending, with us, their six children. They also instilled in us an ethic of work and generosity that is weakening with each succeeding generation and needs to be reclaimed if we are going to redeem postmodern capitalism.

Redeeming Work

For most people, work is viewed as either a burden to be tolerated, a necessary evil of sorts, or a means to an end, that end being the accumulation of as much personal wealth as possible. As we have seen, those views are distortions of the traditional view of work that gives both meaning and purpose to people's lives and allows them to flourish in the process. Work that is burdensome is bound to be unsatisfying, and work that is radically self-centered is bound to be unhealthy.

A recent (2016) study of workers in Australia, commissioned by Reventure, Ltd., gives a fascinating insight into how people experience work today, and it is sobering reading. Less than half (44 percent) are "extremely" or "very" satisfied with their work, while the other half (49 percent) will "likely" look for a new job over the next year. Half "have experienced one or more serious incidences of conflict or other negative impacts at work."[1] Nearly a third (29 percent) feel "a high amount of stress at work,"[2] and more than half (54 percent) "of millennials are experiencing technology-related stress."[3] The study goes on to say:

> Over half of Australian workers agree with the reality of increasing change and complexity at work. Agreement with this statement is correlated with job dissatisfaction and more frequent high levels of stress at work.[4]

Lastly, the study observes that

> ... cynicism and negativity at work have a significant effect on job dissatisfaction and low productivity ... [and] stress, depression, and anxiety are having a negative impact on productivity.[5]

This cocktail of dissatisfaction is bad for business and bad for the economy, but it is not entirely surprising. First, many economists see work as a disutility. That is to say, if a business could achieve the same level of production without the cost of labor as with it, it would logically eliminate labor from the process. Second, tension has always existed between workers and employers, based largely upon the problem of agency theory highlighted by Eve Poole in chapter 7.

At its most basic, agency theory involves the relationship between principals and agents. It is based upon the assumption that ethical egoism is the dominant framework through which people make business decisions. In the case of employer-employee relationships, it also presumes a logical imbalance between parties. The problem, though, is that its strictly utilitarian bias needlessly presumes that those relationships must be adversarial in nature, thereby eroding trust and reducing work-related relationships to contractual arrangements. There are other options.

From Contract to Covenant

Simply put, covenants are sacred oaths of mutual interdependence and fealty between two parties dedicated to a common cause. The biblical metanarrative is built around them. The Old Testament word for covenant is *berith* and the New Testament word is *diatheke,* and they range from the covenants between God and Adam, Noah, and Abraham, to the covenant between God and the people of Israel at Mount Sinai, to the new covenant instituted by Jesus at the Last Supper, to the more common and very well-known covenant of marriage.

These covenants with God were based upon the suzerain-vassal treaties of the ancient Near East, which also deal with unequal power relationships. Unlike contracts, which are based upon suspicion and anticipate violation,

covenants are built upon mutual respect and trust and presume cooperation. The overriding ethic is deontological, not utilitarian, so agency theory
becomes a moot consideration. Covenantal relationships are risky, because
they presume mutuality. But examples do exist of companies that treat their
employees and their suppliers with mutuality, not only in cooperatives but in
more traditional businesses as well.

At a 2016 forum held at Oxford University's Saïd Business School, several
case studies were presented that explored ways in which large companies have
worked to create environments of mutuality across their entire supply chain.
The example of one such company, Mars Corporation, explored how the development of new performance metrics that measure more than just financial results can help foster flourishing microbusinesses and their surrounding
communities. By measuring such things as human capital and social capital, in
addition to traditional financial capital, they created a hybrid value chain that
encourages all participants to see the total value of their labor, not just its economic value. The presenters described the change as "a set of . . . metrics that
drive impact and that measure business performance across people, planet,
and profit."[6] The results were impressive indeed as employment in some areas
were set to double in just two years, while the micro-businesses worked with
local churches and other community groups to improve employee well-being
and social cohesion.

In businesses that seek mutuality, employers and employees, customers
and suppliers alike, recognize that they simply cannot function without each
other. Their mutual benefit far outweighs any consideration of one gaining
an advantage over the other. At the root of mutuality there must be an ethic
of "fairness," but as recent research has demonstrated, "fairness" as a concept
can be difficult to express theoretically and to implement practically.

In a paper delivered at the aforementioned business forum in Oxford,
researchers Ruth Yeoman and Milena Santos noted that:

> Fairness is complex and it can be approached from both normative
> (how we should act) and behavioral (how we do act) perspectives. To
> break down the concept, it can be useful to look at fair outcomes, fair
> processes, and fair interactions. When employees perceive that they
> are fairly treated, this can improve their willingness to work hard and
> *collaborate—both key for success.*[7]

While developing an ethos of fairness may be difficult at times and may require new paradigms for how businesses think about their employees and their suppliers, and vice versa, research has shown that

> ... there is strong evidence to indicate that larger ... companies with codes of ethics, e.g. those who are explicit about business ethics, out-perform in financial and other indicators those companies who say they do not have a code.[8]

Why this is true is a matter of some speculation, but the general consensus has to do with two primary factors: first, ethical companies build reputations of trustworthiness that set them in good stead in the marketplace, and second, people who are treated fairly at work are generally happier and more moti-vated to perform to a high standard. In short, ethical companies that exercise mutuality bring a sense of purpose to the workplace.[9]

From Professional to Purposeful

The evolution of work from class-dominated, subsistence work, to calling and vocation, to specialization and professionalism has had both positive and negative consequences. On the one hand, people have more freedom to choose their vocation than ever before, and opportunities for high-level training abound. On the other hand, though, too great an emphasis has been placed on technical excellence and less on the psychological, emotional, and spiritual needs of people in the workplace.

In a follow-up to the aforementioned Reventure, Ltd. study entitled *Delivering Purpose and Meaning* (2017), Lindsay McMillan has found that "purpose and meaning are playing an increasingly important role in the contemporary workforce."[10] Millennials especially want their work to have purpose and meaning beyond their own economic enrichment. They are in-terested in three primary areas: the social context of their work; their sense of personal fulfillment at work; and virtuous leadership at work. People who find a combination of these factors are more likely to remain engaged and to create environments where all stakeholders have an opportunity to flourish.

Citing several case studies, the report concludes that in order to create cultures that deliver purpose and meaning, businesses must

> foster employee participation and inclusion, ... communicate the alignment between individual roles and organizational goals, ... encourage autonomy and active engagement, ... provide resources and information, ... serve a greater purpose, ... and reinforce engagement.[11]

This may include involving rank-and-file employees in strategic decision-making and the formation of a company's goals and objectives. It may include training managers to communicate with individuals as people, not merely employees, and make them more sensitive to individuals' needs. It may involve taking some risks to allow employees enough individual responsibility to make decisions without fear of being chastized for minor errors. It would also mean giving people the resources and information necessary to make difficult decisions, being transparent with them regarding the company's overall objectives, and ensuring those objectives involve more than just maximizing shareholder return. Last, it would involve helping employees craft their own career paths and providing the resources necessary for them to achieve their goals, such as mentoring and other developmental tools.

There is no guarantee that everyone will find meaning and purpose at work, but when one considers how much of one's time is spent at work, it is a path worth pursuing. Yet many companies refuse to see the benefits associated with releasing their employees' human and social capital, and even fewer still, their spiritual capital, even though it is a treasure trove of virtue and goodwill from which all stakeholders could benefit.

From Economic Capital to Spiritual Capital

In his widely read book on the subject, T. R. Malloch defines spiritual capital as "[t]he effects of spiritual and religious practices, beliefs, networks, and institutions that have a measurable impact on individuals, communities, and societies"[12]—in other words, the measurable impact of people's core beliefs about the meaning of life, their values, their ethics, and how they express those beliefs in praxis. Considering that the overwhelming majority of people on the planet hold religious beliefs and practice religion in some form or another, it is probably the most powerful and accessible form of capital there is, yet it is grossly undervalued and underutilized.

One reason for this lack of appreciation for the power and usefulness of spiritual capital is a genuine concern for the misuse of religion in the workplace, which in most cases must remain non-sectarian in nature. That genuine concern without a deeper understanding causes severe issues. A religiously neutral environment does not necessitate the denial of people's personal beliefs, any more than a gender-neutral environment requires the denial of one's masculinity or femininity. Beliefs are part of how one defines oneself and they are as ontological as a person's nationality, race, or sexual orientation. Furthermore, we live in an increasingly postsecular time, as demonstrated by people insisting on the rights to wear religiously inspired clothing and jewelry and to observe reasonable religious practices in the workplace.[13]

Spiritual capital is there whether we use it or not, and it is to the detriment of companies and the economy in general when that capital is not incorporated or considered in its many benefits. Spiritual capital, properly employed, can harmonize both cult and culture and allow each to inform the other. It is a universal phenomenon that builds on universal truths and ethical codes of all religious traditions.

In my own faith tradition, work is seen as something holy and intrinsically valuable that contributes to the overall health of the corpus. As the apostle Paul says, in speaking of the church:

> There are different kinds of gifts, but the same Spirit distributes them. There are different kinds of service, but the same Lord. There are different kinds of working, but in all of them and in everyone it is the same God at work. . . . Just as a body, though one, has many parts, but all its many parts form one body. (1 Cor. 12:4–6, 12)

The same, of course, could be said of companies. There are many different employees and each one has different gifts, but they all serve the same purpose. Together they work toward the common objectives of individual, corporate, and societal flourishing. They treat each other and all stakeholders with dignity and respect; they act with integrity; they exercise trust and mutuality;

they respect the environment; they act with prudence, justice, courage, and temperance; and they model faith, hope, and love in all that they do.

The redemption of work cannot happen in a vacuum, though. The redemption of work must be part and parcel of redeemed business cultures.

Redeeming Business Cultures

As important as our consideration of work is, we must not ignore the fact that work is usually done within the framework of a business, and it is highly unlikely that a high view of work will prevail in a business if it is not a virtuous business. Consider for a moment what Karl Marx had to say about the relationship between labor and anarchical businesses:

> The capitalist mode of production, while on the one hand, enforcing economy in each individual business, on the other hand, begets, by its anarchical system of competition, the most outrageous squandering of labor-power and of the social means of production, not to mention the creation of a vast number of employments, at present indispensable, but in themselves superfluous.[14]

Marx was correct, which is why his work resonated with so many people who were employed by businesses that were not virtuous and that treated workers as "wet machines." But while the Dickensian image of the heartless business owner who treats employees with contempt and values profit above all else is a popular one, it is not the only model available to us. As we have discussed, while greed, avarice, and exploitation still abound, many people of good conscience and good will wish to see an economic system rooted in personal morality and social responsibility.

As John Dienhart notes in his book *Business, Institutions, and Ethics*, social institutions serve a variety of functions, including "pursuing self-interest . . . developing familial relationships . . . establishing formal groups . . . [and] pursuing fairness, justice, human rights, and the good of all."[15] This is also true of businesses. In fact, most businesses go through an evolution from self-interest (that is, the decision of an entrepreneur to take the risks necessary to start a business in order to reap future financial rewards), to familial consid-

erations (that is, second-generation growth of the business), to group considerations (that is, creating shareholder value). But not all of them evolve to the
fourth level of pursuing "fairness, justice, human rights, and the good of all."

Creating an economy in which the fourth level becomes paramount is
what redeeming capitalism is all about, and that can happen only if corporate
cultures are aligned with these virtues.

Virtues as Corporate Values

For the sake of simplicity, let us assume that there are three rudimentary
building blocks to any culture: common values, common language, and a
shared history. Based on that rudimentary definition of culture, let us consider how society might go about establishing and nurturing virtuous business
cultures.

Companies often talk about their "corporate values"; however, those values are usually associated with their mission statements, properly betraying
them as merely teleological (that is, necessary for the company to survive).
They usually include such things as leadership, diversity, passion, and commitment to quality.[16] While these are all admirable qualities, they could just
as easily be applied to malevolent organizations as benevolent ones.

Values must be rooted in something more imperative than mere character
traits or personal attributes; they must be grounded in objects of belief and
conviction. For instance, when Thomas Jefferson famously penned the words
of America's Declaration of Independence he began with what can only be
called a statement of faith: "we hold these *truths* [emphasis mine] to be self-
evident, that all men are created equal, that they are endowed by their Creator
with certain unalienable Rights," a faith statement if ever there was one. He
followed that statement with a litany of values: "that among these are *Life,
Liberty* and the *pursuit of Happiness* [emphases mine]."[17] These values have
intrinsic worth beyond any sense of utility; they are something people can
believe in and aspire to, not because they are generally appealing, but because
they resonate with our deepest desires as human beings.

If that presumption is true, what better set of core beliefs could a company have than the cardinal virtues? They resonate with our deepest desires as
human beings as well as our *sensus divinitatis* and the *imago dei*. The corporate

values of every company would theoretically be very similar, that is, some combination of prudence, justice, courage, and temperance (not to mention faith, hope, and love). If they were, one suspects that corporate cultures would be dramatically different from what they are today. But how might those virtues be translated into business values in praxis?

In a properly functioning economy full of healthy businesses, *prudence* would stand as *primus inter pares*, first among equals, among all corporate values, because companies do not operate in a sociological vacuum. They are part of the communities in which they operate and depend on those communities for everything from skilled workers to municipal services. Prudence becomes a corporate value when companies take seriously their responsibility to be good corporate citizens, locally, nationally, and internationally. That means making decisions based upon the long-term best interests of all its stakeholders, not merely the whims of the market or the short-term expectations of stock analysts. It means contributing to the wellbeing of society in the same way individual citizens do. It means being a good neighbor, respecting the environment, considering the macroeconomic impact of its business decisions, and always doing what is right, even if it is not always expedient to do so.

Because commerce cannot properly function without a presumption of fairness and trust at its core, *justice* stands not only as a core corporate value but a core economic value. Justice also cuts both ways and is embodied in the Golden Rule. Justice as a corporate value must include fairness internally, including payment of fair (also known as "living") wages; just employment policies; and provision of a workplace free from danger and discrimination. A virtuous company must also create a culture of fairness externally, including dealing fairly with suppliers and customers alike.

Next is *courage*. While we might expect courage to be viewed as a highly regarded corporate value, as we have seen throughout this book, courage, ironically, seems in short supply. Starting a business takes phenomenal courage, yet once businesses become established they seem to lose the ability to stand firm in the face of adversity and begin to operate more out of fear than fortitude. Companies formed by and through this growing list of values are called to resist the temptation to conform to illicit business standards, cut corners, "massage" the numbers, turn a blind eye to immoral behavior, or be naïve about the negative impact of their business decisions or the moral turpitude of their own employees.

Next, *temperance*, the scarcest of all the virtues, is essential as a corporate value. For far too long companies have bought into the Friedman doctrine and convinced themselves that pursuit of maximum profit is the only moral responsibility they have, when the question companies need regularly to ask themselves is, "How much is enough?"

Faith is an intrinsic corporate value because our entire economic system is based on faith. As we will explore in the next section of this chapter, money and markets both rely solely upon faith for their very existence. Without faith, capitalism cannot be sustained. But faith goes far beyond just believing in money and markets; it also involves believing in things beyond ourselves and in each other.

And what of *hope*? The Scottish historian Thomas Carlyle is said to have described economics as "the dismal science," for reasons that are not entirely clear. The sobriquet has stuck, though, and it may have to do with economists' attempts to dehumanize economic decision-making by applying the presumption of John Stuart Mill that all economic decisions are both selfish and rational. If history has proven anything, it is that people have an uncanny ability to make decisions that are not always selfish or rational, which is why hope has such great potential as a motivating corporate virtue. Hope is not the same thing as the irrational exuberance that sometimes drives the stock market, but it is a belief that human beings are capable of doing some extraordinary things, and business has often been the catalyst behind those extraordinary things. Where there is economic activity, there is hope for the discovery of new things, the betterment of society, and the flourishing of humankind.

Finally, *love* can create a framework for all the other corporate values. Beyond trivialization and mere sentiment, love is genuine concern for others. Any business that does not have love at its core must be, by definition, malevolent. Postmodern capitalism has grown devoid of love, more than any other virtue, and in redeeming postmodern capitalism, love's place must be front and center.

If culture is more than just shared values, if it also involves shared language, the same must be true of business cultures. Properly employed, language has not only the ability to define corporate values but also the power to give them agency.

Virtues: Talking the Talk

Similar to shared values, every company has a common language, a vocabulary of its own. Sometimes it is full of acronyms that are only known to insiders; at other times it is full of "business-speak" and other popular catch phrases. More often than not, though, it has a language that reflects the company's true values. For instance, if a company is customer-focused, their corporate language will be full of phrases and acronyms relating to customer satisfaction, such as OTIF (on time, in full), semantic differentials, CSI (customer satisfaction index), CRM (customer relationship management), feedback analysis, and so on. If they are efficiency-focused they are likely to use terms such as lean manufacturing, Six-Sigma,[18] 5S, kanban, kaizen[19], SMED (single-minute exchange of die), JIT (just in time), and the like. Companies that are focused primarily on financial results will employ a series of KPIs (key performance indicators) that measure GM (gross margin), COS (cost of sales), OP (operating profit), ROIC (return on invested capital), EPS (earnings per share), EBITDA (earnings before interest, taxes, depreciation, and amortization), WC (working capital), FCF (free cash flow), and a host of other measurements.

Corporate language exists in two distinct yet related forms. The first is the company's *lingua franca* or local vernacular. It has no specific origin and constantly evolves over time, but it is greatly influenced by the second form of corporate language, corporate messaging. It is through corporate messaging, both internally and externally, that businesses reveal what is truly important to them. Their brands, taglines, rally cries, mottos, slogans, message boards, newsletters, websites, and tweets all say something about what a company values. For example, IBM's motto is simply "Think," reflecting the company's understanding of a computer as an extension of one's mind. But Apple Computer's motto, until 2002, was "think different," perhaps representing founder Steve Jobs's commitment to differentiate Apple from IBM and more importantly his purported belief that a computer could be an extension of one's self. US supermarket giant Walmart, on the other hand, has a very simple and straightforward motto: "Save money. Live better." This is strikingly similar to UK supermarket Tesco's motto "Every Little Helps." Both convey the fact that they are price-driven retailers who will presumably improve the lives of their customers by saving them money.

In these and countless other examples, the language employed by a company not only reveals the company's values, but it also shapes the company's values. The language reinforces attitudes and informs behavior. Therefore, a company that wishes to be virtuous would need both to adopt a vocabulary and create messaging that celebrate and encourage virtue.

Imagine a company whose motto is "seek the common good," or "always do the right thing," or "be courageous," or "resist greed." (I admit that Google's motto, "don't be evil," is a step in the right direction, but one suspects that a virtuous society could produce businesses with more uplifting messages.)

Interestingly, some of the most inspiring mottos have come from the nonprofit sector, which may say something about their motives. The United Negro College Fund, for example, had the simple motto "A Mind Is a Terrible Thing to Waste." While it had a negative overtone, it got to the heart of the matter. For far too long, people of color were denied access to higher education, and even today there are more African American men in prison in the United States than there are in college. This simple but highly effective motto laid bare a political and moral scandal that needed to be addressed. Similarly, back in the 1970s when New York State was getting a bad reputation for crime and pollution, the state's tourist board embarked on a heartfelt plea to both fellow New Yorkers and potential visitors to give their beloved home a try before writing it off, and the "I Love New York" motto was born.

Words matter and the messages they convey will affect both people's attitudes and their actions, but it is the actions of companies that will ultimately define whether or not they are virtuous businesses.

Virtues: Walking the Walk

With all the good intentions in the world and with a vocabulary of virtue on the lips of every employee, a business cannot be said to be virtuous until it acts in a virtuous manner, both internally and externally, both visibly and invisibly. Boards need to make decisions that reflect more than just the interests of shareholders. They need to consider the bigger picture and the wider community of stakeholders. While there are limits to innovative practices such as triple bottom line accounting,[20] there are no limits to virtuous behavior. Just as companies expect their employees to obey the law, nothing stops them from insisting that employees consider the ethical consequences of every policy they adopt and every decision they make. Companies can instill in their employees a belief that what is good for all is also good for them, rather than the reverse. They can also seek to do the right thing and be fair, as well as honest, in everything they do. They need not accept the "I win, you lose" mentality that permeates much of our economic intercourse, when win-win scenarios are nearly always available. Businesses can also act with courage in the face of adversity and take the tough decisions necessary for the long-term benefit of a company and its stakeholders. They can also, contrary to popular belief, make healthy profits and produce solid returns for their shareholders without succumbing to greed and avarice.

It is that win-win attitude that is the central theme of this book and a call to see society's need for a single, over-arching ethic of virtue to undergird, guide, inform, and even inspire our economic activity. Without it, we suffer the unrelenting effects of postmodern capitalism. With it, we have the possibility of redeeming capitalism for the glory of God and for the benefit of humankind.

Establishing and nurturing virtuous business cultures will be a difficult task indeed and will take at least a generation to accomplish. But we can see signs that people are ready for this endeavor. The global financial crisis has caused even the most ardent supporters of capitalism to stop and ask hard questions about how we create wealth, the relationship between wealth and money, wealth distribution, fair trade, debt, usury, corporate social responsibility, executive compensation, shareholder rights, globalization, tax avoidance, corporate governance, and a host of similar issues. But it will simply be impossible for us to redeem postmodern capitalism, if we do not also redeem money and markets.

Redeeming Money

Money is a uniquely human contrivance and has been in existence for over ten thousand years. Contrary to popular belief, money is not the same thing as wealth, although for some it may be a reasonable representation of wealth. At its core, money is, first and foremost, nothing more than a mutually agreed-upon standard of exchange. In a fascinating little book entitled *The History of Money*, Jack Weatherford provides readers an accessible description of the evolution of money from the commodity money (such as coca beans, shells, salt, and tobacco) of prehistoric times to the specter of electronically based private currencies[21] available today.

The evolution of money to something similar to what we would recognize as legal tender today began with the emergence of proto-money (that is, precious metals and stones) as an organic currency used by international traders prior to the establishment of minted coins in the sixth century BCE. The coins became the new standard because they were much more convenient than raw metals and stones. Coins could be standardized in terms of size and denomination, and their purity could be authenticated by the imprimatur of an emperor.

While this standardization did not completely prevent merchants or sovereigns creating counterfeit currency (Weatherford mentions Nero's debasement of Roman coinage as a particularly egregious example), it did provide a relatively stable and trustworthy system for conducting commerce and collecting taxes.

With the fall of the Roman Empire, though, money was temporarily replaced by the introduction of feudal rents and tithe barns, and the widespread use of gold did not significantly make a comeback until the early Middle Ages, when the Knights Templar became Europe's first international bankers. The combination of their reputation as fierce military men, their ability to offer safe passage to pilgrims traveling across the continent (often en route to the Holy Lands to fight in the Crusades), their strategically placed castles, and their reputation for chivalry, noble elites could entrust their wealth to the care of the Templars, who would extract a small fee in exchange for their services.

By the beginning of the fourteenth century, when the Crusades ended badly for the Christian princes, the pope grew suspicious of the Templars. They were disbanded and their leaders were executed, but their banking practices were replaced by a combination of Jewish moneylenders and Italian merchant families, whose bills of exchange made commercial finance possible without falling afoul of the Catholic Church's ban on usury. With the introduction of Arabic numbers and the birth of double entry accounting, even small shopkeepers could conduct business and keep accounts in a way that we would recognize in modern times.

As Europe emerged from centuries of war and plague, and as the feudal system gave way to the rise of the nation-state, populations began to rise and Europeans began to look beyond their shores for opportunities to create wealth. As explorers from Spain and Portugal brought back gold and silver from the New World, the scale of economic activity rose to unimaginable levels, and with it came the use of gold and silver as universally accepted currencies, including the use of silver coins, minted in the Bohemian town of Jáchimov, known as *tallers*, translated into English as "dollars." Now everyone could participate in a monetized economy, from the largest corporations, such as the Dutch East India Company, to the local butcher. Yet another innovation would soon replace the convenience and ubiquity of minted coins, namely government-backed paper money.

Paper money, while invented by the Chinese nearly two thousand years ago, owes it current iteration to none other than the previously mentioned philosopher and statesman Benjamin Franklin. Franklin was in the printing business, and his knowledge of experiments in England and France, where private banks issued paper notes in order to improve general liquidity, convinced him that governments should do the same. As Weatherford notes, the "American Revolution has the distinction of being the first war to be financed with paper money."[22] Unfortunately, the experiment did not go very well, and while the original currency, a dollar bill known as a Continental, was backed by a reserve of Spanish silver dollars, the cost of the war was so great that the currency devalued by nearly 99 percent, and dollars were eventually redeemed by the government for a government bond worth one penny each.[23]

For about the next one hundred fifty years, governments struggled with the relative merits of a monetary system backed by precious metals, such as the gold standard, and the issuance of money backed only by the taxing power of the state (that is, fiat money). The pros and cons were obvious. A gold standard enforces discipline on governments to manage their affairs according to their actual wealth in reserve. If they choose to live beyond their means, they are free to do so, but the result may be a devaluation of their currency or inflation or both. Conversely, if they do not increase their money supplies at strategic times, that lack of flexibility could restrict their ability to meet their other needs, including the ability to wage war.

Through the start of the twentieth century, nation-states fluctuated between commodity-backed currencies and fiat currencies. Germany's Weimar Republic chose the latter at great cost to its people and its sovereignty.

When Germany entered the Great War (World War One), it made a deliberate calculation that financing the war through fiat money and national debt was worth the risk of devaluing its currency. But when it lost the war, it was further saddled by the ignominy of having to pay its war reparations to the Allies in hard currency. The result was unprecedented hyperinflation, economic meltdown (including a default on its sovereign debt), political turmoil, and the rise of National Socialism and the Nazi Party. Bankruptcy always results in collateral damage, but when a sovereign debt crisis arises, it can cause widespread suffering on a massive scale.

The United States was not immune from the global downturn now known as the Great Depression. The worldwide contagion took years to recover from. As people lost faith in the entire financial system, many people took their US dollars to local banks and insisted they be converted into gold bullion, as they had been promised. This phenomenon was known as a run on the bank. To stop this practice, President Franklin Delano Roosevelt nationalized the entire country's gold reserves. Private citizens were required to surrender all of their gold coins and gold certificates[24] to the government in exchange for US dollars, allowing the government to print more money and help alleviate the effects of the Depression. A vault was created at Fort Knox, Kentucky, where the surrendered gold was melted into gold bars, and the policy forbidding private citizens from hoarding gold remained in effect for forty years.

This and a series of other measures known collectively as the New Deal ushered in a time of unprecedented government intervention into the economic affairs of the United States that, along with the onset of World War Two, thrust the United States into a level of debt not previously seen in modern times. The war did have one positive outcome for the United States: it emerged as a global military and economic superpower that would use its newfound confidence and technological prowess to power an economic engine the likes of which had not been seen since the Industrial Revolution. So much wealth was created after the war that the national debt as a percentage of GDP soon began to recede and the American economy became the largest and most productive in the world.

Something else happened after the end of World War Two—a meeting in Bretton Woods, New Hampshire, attended by representatives of over forty countries. There it was agreed that, in order to ensure economic stability worldwide, the US dollar would be pegged at a value equivalent to .028 (1/35) of a troy ounce of gold (and vice versa), and most other currencies would then peg their currencies against the US dollar, essentially putting the entire world back onto the gold standard. This worked well until the age-old problem of flexibility reared its head and President Richard Nixon took America off the gold standard in 1971 to help fund the highly unpopular Vietnam War.

The "Nixon shock,"[25] as it has become known, was not unjustified. There were several valid reasons besides the Vietnam War for America to abandon the gold standard. Germany had already left the gold standard, as had Switzerland, and other countries were calling into question the Bretton Woods mechanism. Additionally, the overvalued US dollar was hurting US exports, creating a large trade imbalance and slowing down the overall economy. Last of all, other countries held billions of US dollars in their national reserves, and wholesale demand for convertibility to gold could have caused the equivalent of a run on Fort Knox. In its immediate aftermath, going off the gold standard proved to be a wise move, with one unintended consequence: the wide-scale disassociation between wealth and money.

The GDP of the United States in 1971 was approximately $1.2 trillion at a gold standard rate of one dollar to .028 troy ounces of gold. The current GDP of the United States is just over $19 trillion, but a dollar itself is now worth only .0008 troy ounces of gold.[26] That means in gold-standard dollars, the US economy has shrunk by 60 percent in real terms and has grown only nominally in relative terms. One might ask, which, then, is a true reflection of US output?

Similarly, since 1971, US national debt has gone from $400 billion (33 percent of GDP) to $19 trillion (104 percent of GDP), a forty-eight-fold increase. Additionally, 78 percent of the US economy is now in the service sector, including financial services, which have gone from somewhere between three to four percent of GDP to more than seven percent. There has also been a further concentration of US wealth as one percent of US households hold 32 percent of the wealth, and two percent of US households hold another 50 percent of the wealth.

While this phenomenon has been evolving for years, for a brief period during the 1990s the US economy was growing significantly and the national debt was going down. In the aftermath of the global financial crisis, however, things have steadily gone from bad to worse. As we noted before, since the start of the crisis alone the government has added $10 trillion to the national debt and "printed"[27] $4.5 trillion in new money through its program of quantitative easing. Over the same period of time GDP has gone from $14 trillion to $19 trillion. That is a bit like a CEO telling his or her shareholders that in order to add $5 billion over eight years to the P&L account, they had to take $14.5 billion off the balance sheet! I am pretty sure the shareholders would not be happy, but that is exactly what our government has done to "America, Inc.," except it is in the trillions, not billions, of US dollars.

Where this will all end, no one can be sure. It is not unprecedented for governments to default on their debts, causing widespread devastation. Even the fourteenth-century Italian families fell victim to similar government profligacy. As Weatherford notes:

> The Italian bankers thrived, but like the Templars before them, they were ultimately undone as a result of their success and their dealings with government. . . . The entire system of money based on bills of exchange ultimately rested on the honesty and goodwill of the participants, but when the government became too burdened by debts, it had the power to cancel them, thereby destroying the system.[28]

US national debt currently stands at 104 percent of GDP. This is unprecedented in peacetime, and there are signs that many of the practices that led to the global financial crisis, such as irresponsible mortgage lending and low-rate adjustable mortgages, are driving up housing prices to precrash levels. Additionally, serious talk continues about repealing the Dodd-Frank Act, which was passed in the aftermath of the global financial crisis to safeguard against a similar event.

Interest rates are beginning to rise and may have an inflationary effect on the economy. If rates rise too quickly and people cannot adjust to higher mortgage rates, another crash in the housing market could result, not to mention a crisis in the bond market.[29] If proposed tax cuts and increases in military spending and infrastructure result in increased debt levels, there is simply no way of knowing how international markets will react. A US sovereign debt crisis would be catastrophic, not just for the United States, but also for the entire global economy.

We might reasonably ask then, why is the stock market doing so well? The answer is simple: the stock market is not a good measure of economic health. But it is a good barometer of short-term opportunism. In anticipation of lower corporate and personal tax rates, speculators are investing heavily in equities, and they are making a lot of money in the process. Whether there is any correlation between the amount of money being made and the actual wealth being created is questionable. The sustainability of the current bull market is also doubtful. More probably, another dangerous economic bubble is in the making, and when it eventually bursts, the people at the bottom of the economic ladder are the ones who will feel most of the pain.

If capitalism is going to be redeemed, the disconnect between money and wealth will have to be addressed, as will the profligacy of national governments and the unbridled recklessness and greed of those who control both the world's money supply and the world's markets.

Redeeming Markets

Markets have existed since time immemorial. They are places of exchange where those with a surplus of goods or capital can trade with others who have a surplus of goods or capital of their own. From the barter systems of the ancients, in which necessary goods were exchanged for other necessary goods, often by nomadic traders, to later stationary markets, where buyers and sellers regularly exchanged goods for money, the nature of markets has not changed much for millennia.

With the dawn of the Reformation, though, and the emergence of benevolent usury as a stimulus for credit-based transactions (including capital investment), the paper-based banking system, an influx of goods from the New World, better transport systems, relatively stable governments, and the rule of law, market economies began to emerge across Europe and North America. Businesses evolved from sole proprietorships to companies and from companies to corporations, with ownership shared among groups of investors.

The shift to shared ownership created the need for a market in shares themselves whereby businesses needing to raise capital could find investors willing to risk their money in exchange for shared ownership of said businesses.

Most believe that the Dutch East India Company (1602) was the first to offer shares to the general public, thereby creating the Amsterdam Bourse (Exchange), which was followed by similar exchanges in London and Paris.

The formula was straightforward: in exchange for providing finance, a private investor could expect a dividend (share of the profits) to be paid when the company successfully executed its plans to import goods from afar and sell them locally. Their liability was limited by the size of their investment, so their risk was reasonable in comparison to their potential gain.

The demand for shares and their ultimate price were determined by two factors: the reputation of the company for success, and the availability of capital to be invested. A good reputation or competition for shares drove prices up; a bad reputation or little available capital drove prices down. The onus was on the companies to prove their value to potential investors and on the investors to do their due diligence on the companies. The markets acted simply as intermediaries between the parties, for which they would extract a modest fee. It was a simple model, and it remained relatively unchanged for centuries. But, as with every other aspect of capitalism, it was transformed beyond recognition by the Industrial Revolution.

As the New World began to produce opportunities for wealth creation and investment, stock exchanges, as they had become known, emerged in Philadelphia and New York. Originally, the New York bourse was just a band of gentlemen who traded with each other exclusively at the Tontine Coffee House on Wall Street under a charter known as the Buttonwood Agreement (1792), where they pledged, somewhat ironically, not to accept a commission rate "less than 0.25%"[30] of the value of their transactions. This rather quaint agreement and the coffee house where they met served the traders well until the size of their operation and the demand for stocks became so intense that they had to formally reorganize in 1817 to become the New York Stock and Exchange Board and move to more permanent quarters.

Over the succeeding years, the New York Stock Exchange has grown to become the largest in the world, with a market capitalization over $20 trillion, but the road has sometimes been a bumpy one. Whether one subscribes to the notion that economic cycles are the result of inefficient monetary policies (as taught by the Austrian School) or the result of a lag between growth and wages (the Keynesian School), most economists agree that some level of economic fluctuation is natural and can be sufficiently managed (the Freidman School). Real problems occur, though, when markets are manipulated or when irrational exuberance is followed by market panic, such as occurred during the Railroad Bubble (1840s), the Crash of 1929, Black Monday (1987), the Dot-Com bubble (1990s), and the Global Financial Crisis (2008). In these instances, markets seem to defy the efficient market hypothesis (EMH), which posits that markets should react rationally to business data. When they do not, and people fall victim to greed and fear, irrational behavior causes huge swings in the market, resulting in financial collapse, societal grief, and personal calamity.

Bubbles and crashes happen for many complex reasons, but one concern today is the over-expansion of the financial sector itself. In the last ten years, technology has led to increases in both speed and volume that make investing according to business fundamentals seem quaint by comparison. At one time, stock markets were driven by traders investing rationally in companies, but no more. Now, with an exponential increase in hedge funds, derivatives trading, naked short-selling, and a host of other practices that increase opportunities for market manipulation, markets are being driven by traders investing speculatively in products with no regard for the traditional relationship between stock ownership and company performance. This has been further exacerbated by the increase in institutional investing. As Gregg E. Berman of the Securities and Exchange Commission recently noted,

> ... modern market structure has evolved to the point where liquidity takers, including buy-side participants, focus their trading efforts on nothing more than what's available at the NBBO (National Best Bid Offer).[31]

When traders no longer act as intermediaries but focus primarily on their own accounts (so-called prop traders), computer programs are designed to make trades in milliseconds based upon predetermined models, and the entire system has essentially been dehumanized, it is no surprise that some of the market's greatest critics are also some of its most seasoned veterans.

Take, for instance, what George Soros, chairman of Soros Fund Management, has to say about markets and institutional investors:

> Every bubble consists of a trend that can be observed in the real world and a misconception relating to that trend. The two elements interact with each other in a reflexive manner. ... The trouble with institutional investors is that their performance is usually measured relative to their

peer group and not by an absolute yardstick. This makes them trend followers by definition.[32]

Or Warren Buffet, who says this about models:

> Investors should be skeptical of history-based models. Constructed by a nerdy-sounding priesthood using esoteric terms such as beta, gamma, sigma and the like, these models tend to look impressive. Too often, though, investors forget to examine the assumptions behind the models. Beware of geeks bearing formulas.[33]

Markets were designed by business people for the purpose of facilitating exchange to benefit all stakeholders, based on a mutuality of risk and reward. Unfortunately, they have become a kind of Frankenstein's monster, affirming the saying of earth scientist and alternative energy pioneer Amory Lovins: "The markets make a good servant but a bad master, and a worse religion."[34]

As CNBC business editor Heesun Wee rightly notes, the problems facing the markets are not only structural but also ethical, and every economist worth his or her salt knows this:

> Some ethics experts and Wall Street watchers argue that the seeds of another catastrophic meltdown or massive taxpayer-funded bailout don't lie in bank capital requirements or regulations. It's about ethics. Values, . . . any economist will tell you, individual perceptions about the economy, perceived opportunity and whether you can get a fair shake do influence consumer consumption and economic output.[35]

Most people, though, automatically call for regulatory responses to economic challenges, and while regulatory mechanisms are essential to staving off the worst excesses of the market, our underlying problems are moral and can be addressed only by philosophical, theological, and cultural responses. If capitalism is going to be redeemed, hard questions will have to be asked about how markets operate, for whom they operate, and what alternatives to the publically listed company (PLC) model exist.

Pierre-Yves Néron, professor at the Catholic University of Lille, asks whether our entire understanding of "egalitarian economics" is not skewed

toward distribution at the expense of relational considerations[36]—a philosophical question with practical implication if ever there was one. And it is not
only philosophers who care about such things. Some actors in the marketplace
are not merely asking those questions, but they are providing answers, and
the results, while modest, are noteworthy. For instance, the number of people currently enrolled in employee stock option plans (ESOPs) has increased
significantly in recent years, with fourteen million participants holding $1.3
trillion of company assets.[37] While this is a fraction compared to the assets
of publically traded companies, the trend is growing and reflects a desire to
reintroduce the relationship between stock ownership and economic activity.

The market has also seen a dramatic increase in the amount of money earmarked specifically for impact investing—investing in companies dedicated
to a specific social or environmental purpose. According to Durreen Shahnaz
of Impact Investment Exchange, "There's about $8.7 trillion in the US that is
earmarked for . . . impact investing . . . up 33 percent from 2014,"[38] a figure that
cannot be ignored by traditional market participants. Once again, this trend
reestablishes the relationship between capital and the greater good of society.

As noted earlier, markets have been around for centuries and there are no
quick fixes available to those seeking to redeem them. What the markets eventually become, how they eventually work, and for whom they ultimately exist
will, at least in part, be the result of how they are informed by philosophical,
theological, and cultural voices. That said, some of the possible antidotes to
the excesses of the market need not come from particularly erudite sources.
They may, instead, come from sources both ancient and timeless, and they may
be as simple to understand as the homespun wisdom of Benjamin Franklin,
who was particularly keen on one economic virtue above all others: thrift.

Thrift—An Antidote to Economic Excess

Contrary to popular opinion, thrift is not about parsimony but about stewardship. In the Genesis narrative of creation, the word for *cultivate* is, in fact
derived, from the Hebrew word *abad,* which literally means to serve, and the
image of Adam is one of a servant who treats all of creation reverently, yet
thankfully, as a source of life and nourishment. Such stewardship is about
taking the creation mandate seriously and applying our God-given talents to

the cultivation of the Earth in a way that serves the creation while glorifying the Creator.

Peter Heslam, in his book entitled *Transforming Capitalism: Entrepreneurship and the Renewal of Thrift*, gives the etymology of the word *thrift* itself:

> From an Old Norse word meaning "to thrive," thrift literally means prosperity or well-being, in the sense of wholeness. These meanings are encompassed . . . in the Hebrew notion of shalom, which embodies the broader understanding of wealth . . . which is central to the scriptural theme of redemption.[39]

Going on to explain the redemptive nature of thrift, he says that

> . . . thrift is able to work redemptively . . . in preserving resources. . . . While profligacy wastes resources, . . . thrift is an amalgam of attitudes and habits that help people thrive because it involves the wise and grateful stewardship of the resources with which human beings are entrusted. . . . It is a form of well-being that leads to the human flourishing and happiness that is characterized by fulfillment rather than by hedonistic pleasure.[40]

Within the context of redeeming capitalism, thrift means living within one's means instead of beyond one's means, which requires a burden of debt. It means preserving capital for useful purposes, accumulating interest instead of paying it, investing for the long-term, reducing waste, respecting the environment, and rejecting the lure of conspicuous consumption. Thrift encourages people to have a healthy work/life balance and guards against the desire to succeed degrading into workaholism or other excesses. Thrift is at the heart of proper stewardship of resources, sound financial management, continual improvement, maximization of assets, and good corporate citizenship. Thrift at the government level would ensure the development of a monetary standard that enshrines a genuine relationship between wealth and money, government accountability, and personal financial responsibility. In the markets, an ethos of thrift would naturally shun financial churn, ensuring that markets serve people and society, not vice versa.

Redeeming capitalism is not an economic exercise; it is a cultural mandate. It begins from the bottom up, as individuals, families, churches, communities, companies, multinational corporations, local, state, and national governments, aid organizations, and international regulatory agencies begin to realize the limits of ethical egoism and dare to explore ideas and actions that align individual economic activities with the common good. But redeeming capitalism must also work from the top down, as we will explore in the next chapter.

13

Redeeming Capitalism
from the Top Down

And I saw a new heaven and a new earth; for the first heaven and the first earth passed away.
                                              REVELATION 21:1A

The capitalism we have, as I have said before, is the capitalism we have created. It has evolved over the centuries from the capitalism described by Adam Smith in the eighteenth century, to the modern capitalism observed by Max Weber in the early twentieth century, to our current postmodern form of capitalism. Then and now, capitalism reflects cultural values. If we want a different kind of capitalism—virtuous capitalism—to emerge, we need to begin to change the social, political, theological, and ethical drivers that have formed our economic system from the beginning (see figure 1 below). We cannot do this simply by changing the laws that govern our economic activities, although some changes would no doubt result from such efforts. Capitalism can be changed only through a wholesale change of hearts and minds as people consciously seek to create an economic system that serves the common good.

Figure 1. Capitalist Forms in Comparison

Driver	Traditional	Modern	Postmodern	Virtuous / Redeemed
Purpose	Subsistence	Acquisition	Consumption	Well-being / Human flourishing
Capital	Means	Credit	Debt	Thrift
Nature of Work	Class	Calling	Professionalism	Spiritual / Work as worship
Method of Work	Rhythmic	Regimented	Compartmentalized	Holisitc
Ethic	Orthodoxy	"In" the world	"Of" the world	Common grace
Accountability	God is watching	Self-monitoring	No one is watching	Covenantal / Mutuality
Ontology	Saved by works	Predestined	Temporal	*Imago dei* / *Missio dei*
Theology	God is remote	God is active	God is dead	God is present / God is accessible
Geography	Local	International	Global	Think globally / Act locally
Epoch	Agrarian	Industrial	Informational	Interconnected
Output	Necessities	Products / Services	Brands / Images	Added value
Sociology	Homogenization of cult and culture	Homogenization of cult / Marginalization of culture	Marginalization of cult / Homogenization of culture	Harmonization of cult and culture

The Purpose of Virtuous Capitalism

At its most basic, the driving force for the development of traditional capitalism was framed by a desire to emerge from the drudgery of subsistence living. Now, it is easy to lose sight of just how difficult basic survival was for most of human history. With the establishment of nation-states, emergence of an accessible banking system, improvements in the division of labor, international commerce, laws of incorporation, increases in population, and newfound political and religious freedoms, a postsubsistence existence became a distinct possibility.

Free markets provided a vehicle for enterprising individuals and companies to create the wealth necessary for people to enjoy life, not merely to survive it. For the first time in history, education, healthcare, the arts, democratic government, and countless other benefits were available to large portions of the population and not just the landed gentry. It was a noble purpose and led to economic, technological, and social advances, many of which are still enjoyed today.

As technology advanced at breakneck speed, though, and as the Industrial Revolution brought about previously unimagined improvements in production, the ability for some people to accumulate vast amounts of personal wealth became the primary purpose of modern capitalism. While many of the wealthiest industrialists chose, primarily for religious reasons, not to enjoy the fruits of their wealth, they nevertheless fed the economic ethos that would lead to postmodern capitalism's insatiable appetite for conspicuous consumption. The avarice and hedonism that drives much of capitalism today has led to huge disparities of wealth and an almost palpable contempt for the poor. Supported by a narrative that distorts liberal economic orthodoxy, governments have colluded with the super-rich to perpetuate the false notion that wealth concentration and economic excesses are necessary evils to be tolerated in order to ensure the efficacy of the free market. This is a completely false notion. While closed economic systems may indeed be less efficient than free-market capitalism, markets themselves are far from infallible and require ethical—and sometimes regulatory—constraint. As fund manager George Soros rightly said:

> If we care about universal principles such as freedom, democracy, and the rule of law, we cannot leave them to the care of market forces; we must establish some other institutions to safeguard them.[1]

The general purpose of virtuous capitalism, then, is neither wealth accumulation nor conspicuous consumption but a genuine desire to see the power of free markets used for the purpose of human flourishing. By flourishing I mean wellbeing in all of its forms—economically, socially, spiritually, physically, and politically. In other words, capitalism would once again be the servant, not the master, of humankind. Virtuous capitalism would be free enough to create wealth sufficient to benefit all of humanity, while still rewarding those who take reasonable risks, work hard, innovate, and are motivated to succeed. Benefits for the common good would be achieved, not by imposing a utopian egalitarianism or an arbitrary redistribution of wealth, but by creating a new narrative around the purpose of wealth-creation and the development of an ethos of generosity.

Believing that we are all in this together certainly is not a new concept. At the end of the Fourth Gospel, Jesus tells his disciples that if they truly love him, they must "feed [his] sheep" (John 21:15–19). While it is reasonable to suggest that Jesus was speaking of spiritual food in this passage, we cannot ignore the obvious connotation that his disciples were also responsible for the material wellbeing of their neighbors, as demonstrated by the early church's communal environment (see Acts 2 and 5). At the very least, maintaining a just and properly functioning economic system is paramount to following Jesus's admonition.

Capital in a Virtuous System

Traditionally, access to capital was based upon one's own means. While there have always been moneylenders of one sort or another, people generally believed that money begets money, and entrepreneurs without their own capital had to sell shares in their businesses in order to raise it. During the modern era, though, as the new wealth generated by industry made capital more readily available and the banking system became more sophisticated, the use of credit became more widely accepted. With strict laws still in place against usury, access to capital was fairly limited. Now, money is relatively easy to come by, and postmodern capitalism is built upon mountains of debt. Usury laws have been dramatically liberalized, and individuals assuming massive amounts of personal debt have made conspicuous consumption itself possible. Despite an availability of credit for some, access to capital for the poor, especially people of color, and for entrepreneurs in the developing world remains highly restricted and very expensive.

Virtuous capitalism cannot be built upon irresponsible lending, profligate government spending, and the collusion of central banks. Instead, it must build on thrift and responsible monetary policies, as well as the further development of banking models designed specifically to help the poor.

Recently in the UK, community banks have been developing in a form not dissimilar from traditional models. One such bank, Swan Credit Union, exemplifies how a small institution can make a big difference in a community. Unlike most credit unions that rely on an ever-decreasing amount of support from government grants, the Swan Credit Union is run like any business in that it is self-sustaining. Its business model is similar to that of traditional savings and loan companies, with a broad base of small depositors supporting small loans to its members on a very modest loan-to-asset basis. Their business plan is as thorough as corporate entities of far greater size and is available for public scrutiny.[2] Even more impressive are their stated mission and ethos. They exist to provide ethical banking services and loans to people who are often left out of the traditional banking sector. They run their business according to their stated values of "openness, trust, fairness, and mutuality."[3] How, one may ask, does this bank serve their community? The answer is simple: they treat their members as people, not numbers, and they provide an alternative to the predatory practices of payday loan companies, doorstep (home-equity) lenders, and loan sharks. While Swan is a not-for-profit enterprise, it is not a charity and it proves that banking can be both virtuous and successful.

A similar movement is afoot in the area of microfinancing. As Chris Horst and Peter Greer note in their book *Entrepreneurship for Human Flourishing*, the microfinancing movement was started in the 1970s by Muhammad Yunus of the University of Chittagong in Bangladesh. The story goes like this:

> He [Yunus] met poor women who were leading very small businesses. Over time he learned that if they had an initial investment in their grassroots businesses, their profits would increase dramatically. Yunus created Grameen Bank . . . to ensure access to small loans. . . . Instead of requiring physical collateral, he used a group guarantee. . . . Defying expectation, they repaid their loans on time. And the modern microfinance movement was born.[4]

This exercise of grace and courage led to a global phenomenon that has made entrepreneurship available to poor people all over the world. Yunus was even awarded the Nobel Peace Prize for his efforts. The movement has done more than just provide capital, though. Thanks to the mutuality of the loan guarantees and the close-knit nature of the businesses themselves, it has also helped to empower women (for most of the loans go to women-run businesses) and foster a greater sense of pride and purpose in their communities. Thrift relieves the burden of debt and enhances human flourishing, something that needs to be reinforced by those of us who seek virtuous capitalism.

The Nature of Work in a Virtuous System

As we saw previously, for most of human history one's social class or station determined where and how one worked. It was not until the modern period that the Reformation concept of calling gained credence. This higher notion of work being related to divine providence soon gave way, though, to an emphasis on technical excellence or professionalism. While there is nothing intrinsically wrong with professionalism, there are limits to its usefulness.

Professionalism tends toward utilitarianism. The more proficient one is at his or her job the better. Still, it is quite possible for a person to be extremely proficient, but in a malevolent manner. If professionalism in the medical sciences, for instance, leads one down the path of eugenics, that particular expression of professionalism clearly poses a threat to society and is wicked. If one is proficient in biology, or chemistry, or physics, and that person develops a technology that may be used as a weapon capable of posing an existential threat to humanity, that expression of professionalism is corrupt and dangerous. In fact, when anyone in any profession puts the purity of craft before the welfare of neighbor, that expression of professionalism becomes potentially dangerous and can also lead to the elevation of work to the status of an idol.

As Tim Keller and Katherine Leary Alsdorf note: "Work is not all there is to life. . . . [I]f you make any work the purpose of your life . . . you create an idol that rivals God."[5] Yet any work, done for a noble purpose, no matter how modest, is by definition good work.

I recently visited an art museum in Melbourne, Australia. Its collection of Baroque masters was truly exceptional, and many of the scenes depicted stories from the Bible. Whether or not the artists themselves were believers matters little to onlookers three hundred years later, but their work was divine nonetheless, and it no doubt stirred the hearts and souls of everyone who had the privilege of seeing it. I must confess that I get a similar feeling whenever I view great architecture, whether it is a Gothic cathedral, the Great Wall of China, or a Roman aqueduct. There is something deeply moving about the work itself, especially when one considers the limits of ancient technology.

The question is, why shouldn't we be similarly moved when we see a perfectly polished floor or a beautifully mown lawn or eat a delicious pizza? The answer is, we should feel that way about any work that is done beautifully with a virtuous purpose, because in the overall scheme of things, what matters most to God is not what we do, but how we do it. That is the essence of work as worship, and if capitalism is to become truly virtuous, work must become worship for all of us. For people of faith, that means God-directed work, whether creative or mundane, sacred or secular, but even for nonbelievers, work can and should be inspiring and uplifting, if the fruits of our labor are going to be more than just a means to an end and if our work is going to be for the common good.

The Method of Work in a Virtuous System

Traditionally, economic activity—work—was rhythmic in that it reflected humankind's relationship to the natural world, the seasons of the year, and the seasons of life. It was also family- and community-based and intergenerational, and it was viewed within the greater context of life itself. It was a time of apprenticeships and civic societies, church fetes and almshouses. Not until the modern era did work become far more regimented, as workers became seen as extensions of their machines and work itself was dehumanized.

In the postmodern era, this regimentation has given way to compartmentalization: people are more likely to live their lives in virtual silos. Business and family do not mix; neither do civics and religion, recreation and work, money and community. Compartmentalizing one's life makes it easier to profess compassion for the poor on Sunday but to oppose welfare on Monday or to "beggar thy neighbor" on Friday and host a neighborhood barbecue on Saturday. In an era of 24/7 electronic communication, compartmentalization also fuels the fire of workaholism, as people fearful of losing their jobs or being passed over for promotions allow themselves to be virtually at work all of the time—and at great personal, familial, and societal costs.[6] Postmodern capitalism has taken the proverbial rat race to new depths, and its redemption will depend upon a renewed appreciation for the importance of integrating economic activity with life's other requirements.

Maslow's classic hierarchy of needs demonstrates the vast array of human wants from physiological to self-actualization.[7] But our current system, with its emphasis on economic excellence, has reduced almost every aspect of self-actualization to the pursuit of nonstop stimulation, whether in the form of information, entertainment, wealth, or pleasure. It does not need to be that way.

In Mark's Gospel, Jesus asks his disciples, "What good is it for someone to gain the whole world, yet forfeit their soul?" (Mark 8:36). What good indeed? Unlike the radical compartmentalization of today, virtuous capitalism would naturally produce a method of doing business that is holistic in nature and that understands compartmentalization as an addiction. The holism of redeemed capitalism recognizes the needs of whole persons and challenges the economic assumptions that work is a "disutility," that employees are "human resources," that people's concerns are not the concerns of the company, that a balanced lifestyle is a sign of weakness, and that business is merely about making money. For people of faith, the concept of "whole life discipleship" is a calling to holistic and redeemed economic activity.

The Ethic of Virtuous Capitalism

While some may not want to admit it, economics has always had a moral impetus. Throughout this book we have looked at religion's significant role in defining the moral drivers of economic systems, especially in what we sometimes refer to as Christendom. Traditionally, that ethic was rooted in the orthodoxy of the Roman Catholic Church and the high church traditions of Anglicanism. The moral code that dominated the economic landscape was built on the Old Testament Decalogue (the Ten Commandments), the Golden Rule ("do unto others as you would have them do unto you"), and what is commonly known as the Double Love Command ("Love the Lord your God with all your heart and with all your soul and with all your strength and with all your mind," and "love your neighbor as yourself"). These basic teachings, known and understood throughout the world, were constantly reinforced by the church, the state, and the culture at large. The general belief, though, was that economic activity was temporal and therefore not particularly important and that the moral code existed merely as a safeguard against injury and avarice.

During the modern era, the emphasis changed significantly, especially in countries where Reformed (especially Calvinist) theology dominated the religious landscape. In addition to those moral codes, the Calvinists took the words of Jesus in John 15:19 and John 17:14–16, where he speaks of his followers as being at enmity with the world, and those of the apostle Paul in Romans 12:2, where he admonishes believers not to conform to the ways of the world, and developed a theological construct of Christians being "*in* the world, but not *of* the world." This construct holds that believers can and should participate fully in economic and other worldly affairs, as long as they hold themselves to a higher moral standard. This provides Christians with the opportunity to demonstrate their righteousness, both in their economic success (that is, as evidence that they have been blessed by God) and in their moral asceticism. As we have seen, as the religious impetus for this thinking receded, the ethic that followed was one informed by moral relativism and self-gratification.

Earlier we looked at a definition of postmodern capitalism as largely "devoid of a moral compass and resistant, if not impervious, to ethical constraint." While this may be accurate at present, it does not preclude the possibility of capitalism finding a moral compass rooted in common grace and thereby becoming virtuous. The postmodern mood is nothing if not open to new ideas or even fresh expressions of old ideas, including those grounded in religious faith.

We looked at the numbers before, but it is helpful to review them here: despite the rise of secularism, atheism, and religious pluralism, most people (84 percent) still believe in God and still believe in the need for both public and private morality. The *sensus divinitatis,* which is the cornerstone of common grace, and the spiritual capital now dormant inside businesses and communities are available to our purpose. Unless we use them to reanimate a universal moral compass, virtuous capitalism is impossible to achieve. But if we are successful, virtuous capitalism is a certainty.

Accountability under Virtuous Capitalism

Of course we cannot discuss morality without also considering accountability. Who, finally, decides whether someone is acting ethically? Who will be the judge of our conduct? And what will adhere that conduct to conscience when no one else is watching? In the days of traditional capitalism, most people believed that God was the one watching and that God ultimately decided (and made judgments about) whether or not one's conduct was ethical. The Roman Catholic system maintained a strict hierarchy of sins, and certain offenses required specific acts of penance or purgatorial atonement. In the modern, Protestant era, though, no such system existed, and accountability was not unlike Adam Smith's "impartial spectator" or "man within the breast"[8] who determined whether or not one's conduct was moral. In this system, each person was responsible for his or her own behavior based on the exercise of his or her own conscience and the conviction of the Holy Spirit. There was no confessional, no earthly penance, and no purgatory, only the believer's duty to be holy as God is holy, in grateful response to the all-encompassing atonement of Christ on the cross.

Fast-forward to postmodern capitalism, where those vestiges of accountability have given way to a moral relativism and a focus, to the detriment of common good and common grace, on personal freedom. If something in this system is legal, it might be assumed to be moral, and even if it were not legal, the only crime would be getting caught. With a lessening of accountability in postmodern capitalism, a belief that no one is watching, and the absence of a religious or common good consensus, from where will this accountability come? With the word *common* at the center of this redeemed capitalism, the answers are covenantal relationships and mutual accountability. In today's postmodern setting, economic activity has become purely transactional with only the blunt instrument of law holding agents accountable for their actions. In a virtuous, redeemed system, economic intercourse would be relational, based upon the covenantal model of mutual interdependence and fealty, expressed through a spirit of mutuality.

We looked previously at mutuality as fundamental to virtuous capitalism. Mutuality enables us to define the very nature of our business relationships and determine whether we treat each other with dignity, respect, and fairness or continue down a path of economic self-destruction. Mutuality is the basis upon which we hold each other accountable for the morality of our economic actions. This mutual accountability is not merely from the bottom up (that is, in our day-to-day dealings) but also from the top down (that is, in how we construct economic models and devise economic systems for the common good).

The Ontology of Virtuous Capitalism

Issues of morality, of course, are not merely theoretical; they are ontological. That is to say, they are indelibly associated with who we are, or at least who we perceive ourselves to be as human beings created in the *imago dei* and yet estranged from God. Were it not for human sin and frailty, there would be no need for morality or ethics; everyone would simply conduct him- or herself in harmony with the divine. Unfortunately, that is not the way things are, and we must consider our moral codes and our conduct within a soteriological framework.

In the case of traditional capitalism, the orthodox (Roman Catholic) construct presumed that one was judged according to his or her good works (or lack thereof), but this was not the case in the modern (Protestant) era. Calvinist belief in predestination disassociates one's behavior from one's state of grace, at least in terms of agency, and ethics are seen not as a means to an end but as a process of spiritual refinement and a dutiful response to grace. This thinking drove the nature of modern capitalism, including the belief that one's economic activity had a divine purpose. In a postmodern era, however, all of life, including economic activity, is viewed as exclusively material and temporal, with a lessened or nonexistent concern for things spiritual and eternal because no such realms exist. Hence, in this era we have discovered a resistance to ethical constraint, barring that which may be viewed as having utility.

Virtuous capitalism—the capitalism of common grace and common good—requires an ontology rooted both in the *imago dei* and the *missio dei*, even among those who do not profess religious belief. The existence and the work of God are not dependent upon the assent of humankind. They exist, acknowledged or not. Even the most hardened nonbeliever can accept the brute fact that despite human reason and intellect, people are capable of immoral and unethical behavior requiring constraint. While this realization may contradict a norm they perceive to be true about the inherent goodness of humankind, people across all faith, cultural, and societal traditions can understand these things on an ontological basis and apply them to questions of morality and ethics in economics and business.

The Theology of Virtuous Capitalism

These considerations come down to our theology of economics and the relationship between our understanding of God—the divine—and our understanding of why human beings exist in the first place.

In the era of traditional capitalism, God seemed remote. God existed, whether in a theistic or deistic sense, but God was not personally active in the everyday operation of the world. For deists, God is nothing more than a prime mover, a force responsible for the existence of things, but not a being with personal attributes. All things are subject to the universal laws of nature, and morality is determined by one's own conscience, within the constraints of personal and group utility. For theists, the God of the Bible is real and personal but not involved in human activity; that is the sole preserve of free will. Consequently, every person is responsible to God for the morality of his or her decisions, based upon a person's relative adherence to divine precepts. In the era of traditional capitalism, there was no real conflict between those who subscribed to orthodox Christian teaching and those who did not, because the latter generally accepted the benefits of Judeo-Christian ethics. It was merely their source that was debated, not their efficacy.

In the modern era, this thinking gave way to a "God is active" mentality, based not only on a literal interpretation of Matthew 10:29–30 ("Are not two sparrows sold for a penny? Yet not one of them will fall to the ground outside your Father's care. And even the very hairs of your head are all numbered"), but also on the Calvinist doctrine of the absolute sovereignty of God. If God is sovereign, then God will have his way and human beings are powerless to frustrate his will. Therefore, ethics are not a matter of utility or adherence to a moral code; they are judged to be right or wrong based upon one's obedience to the sovereign will of God. Max Weber was correct in assuming that this belief had a psychological effect on how modern capitalists viewed the nature of their work, but he was incorrect in assuming it had anything to do with fear of not being "saved." Calvinists worked under the presumption that they were saved; hence, their economic activities and their moral behavior were aligned not out of fear, but out of obedience to God.

What then of postmodern capitalism and its indifference to theology and its propensity for nihilism? The most obvious answer is that "God is dead," at least in terms of God's relevance to economics. God and religion, at least in Christian and post-Christian societies, have become completely divorced from both economic decision-making and public policy. To quote Alistair Campbell, former spokesperson for British Prime Minister Tony Blair, "We don't do God," and few in the City of London or on Wall Street would have demurred.

For some, we seem to be at an impasse between those indifferent to theology and those working to implant a redeemed capitalism. Yet, as Paul Fiddes notes, there is room for dialogue between postmodernism and theology:

> What is our place in the world? It is to live in an open space, through wisdom, in which we can know a God who is hidden but not absent.... Heidegger prompts us to see the way in which a place can become, or fail to be, a space in which to live fully, while Derrida and Kristeva alert us to the transformative power of the "no-place." A wisdom theology for today will maintain that at any moment, anywhere, any place can become holy. It can become the "no-place" where wisdom is encountered, opening up a space in which there is room to dwell.[9]

What may appear to be the absence of God in postmodernism may actually be the mystery of God being hidden from those unwilling to encounter the divine. Virtuous capitalism calls for a realistic look at the destruction caused by utilitarian economics and accepts postmodernity's implicit invitation to speak into this space with the good news that God is indeed present and accessible to all who seek him.

One example of such a dialogue is the relationship between the United Nations Global Compact, a secular initiative devoted to corporate sustainability, and the Religious Freedom and Business Foundation, a faith-based initiative that promotes religious freedom in business and society. While beginning from diverse motives and perspectives, they share many of the same goals and objectives, especially in the areas of human rights, poverty alleviation, and business ethics. The result has been a renewed appreciation for the place of religious belief in economic discourse and an openness to talk of redemption in economic circles.

The Geography of Virtuous Capitalism

A theology of a God who is everywhere at all times is essential to understanding this model of redeemed capitalism because economics is no longer a local matter, as was traditionally the case, or even international, as was the case in the modern era. Economics is indeed a global concern, and not just in our current postmodern context, but in all future contexts as well. The resistance of nationalists and those who gnash their teeth over the corruption and inefficiencies of both corporate and governmental pan-national organizations notwithstanding, railing against globalization is akin to howling at the moon. The world is small and through interconnectedness getting smaller every day. The challenges facing our economies, political structures, and environment are becoming ever more complex and intertwined. To become a force for good in the world, virtuous capitalism cannot be based on a beggar thy neighbor mentality or the weaponization of economic policies designed to give one country an advantage over others. It must be based on a think-globally-act-locally mentality and an ethos of shared responsibility for each other and for the planet we all call home.

Since the end of World War Two, much of the wealth disparity between the global north and the global south has been the result of wealthy countries taking economic and political advantage of poorer countries. It simply has to stop. Similarly, the environmental damage done by wealthy countries often takes a disproportionate toll on the health, wellbeing, and security of poorer countries. This too must stop. "The human environment and the natural environment deteriorate together," Pope Francis said recently, adding that

> . . . we cannot adequately combat environmental degradation unless we attend to causes related to human and social degradation. In fact, the deterioration of the environment and of society affects the most vulnerable people on the planet. . . . Politics must not be subject to the economy, nor should the economy be subject to the dictates of

an efficiency-driven paradigm of technocracy. Today, in view of the common good, there is urgent need for politics and economics to enter into a frank dialogue in the service of life, especially human life. . . . The financial crisis of 2007–08 provided an opportunity to develop a new economy, more attentive to ethical principles, and new ways of regulating speculative financial practices and virtual wealth. . . . The problem of the real economy is not confronted with vigour, yet it is the real economy which makes diversification and improvement in production possible, helps companies to function well, and enables small and medium businesses to develop and create employment. . . . Here too, it should always be kept in mind that "environmental protection cannot be assured solely on the basis of financial calculations of costs and benefits. The environment is one of those goods that cannot be adequately safeguarded or promoted by market forces."[10]

With a unique perspective from which to consider these issues, the pope is a man who has spent his entire life serving God among some of the poorest communities in the world. Now he is the head of one of the largest and most influential organizations in the world. One does not need to be the pope, though, to recognize the problems inherent in a global economic system that is fundamentally unfair. It violates the very precepts of natural justice and requires all people of goodwill to speak out against it and work toward its redemption.

The Epoch of Virtuous Capitalism

Concerns about globalization and the environment were not of concern to people during the days of traditional capitalism. Economic activity was largely agrarian, as shown by Adam Smith's emphasis on the primacy of the country over the city in *Wealth of Nations*. Not until the Industrial Revolution was in full swing did modern capitalism take shape and with it the social concerns addressed by Karl Marx and others. While modern capitalism was about goods and services, the emphasis was very much on the former, and wealth was generally created by industrialists who used technology to magnify the division of labor to heights unimagined by Adam Smith. Postmodern capitalism, though, is driven neither by agriculture nor industry; it is driven by information.

The information economy is a curious thing because information itself has no intrinsic value. Information is merely data and has value only once it has been applied to some other use. The various uses of information are numerous, and the information economy produces genuine wealth across a wide range of sectors, including product design, manufacturing, marketing, telecommunications, retail, and, of course, financial services. The information economy also has produced wild speculation about its unlimited potential, resulting in the boom and bust of the dot-com bubble in the late 1990s, but overall the pros have far outweighed the cons. Still, information in the wrong hands is a dangerous thing, and information also must be subject to ethical constraint.

Information is powerful, and the tools we have designed to give virtually everyone access to it—unfiltered and unverified—pose the risk that it, too, will be weaponized, as appears to have been the case with Russia's involvement in the 2016 US presidential elections. How we handle information, who has access to it, how it may be disseminated, who is responsible for its accuracy, and who owns it are all questions that have not been adequately addressed, even though they pose serious ethical questions.

The unintended consequences of otherwise benevolent applications of information technology could have potentially devastating effects on the economy and society as a whole, including the widespread use of both artificial intelligence (AI) and robotics. Some estimates claim up to 40 percent of jobs currently performed by people may be made obsolete by robots with the ability to think (that is, process data, consider alternative responses, and act accordingly) by the year 2030. These are not just menial tasks. The entire transport sector could become obsolete; manufacturing and order fulfillment could become totally automated, as could food services, financial services, and even medical services. Why would a person see a doctor, who is as prone to error as any other professional, for a medical diagnosis when a thinking computer, accessed from the comfort of home, will be able to process all of one's medical data in seconds and make a diagnosis that is 99 percent accurate?

Virtuous capitalism is not only an option but also a complete necessity for an information-based economy to become an interconnected economy. In such an economy, the ramifications of the changes about to affect us must involve thought-leaders and policy-makers from all related disciplines who take a common-good focus and operate in an open and transparent manner.

Virtuous capitalism will not function in silos. The problems facing us are too great and too important to be left to the technicians alone. If we are going to navigate the waters of economic uncertainty more effectively than our forbearers handled the Industrial Revolution, ethicists, religious leaders, and philosophers will also need a place at the table of economics.

Output under Virtuous Capitalism

All economic systems create output. The traditional capitalism observed by Adam Smith focused on the efficient production of life's necessities, along with a smattering of modest luxuries. The modern capitalism of the Industrial Revolution gave us a wide array of goods and services, some of which were necessary, but most of which were designed to enhance life. The necessities produced were more plentiful and less expensive than ever before, as were the luxuries that once seemed beyond the reach of most working people. The middle class had disposable income that their ancestors would have never dreamt of, and they used it to purchase homes, cars, appliances, fashion items, and more. Quality of the products, their durability, their price, and their availability were emphasized. Sales and marketing focused on the features and benefits of individual products, and distribution was the key to success.

Postmodern capitalism is quite different. It is not about features and benefits, distribution, or products at all, which it understands as a given. Postmodern capitalism is about brands and images. Businesses focus on how they can make an association between a person's desires and their brand, asking, "How can I make doing business with my company an enjoyable experience? How can I exploit the way people want to feel? How can I turn people's wants into their perceived needs, and how can I capitalize on those wants and needs, as it relates to their egos?" Postmodern capitalism has quickly morphed into a world of promises and propositions, hopes and dreams, fantasies and delusions. It is more about the messaging than the message, and through this postmodern capitalism has become an economic deceit.

Virtuous capitalism must be built on something very different. It must have the potential to genuinely add value to people's lives, not by seducing consumers into buying things they neither need nor want, but by encouraging them to invest in things that help them and their communities flourish. As Flint McGlaughlin notes, " . . . [B]rand awareness is a result; the value proposition is a cause."[11] Creating products and services that help people climb the pyramid of higher-order needs instead of sliding down its slippery slope is far more satisfying for producers and consumers alike, and it is ultimately much better for society. Our planet simply cannot sustain the relentless production of ever cheaper, less useful, disposable products, and our economy cannot sustain the mountain of debt that continues to prop it up. A redeemed economy would produce life-enhancing products and services that alleviate poverty, do no harm to the environment, and stop the cycles of conspicuous and insatiable consumption.

The Sociology of Virtuous Capitalism

In eighteenth-century Europe, when traditional capitalism was just beginning to emerge from the mercantilism of the previous era, no one knew that the economic landscape was changing forever. There was no thought of economic epochs or sociological phenomena. We who study these things have the benefit of hindsight to describe them in terms that meet our needs, regardless of whether the people of that time would have agreed with our assessments. Looking back on that century, we see quite clearly that when it comes to the relationship between economics and theology, business and ethics, there simply was no distinction made between cult and culture; they were genuinely homogenized. Society based its laws on church teaching, and the rhythm of economic life mirrored the church calendar, which itself reflected a combination of the natural seasons and the lectionary.

During the modern era, though, things became very different, especially in America, where the separation of church and state, while not nearly as pronounced as it is today, was nonetheless enshrined in law. As noted by Max Weber, Protestant sects dominated the economic landscape, and while the cult became homogenized, culture became marginalized. Calvinists especially were happy to be in the world but not of the world, and they ran their businesses unabashedly according to their religious convictions. In our current postmodern era, though, the opposite is true. Religion has been pushed to the margins, and culture has become homogenized around moral relativism and economic excess. Virtuous capitalism is neither of these things.

Virtuous capitalism will work because it will harmonize cult and culture in order to genuinely serve the common good. In our pluralistic, globalized economy, it is essential that society do the same. To bring about virtuous capitalism, there will need to be a dialogue between all stakeholders—public and private, large and small, rich and poor, secular and religious. The economic problems we face are legion and cannot be solved quickly or coercively. This is a multigenerational project that requires the humble commitment of like-minded people who see the current landscape as both unsustainable and undesirable. Even without religious consensus, religious voices are part of the conversation and can effectively inform the discussion by plumbing the depths of our spiritual and moral reservoir.

Epilogue

The monumental task of redeeming capitalism will likely begin—and in some respects has already begun—in the religious sector. So we might logically ask, how are people of faith to bring it about? That question, while perfectly reasonable, is beyond the scope of this book. While I have given many examples throughout of virtuous companies and innovative approaches to business and economics, this is a can-do book, not a how-to book. It is more a rallying cry than a playbook. This book is not the manifesto of a movement, but it is the credo of a community that refuses to underestimate the power of God to do the impossible against great odds.

Redeeming capitalism is not a project; it is a mission. Missions take faith, time, and commitment, and history has shown these models to be successful. Missionaries understand a high calling from God and use the tools necessary to make their calling a reality. The tools at our disposal are powerful: faith, hope, love, prudence, justice, courage, temperance, wisdom, and, of course, common grace. But they will only be as effective as our willingness to use them. As Aristotle and Aquinas both remind us, there is no recipe for the attainment of virtue—it is forged in the crucible of practice—and there is no substitute for a relentless appeal to conscience and empathy.

The process of redemption begins by constantly reminding ourselves that it *can* be done and that it *must* be done, or as the Lord himself reminded the people of Israel when he gave them his commandments:

> Fix these words of mine in your hearts and minds; tie them as symbols on your hands and bind them on your foreheads. Teach them to your children, talking about them when you sit at home and when you walk along the road, when you lie down and when you get up. Write them on the doorframes of your houses and on your gates. (Deut. 11:18–20)

Redeeming capitalism is a journey, not a destination, but if, like the Israelites, we follow the teachings, values, and commands that have provided the common ground for a values-based culture, we can escape the desert of postmodern capitalism and let those principles pave the way to a new economic promised land.

BIBLIOGRAPHY

Appleby, J. *The Relentless Revolution: A History of Capitalism*. New York: Norton, 2010.

Aquinas, Thomas. *Summa Theologiae: A Concise Translation*. Edited by T. McDermott. Notre Dame: Ave Maria, 1989.

———. *Summa Theologiae*. Edited by K. Knight. New Advent, 2009. http://www
.newadvent.org/summa/index.html

Augustine. *City of God*. Edited by K. Knight. New Advent, 2009. http://newadvent
.org/fathers/1201.htm.

———. *On the Morals of the Catholic Church*. Edited by K. Knight. New Advent,
2009. http://newadvent.org/fathers/1401.htm.

———. *On the Works of Monks*. Edited by K. Knight. New Advent, 2009. http://
newadvent.org/fathers/1314.htm.

———. *Sermons on Selected Lessons of the New Testament: Sermon 63*. Edited by
K. Knight. New Advent, 2009. http://newadvent.org/fathers/160363.htm.

Barnes, K. "A Response to M. Volf and A. Blair on 'Globalization and the Challenge
of Faith.'" Paper presented at Yale Divinity School. June 23, 2013.

BBC News. "Rolls Royce Apologises after £671 Million Bribery Settlement." January
18, 2017. http://www.bbc.com/news/business-38644114.

Berkshire Hathaway, Inc. "Berkshire's Corporate Performance vs. the S&P 500." In
2001 Annual Report. http://www.berkshirehathaway.com/2001ar/2001letter
.html.

Berman, G. "What Drives the Complexity and Speed of Our Markets." Speech to the
NATA Summit. April 15, 2014. https://www.sec.gov/news/speech/2014-spcho
41514geb#_edn4.

Butcher, S. "Perfect Profiles for Careers at Goldman Sachs, JP Morgan, Deutsche, and

Others." *eFinancialCareers*. September 16, 2014. http://news.efinancialcareers
.com/us-en/140515/perfect-profiles-for-careers-at-goldman-sachs-j-p-morgan
-and-others/.

Calvin, J. *Institutes of the Christian Religion*. Grand Rapids: Eerdmans, 1983.

Congressional Black Caucus Foundation. "Minority Access to Capital and Employment." Washington, DC: Congressional Black Caucus Foundation, 2016. http://
www.cbcfinc.org/wp-content/uploads/2016/01/CBCFMinorityAccessCapital
_FactSheet_final.pdf.

Dienhart, J. *Business, Institutions and Ethics*. Oxford: Oxford University Press, 2000.

Economist Briefing. "Not Always with Us." *The Economist*, June 1, 2013. https://www
.economist.com/news/briefing/21578643-world-has-astonishing-chance-take
-billion-people-out-extreme-poverty-2030-not.

Edleman, R. "Edleman Trust Barometer (Executive Summary)." New York: Daniel J.
Edelman Holdings, 2017.

EEOC. "Religious Garb and Grooming in the Workplace: Rights and Responsibilities."
2017. https://www.eeoc.gov/eeoc/publications/qa_religious_garb_grooming
.cfm.

El Issa, E. "2016 American Household Credit Card Debt Study." *Nerdwallet.com*.
2016. https://www.nerdwallet.com/blog/average-credit-card-debt-household/.

Elliott, C. *Usury: A Scriptural, Ethical and Economic View*. Millersburg, OH: The
Anti-Usury League, 1902.

Elliott, D. *Wall Street Pay: A Primer*. Washington, DC: Brookings Institution, 2010.
https://www.brookings.edu/research/wall-street-pay-a-primer/.

ERisk. "Barings Bank: Case Study." October 17, 2007. https://web.archive.org
/web/20071017041450/http://www.erisk.com/Learning/CaseStudies/Barings
.asp.

Fannie Mae. "Selling Guide." July 2017. www.fanniemae.com/content/eligibility_in
formation/eligibility-matrix.pdf.

Farley, R. "Is Trump's Tax Plan Revenue Neutral?" *FactCheck.org*. October 1, 2015.
http://www.factcheck.org/2015/10/is-trumps-tax-plan-revenue-neutral/.

Federal Reserve of New York. "Quarterly Report on Household Debt and Credit."
November 2016. www.newyorkfed.org/medialibrary/interactives/household
credit/data/pdf/HHDC_2016Q3.pdf

Fiddes, P. S. *Seeing the World and Knowing God: Hebrew Wisdom and Christian Doctrine in a Late-Modern Context*. Oxford: Oxford University Press, 2013.

Flanagan, K. and P. Jupp. *Postmodernity, Sociology and Religion*. London: MacMillan Press, 1996.

Forbes, S. and J. Prevas. "The Price of Arrogance." *Forbes*, June 18, 2009. https://www .forbes.com/2009/06/18/alexander-great-hubris-leadership-power.html.

Francis I. *Laudato si'*. 2015. http://w2.vatican.va/content/francesco/en/encyclicals /documents/papa-francesco_20150524_enciclica-laudato-si.html.

Francis, James M. *Reflections on Non-Stipendiary Ministry as Ministry in Secular Employment: Collected Papers (1989–1996)*. Sunderland, UK: University of Sunderland, 1996.

Friedman, M. *Capitalism and Freedom*. Chicago: University of Chicago Press, 1962.

Friends of Bernie Sanders. 2017. https://berniesanders.com/issues/income-and -wealth-inequality.

Gallup, Inc. *Gallup-Hope Index 2015*. Washington, DC: Gallup, Inc., 2016. https:// www.operationhope.org/images/uploads/Files/OperationHope_Final_2015.pdf.

Gelles, D. "Top CEO Pay Fell—Yes Fell—in 2015." *New York Times*, May 27, 2016. https://www.nytimes.com/2016/05/29/business/top-ceo-pay-fell-yes-fell-in -2015.html?rref=collection%2Ftimestopic%2FExecutive%20Pay&action=click &contentCollection=timestopics&region=stream&module=stream_unit&version=search&contentPlacement=10&pgtype=collection.

Gill, D. *It's about Excellence: Building Ethically Healthy Organizations*. Eugene, OR: Wipf & Stock, 2008.

Greenwood, R. and D. Scharfstein. "The Growth of Finance." *Journal of Economic Perspectives* 27, no. 2 (Spring 2013): 3–28.

Hamilton, W. "Lehman Compensation Chart." *Los Angeles Times*, April 27, 2012. http://documents.latimes.com/lehman-compensation-chart/.

Heaton, H. *Economic History of Europe*. New York: Harper and Bros., 1948.

Heslam, P. *Transforming Capitalism: Entrepreneurship and the Renewal of Thrift*. Cambridge, UK: Grove Books, 2010.

Hollinger, D. *Choosing the Good: Christian Ethics in a Complex World*. Grand Rapids: Baker Academic, 2002.

Horst, C. and P. Greer. *Entrepreneurship for Human Flourishing*. Washington, DC: AEI Press, 2014.

Ignatius, A. and G. McGinn. "Novo Nordisk CEO Lars Sørensen on What Propelled Him to the Top." *Harvard Business Review*, November 2015. https://hbr .org/2015/11/novo-nordisk-ceo-on-what-propelled-him-to-the-top.

InsideGov.com. "Compare Top Federal Tax Rates." 2017. http://federal-tax-rates
.insidegov.com.

Institute for Policy Studies. "Income Equality in the United States." 2017. http://
inequality.org/facts/income-inequality/.

InvestingAnswers.com. "50 Quotes from the World's Most Controversial Billionaire." October 18, 2013. http://www.investinganswers.com/education
/famous-investors/50-quotes-worlds-most-controversial-billionaire-2897.

John Paul II. *Crossing the Threshold of Hope*. London: Random House, 1994.

Keller, T. and K. Leary Alsdorf. *Every Good Endeavor: Connecting Your Work to God's
Work*. New York: Penguin, 2012.

Kindleberger, C. *A Financial History of Western Europe*. London: Routledge, 1984.

Knowledge @Wharton. "Why Impact Investing Needs to Go Mainstream." July
26, 2017. http://knowledge.wharton.upenn.edu/article/impact-investing-going
-mainstream.

Kosfeld, M., et al. "Oxytocin Increases Trust in Humans." *Nature: International
Weekly Journal of Science*, June 2, 2005. http://www.nature.com/nature/journal
/v435/n7042/abs/nature03701.html.

Lincoln, A. *Collected Works*. Vol. 6. Edited by R. P. Blaser. New Brunswick, NJ: Rutgers University Press, 1953.

Lovins, A. "This Much I Know." *The Guardian*, March 23, 2008.   https://www.
theguardian.com/environment/2008/mar/23/ethicalliving.lifeandhealth4.

Luther, Martin. *The Babylonian Captivity of the Church*. http://www.lutherdansk.dk
/Web-babylonian%20Captivitate/Martin%20Luther.htm.

———. *Letters of Spiritual Counsel*. Edited by T. G. Tappert. Philadelphia: Westminster, 1960.

———. "On Trade and Usury." Translated by W. H. Carruth. *The Open Court* 11: 1
(January 1897), 16–34.

Maddison, A. *Contours of the World Economy*. Oxford: Oxford University Press, 2007.

Malloch, T. *Spiritual Enterprise: Doing Virtuous Business*. New York: Encounter,
2008.

Mars Incorporated (Mars Catalyst Project). "The Economics of Mutuality." *Responsible Business Forum: Saïd Business School*, May 2016. http://www.sbs.ox.ac.uk/sites
/default/files/research-projects/MiB/10-Maua-and-Bloom-Presentation.pdf.

Marx, K. *Capital: A Critical Analysis of Capitalist Production*. Ware, UK: Wordsworth
Editions, 2012.

Marx, K. and F. Engels. *Selected Works*. Vol. 1. Moscow: Progress Publishers, 1969.

https://www.marxists.org/archive/marx/works/sw/progress-publishers/volume 01.htm.

Maslow, A. H. "A Theory of Human Motivation," *Psychological Review* 50 (1943): 370–96.

McGlaughlin, F. *The Marketer as Philosopher: Ten Brief Reflections on the Power of Your Value Proposition.* Jacksonville, FL: MECLABS Institute, 2014.

McMillan, L. *Delivering Purpose and Meaning.* Melbourne, Australia. Reventure, 2017.

———. *Snapshot of the Australian Workplace.* Melbourne, Australia. Reventure, 2016.

McNeill, J. T. *The History and Character of Calvinism.* Oxford: Oxford University Press, 1954.

Moylan, J. "Rolls-Royce Apologises after £671m Bribery Settlement." *BBC News*, January 18, 2017. http://www.bbc.com/news/business-38644114.

NASA. "Global Climate Change: Vital Signs of the Planet." 2017. https://climate.nasa.gov/evidence.

NCEO. "ESOPs by the Numbers." 2017. http://www.nceo.org/articles/esops-by-the-numbers.

Néron, P. "Rethinking the Very Idea of Egalitarian Markets and Corporations: Why Relationships Might Matter More Than Distribution." *Business Ethics Quarterly* 25, no. 1 (2015): 93–124. doi:10.1017/beq.2015.7.

Nowak, M. "Five Rules for the Evolution of Cooperation." *Science* 314, no. 5805 (December 2006): 1560–63.

OECD. "Household Income Inequalities across OECD Countries." June 2015.

Oxfam Briefing Paper. "An Economy for the Ninety-nine Percent." Oxford: Oxfam, 2017.

Pew Research Center. "Worldwide, Many See Belief in God as Essential to Morality." *Global Religious Futures.* March 13, 2014. http://www.pewglobal.org/2014/03/13/worldwide-many-see-belief-in-god-as-essential-to-morality/.

Pew-Templeton Project. "About the Data." *Global Religious Futures.* 2016. http://www.globalreligiousfutures.org/explorer/about-GRF-data.

Piketty, T. *Captial in the Twenty-first Century.* Cambridge, MA: Harvard University Press, 2014.

Poole, E. "Capitalism's Seven Deadly Sins." *Faith in Business Quarterly* 16:3 (May 2013): 17–24.

———. *Capitalism's Toxic Assumptions: Redefining Next Generation Economics.* London: Bloomsbury, 2015.

Radkau, J. *Max Weber: A Biography*. Cambridge, UK: Polity, 2009.

Rae, J. *Life of Adam Smith*. New York: MacMillan, 1895.

Rankin, J. "Rolls-Royce Missed Several Chances to Fix A380 Engine Problem—Safety Report." *The Guardian*, June 27, 2013. https://www.theguardian.com/business/2013/jun/27/rolls-royce-a380-engine-safety-report-qantas.

Richards, J. *Money, Greed and God: Why Capitalism Is the Solution, Not the Problem*. New York: HarperCollins, 2009.

Rosner, B. *Greed as Idolatry*. Grand Rapids: Wm. B. Eerdmans, 2007.

Scheidel, W., ed. *Cambridge Companion to the Roman Economy*. Cambridge: Cambridge University Press, 2013.

Shen, C. and I. Burton. "Taking Economics of Mutuality into Unexplored Territory: A Business Case of Doing Good & Doing Well . . . at Scale." *Responsible Business Forum 2017: Making Business Mutual*. Said Business School. University of Oxford. 2017. http://www.sbs.ox.ac.uk/faculty-research/research-projects/mutuality-business/responsible-business-forum-making-business-mutual/case-studies-driving-purpose-bottom.

Smith, A. *An Inquiry into the Nature and Causes of the Wealth of Nations*. New York: MetaLibri, 2007.

———. *The Theory of Moral Sentiments*. Oxford: Bennett, 2008.

Sonn, P. and Y. Laythrop. "Raise Wages, Kill Jobs? Seven Decades of Historical Data Find No Correlation between Minimum Wage Increase and Employment Levels." *National Employment Law Project*. May 5, 2016. http://www.nelp.org/publication/raise-wages-kill-jobs-no-correlation-minimum-wage-increases-employment-levels/.

Sperber, J. *Karl Marx: A Nineteenth Century Life*. New York: Liveright, 2013.

Suredividend.com. "Warren Buffett Quotes." 2017. http://www.suredividend.com/warren-buffett-quotes/#crowd.

Swan Credit Union. 2016. http://swancreditunion.org.uk/wp-content/uploads/BizPlan_2016–19_Final.pdf.

Tillich, P. *Dynamics of Faith*. New York: Harper and Row, 1957.

Trading Economics. 2017. https://tradingeconomics.com/united-states/government-debt-to-gdp.

United Nations Population Fund. *Annual Report 2011*. New York: UNFPA, 2012.

Valukas, A. "Examiner's Report in re Lehman Brothers Holdings, Inc. et al., Debtors." *Jenner and Block*. March 11, 2010. https://jenner.com/lehman/VOLUME%201.pdf.

Weatherford, J. *The History of Money*. New York: Three Rivers Press, 1997.

Weber, M. *The Protestant Ethic and the Spirit of Capitalism*. Oxon, UK: Routledge, 2001.

Webley, S. and E. More. "Does Business Ethics Pay?" *London: Institute of Business Ethics*, 2003.

Wee, H. "The Problem with Wall Street Greed Five Years after the Crash." *CNBC*, September 13, 2013. http://www.cnbc.com/id/101022751.

"Why Impact Investing Needs to Go Mainstream." Interview with Durreen Shahnaz. *Knowledge@Wharton*. Wharton School. University of Pennsylvania. July 26, 2017. http://knowledge.wharton.upenn.edu/article/impact-investing-going-mainstream

Wiefek, N. "ESOPs by the Numbers." *National Center for Employee Ownership*. March 2017. http://www.nceo.org/articles/esops-by-the-numbers.

Williams-Grut, O. and L. Brinded. "RBS Is Paying £400 Million over Its 'Dash for Cash' Scandal." *Business Insider*, November 8, 2016. http://www.businessinsider.com/fca-rbs-grg-sme-dash-for-cash-compensation-scheme-2016-11.

Winfield, D. and D. Griffin. "Barclays Traders Fined $487.9 Million by U.S. Regulator." *Bloomberg*, July 16, 2013.

Wolff, Jonathan. "Karl Marx." *The Stanford Encyclopedia of Philosophy*. Edited by Edward N. Zalta. Winter 2015. https://plato.stanford.edu/archives/win2015/entries/marx/.

Wood, J. C., ed. *Adam Smith: Critical Assessments*. New York: Routledge, 1984.

Yeoman, R. and M. Santos. "Fairness and Organizational Performance: Insights for Supply Chain Management." *Mutuality in Business, Briefing* No. 3. Saïd Business School. University of Oxford. November 11, 2016. http://www.sbs.ox.ac.uk/sites/default/files/research-projects/MiB/Fairness_and_Organizational_Performance_Insights_for_Supply_Chain_Management_MiB_Briefings_No_3_HF241116_0.pdf.

Zak, P. and J. Barraza. "The Neurobiology of Collective Action." *Frontiers in Science*, November 19, 2013. https://www.ncbi.nlm.nih.gov/pmc/articles/PMC3832785/.

NOTES

Notes to Chapter 1

1. Berkshire Hathaway, Inc., "Berkshire's Corporate Performance vs. the S&P 500," *2001 Annual Report*, http://www.berkshirehathaway.com/2001ar/2001letter.html.

2. The most comprehensive account of Lehman Brothers's failure is the official Examiner's Report (a.k.a. the Valukas Report) commissioned by and submitted to the bankruptcy court in March 2010. The twenty-two-hundred-plus-page report is available online at https://jenner.com/lehman/VOLUME%201.pdf.

3. NINJA is an acronym for "no income, no job or assets."

4. The business judgment rule determines whether executive decisions are reasonable or reckless to the point of violating management's fiduciary duties, or duties of confidence and trust, to its shareholders. In the case of Lehman Brothers, the court-appointed examiner found that the actions of Lehman Brothers in this regard were not colorable, that is, not intentionally deceptive.

5. This refers to financial transactions between banks that involve one bank selling assets to another with the promise to repurchase those assets at a slight premium. These transactions usually take place overnight and are used to cover a bank's short-term cash requirements.

6. The Examiner's Report cites several interviews with Lehman Brothers executives, as well as internal emails that reveal the deceptive intent of using Repo 105 in this way.

7. A company's liquidity pool is comprised of cash and other assets that may be easily converted into cash, or monetized, in an emergency situation.

8. My criticism of this particular aspect of Friedman's thinking should not be construed as rejection of his entire economic philosophy, much of which is commendable.

9. As its name implies, consequentialism is predicated on the proposition that the morality of any given act is determined solely by its consequences. Classic utilitarianism, or "the end justifies the means," is an example of consequentialism.

10. The importance of the Decalogue and the cardinal virtues is demonstrated by the bas-relief of Moses and the Ten Commandments prominently displayed on the east side of the US Supreme Court building in Washington, DC, and in countless other judicial settings.

11. For an interesting perspective on the relationship between virtue ethics and the release of "spiritual capital" in business, I would direct readers to Theodore Roosevelt Malloch and Whitney MacMillan, *Spiritual Enterprise: Doing Virtuous Business* (New York: Skyhorse, 2008).

12. Thomas Aquinas, *Summa Theologiae: A Concise Translation*, ed. T. McDermott (Notre Dame: Ave Maria, 1989), II-II, Q47, A1.

13. Aquinas, ST II-II, Q47, A10.

14. Aquinas, ST II-II, Q50, A1.

15. Aquinas, ST II-II, Q53–Q56.

16. A. Valukas, "Examiner's Report in re Lehman Brothers Holdings, Inc. et al., Debtors," *Jenner and Block* (March 11, 2010), 4, https://jenner.com/lehman/VOLUME%201.pdf.

17. Aquinas, ST II-II, Q61, A1.

18. Aquinas, ST II-II, Q80, A1.

19. Aquinas, ST II-II, Q77, A1.

20. Aquinas, ST II-II, Q80, A1.

21. Aquinas, ST II-II, Q123, A1.

22. Aquinas, ST II-II, Q129–Q134.

23. Aquinas, ST II-II, Q141, A1.

24. Aquinas, ST II-II, Q161, A6.

25. W. Hamilton, "Lehman Compensation Chart," *Los Angeles Times*, April 27, 2012, http://documents.latimes.com/lehman-compensation-chart/.

26. D. Elliott, *Wall Street Pay: A Primer* (Washington, DC: Brookings Institution, 2010), https://www.brookings.edu/research/wall-street-pay-a-primer/.

27. This is a reference to a sobriquet from Tom Wolfe's book *Bonfire of the Vanities* (1987).

28. The distinction between wealth and money will be explored in a later chapter.

29. Aquinas added the apostle Paul's theological virtues of "faith, hope, and love" (which we will explore in a later chapter), to Aristotle's cardinal virtues.

30. Barclay's Bank was recently fined nearly $1 billion for two separate incidents of price-fixing by relatively low-level traders.

Notes to Chapter 2

1. For a useful insight into the evolution of market economies and their impact on Western culture particularly, I recommend Joyce Appleby's book *The Relentless Revolution: A History of Capitalism* (New York: W. W. Norton, 2010).

2. For the purposes of this book, I will define *economic activity* as the "production and distribution of goods and services."

3. Even the biblical creation narrative refers to the existence of gold in the Garden of Eden (Gen. 2:11).

4. Here I define a *market* as any "place of exchange."

5. Here I define *wealth* as "the product of all economic activity beyond that which is necessary for subsistence."

6. W. Scheidel, ed., *Cambridge Companion to the Roman Economy* (Cambridge: Cambridge University Press, 2013), 13.

7. This particular term for the early Middle Ages (ca. the fifth to ninth centuries CE) is considered by some to be pejorative and unhelpful.

8. H. Heaton, *Economic History of Europe* (New York: Harper and Bros., 1948), 86.

9. A. Smith, *An Inquiry into the Nature and Causes of the Wealth of Nations* (New York: MetaLibri, 2007), 329.

10. Smith, *Wealth of Nations*, 470.

Notes to Chapter 3

1. J. Rae, *Life of Adam Smith* (New York: MacMillan, 1895), 11.

2. Rae, *Life of Adam Smith*, 129.

3. A. Smith, *The Theory of Moral Sentiments* (Oxford: Bennett, 2008), 155–58.

4. Rae, *Life of Adam Smith*, 14.

5. Note that such eighteenth-century writers as Smith and Hume did not make a distinction between *sympathy* and *empathy*, using the former to convey emotions modern philosophers would describe as distinctive from sympathy.

6. Rae provides detailed accounts of Smith's travels across continental Europe, his encounters with leading Enlightenment thinkers, and his disappointment with Oxford University's apparent lack of interest in the "new philosophy."

7. Smith, *Moral Sentiments*, 1. Additional references to this source are given parenthetically in the text.

8. M. Friedman, *Capitalism and Freedom* (Chicago: University of Chicago Press, 1962), 5.

9. I use this term in a generic sense, with no association, explicit or implied, to the work of economist Robert H. Frank.

10. A. Smith, *An Inquiry into the Nature and Causes of the Wealth of Nations* (New York: MetaLibri, 2007), 8. Additional references to this source are given parenthetically in the text.

11. J. C. Wood, ed., *Adam Smith: Critical Assessments* (New York: Routledge, 1984), 776.

Notes to Chapter 4

1. A. Smith, *An Inquiry into the Nature and Causes of the Wealth of Nations* (New York: MetaLibri, 2007), 12.

2. J. Appleby, *The Relentless Revolution: A History of Capitalism*, Kindle ed. (New York: Norton, 2010), loc. 2508.

3. For a detailed account of the life of Karl Marx, see J. Sperber, *Karl Marx: A Nineteenth Century Life* (New York: Liveright, 2013).

4. K. Marx, *Capital: A Critical Analysis of Capitalist Production* (Ware, UK: Wordsworth Editions, 2012), 27. Additional references to this source are given parenthetically in the text.

5. K. Marx and F. Engels, *Selected Works* (Moscow: Progress Publishers, 1969), 1:26, https://www.marxists.org/archive/marx/works/sw/progress-publishers/volume01.htm.

6. Marx and Engels, *Selected Works*, 1:27.

Notes to Chapter 5

1. For more biographical information on Max Weber, readers may refer to *Max Weber: A Biography* by Joachim Radkau (Cambridge, UK: Polity, 2009).

2. M. Weber, *The Protestant Ethic and the Spirit of Capitalism* (Oxon, UK: Routledge, 2001), 3. Additional references to this source are given parenthetically in the text.

3. M. Luther, *The Babylonian Captivity of the Church*, 3.42, http://www.lutherdansk.dk /Web-babylonian%20Captivitate/Martin%20Luther.htm.

4. The term *Reformed* is generally preferred to *Calvinist*, as the former is more inclusive of other voices beyond that of John Calvin alone and also distinguishes between the theology of Calvin and his contemporaries and some later distortions of his followers.

Notes to Chapter 6

1. P. S. Fiddes, *Seeing the World and Knowing God: Hebrew Wisdom and Christian Doctrine in a Late-Modern Context* (Oxford: Oxford University Press, 2013), 40.

2. Fiddes, *Seeing the World and Knowing God*, 55.

3. Fiddes, *Seeing the World and Knowing God*, 56.

4. Fiddes, *Seeing the World and Knowing God*, 45.

5. A. Maddison, *Contours of the World Economy* (Oxford: Oxford University Press, 2007), 382.

6. Economist Briefing, "Not Always with Us," *The Economist*, June 1, 2013, https://www .economist.com/news/briefing/21578643-world-has-astonishing-chance-take-billion-people -out-extreme-poverty-2030-not.

7. United Nations Population Fund, *Annual Report 2011* (New York: UNFPA, 2012), 2.

8. Oxfam Briefing Paper, "An Economy for the Ninety-nine Percent" (Oxford: Oxfam, 2017), 2.

9. Trading Economics, (2017), https://tradingeconomics.com/united-states /government-debt-to-gdp.

10. Federal Reserve of New York, "Quarterly Report on Household Debt and Credit," November 2016, www.newyorkfed.org/medialibrary/interactives/householdcredit/data/pdf /HHDC_2016Q3.pdf.

11. Fannie Mae, "Selling Guide," July 2017, www.fanniemae.com/content/eligibility_in formation/eligibility-matrix.pdf.

12. NASA, "Global Climate Change: Vital Signs of the Planet," 2017, climate.nasa.gov /evidence.

13. ERisk, "Barings Bank: Case Study," October 17, 2007, https://web.archive.org /web/20071017041450/http://www.erisk.com/Learning/CaseStudies/Barings.asp.

14. See http://www.cfr.org/united-kingdom/understanding-libor-scandal/p28729.

15. R. Greenwood and R. Scharfstein, "The Growth of Finance," *Journal of Economic Perspectives* 27, no. 2 (Spring 2013): 4.

16. Greenwood and Scharfstein, "Growth of Finance," 24.

Notes to Chapter 7

1. Friends of Bernie Sanders, 2017, https://berniesanders.com/issues/income-and-wealth-inequality.

2. Early editions of the book and the title of Poole's *Just Share Lecture* (2013) used the expression "Seven Deadly Sins" in favor of the current edition's sub-title "Redefining Next Generation Economics."

3. E. Poole, *Capitalism's Toxic Assumptions: Redefining Next Generation Economics* (London: Bloomsbury, 2015), 19.

4. Poole, *Capitalism's Toxic Assumptions*, 18.

5. Poole, *Capitalism's Toxic Assumptions*, Kindle edition.

6. Poole, *Capitalism's Toxic Assumptions*, Kindle edition.

7. Poole, *Capitalism's Toxic Assumptions*, Kindle edition.

8. M. Nowak, "Five Rules for the Evolution of Cooperation," *Science* 314, no. 5805 (December 2006): 1560–63.

Notes to Chapter 8

1. This is also why Sabbath rest is so fundamental to biblical teaching, as human beings emulate their creator God in the seventh day of rest. Not merely for practical reasons, but as a demonstration of God's solidarity with humankind and vice versa, or as Jesus famously taught, "the Sabbath was made for man, not man for the Sabbath" (Mark 2:27).

2. J. M. Francis, *Reflections on Non-Stipendiary Ministry as Ministry in Secular Employment: Collected Papers (1989–1996)* (Sunderland, UK: University of Sunderland, 1996), 16.

3. Note that in the second creation narrative, the appearance of vegetation was delayed until after the creation of Adam, because until that point there was no one "to till the ground" (Gen. 2:5).

4. Those familiar with the work of Max Weber will recognize the systematic organization of her life as reminiscent of the "ideal type" observed in his study of nineteenth-century American Protestantism.

Notes to Chapter 9

1. Augustine, *Sermons on Selected Lessons of the New Testament: Sermon 63*, ed. K. Knight (New Advent, 2009), para. 4, http://newadvent.org/fathers/160363.htm.

2. Augustine, *On the Works of Monks*, ed. K. Knight (New Advent, 2009), para. 33, http://newadvent.org/fathers/1314.htm.

3. Augustine, *Sermon 63*, para. 4.

4. Augustine, *City of God*, ed. K. Knight (New Advent, 2009), ch. 7, http://newadvent.org/fathers/1201.htm.

5. Augustine, *On the Morals of the Catholic Church*, ed. K. Knight (New Advent, 2009), ch. 15, http://newadvent.org/fathers/1401.htm.

6. T. Aquinas, *Summa Theologiae: A Concise Translation*, ed. T. McDermott (Notre Dame: Ave Maria, 1989), II-II, Q66, A1.

7. Aquinas, ST II-II, Q117, A3.

8. Aquinas, ST II-II, Q187, A3.

9. Aquinas, ST II-II, Q78, A1.

10. J. Calvin, *Institutes of the Christian Religion* (Grand Rapids: Eerdmans, 1983), 3.7.1.

11. Calvin, *Inst.* 2.8.46.

12. C. Elliott, *Usury: A Scriptural, Ethical and Economic View* (Millersburg, OH: The Anti-Usury League, 1902), 74.

13. Elliott, *Usury*, 76.

14. Calvin, *Inst.* 2.1.1.

15. Calvin, *Inst.* 2.8.1.

16. Calvin, *Inst.* 2.8.9.

Notes to Chapter 10

1. J. Calvin, *Institutes of the Christian Religion* (Grand Rapids: Eerdmans, 1983), 1.1.1.

2. Calvin, *Inst.* 1.3.2.

3. Pew-Templeton Project, "About the Data," *Global Religious Futures* (2016), http://www.globalreligiousfutures.org/explorer/about-GRF-data.

4. Pew Research Center, "Worldwide, Many See Belief in God as Essential to Morality," *Global Religious Futures*, March 13, 2014, http://www.pewglobal.org/2014/03/13/worldwide-many-see-belief-in-god-as-essential-to-morality/.

5. Institute for Policy Studies, "Income Equality in the United States," 2017, http://inequality.org/facts/income-inequality/.

6. OECD, "Household Income Inequalities across OECD Countries," June 2015, https://www.oecd.org/std/household-wealth-inequality-across-OECD-countries-OECDSB21.pdf.

7. Congressional Black Caucus Foundation, *Minority Access to Capital and Employment* (Washington, DC: Congressional Black Caucus Foundation, 2016), http://www.cbcfinc.org/wp-content/uploads/2016/01/CBCFMinorityAccessCapital_FactSheet_final.pdf.

8. D. Gelles, "Top CEO Pay Fell—Yes Fell—in 2015," *New York Times*, May 27, 2016, https://www.nytimes.com/2016/05/29/business/top-ceo-pay-fell-yes-fell-in-2015.html?rref=collection%2Ftimestopic%2FExecutive%20Pay&action=click&contentCollection=timestopics&region=stream&module=stream_unit&version=search&contentPlacement=10&pgtype=collection.

9. InsideGov.com, "Compare Top Federal Tax Rates," 2017, http://federal-tax-rates.insidegov.com.

10. A. Ignatius and G. McGinn, "Novo Nordisk CEO Lars Sørensen on What Propelled Him to the Top," *Harvard Business Review*, November 2015, https://hbr.org/2015/11/novo-nordisk-ceo-on-what-propelled-him-to-the-top.

11. T. Aquinas, *Summa Theologiae: A Concise Translation*, ed. T. McDermott (Notre Dame: Ave Maria, 1989), I-I, Q79, A1.

12. Aquinas, ST II-II, Q56, A1.

13. It is interesting to note that modern neuroscience appears to be confirming Aquinas's

assumptions about the habitual nature of moral reasoning. See https://www.ncbi.nlm.nih
.gov/pmc/articles/PMC4166998/.

14. J. Rankin, "Rolls-Royce Missed Several Chances to Fix A380 Engine Problem—Safety
Report," *The Guardian*. June 27, 2013, https://www.theguardian.com/business/2013/jun/27
/rolls-royce-a380-engine-safety-report-qantas.

15. BBC News, "Rolls Royce Apologises after £671 Million Bribery Settlement," January
18, 2017, http://www.bbc.com/news/business-38644114.

16. Aquinas, ST II-II, Q63, A1.

17. S. Butcher, "Perfect Profiles for Careers at Goldman Sachs, JP Morgan, Deutsche,
and Others," *eFinancialCareers*, September 16, 2014, http://news.efinancialcareers.com
/us-en/140515/perfect-profiles-for-careers-at-goldman-sachs-j-p-morgan-and-others/.

18. R. Farley, "Is Trump's Tax Plan Revenue Neutral?," *FactCheck.org*, October 1, 2015,
http://www.factcheck.org/2015/10/is-trumps-tax-plan-revenue-neutral/.

19. Aquinas, ST II-II, Q120, A2.

20. O. Williams-Grut and L. Brinded, "RBS Is Paying £400 Million over Its 'Dash
for Cash' Scandal," *Business Insider*, November 8, 2016, http://www.businessinsider.com
/fca-rbs-grg-sme-dash-for-cash-compensation-scheme-2016-11.

21. E. El Issa, "2016 American Household Credit Card Debt Study," *Nerdwallet.com*, 2016,
https://www.nerdwallet.com/blog/average-credit-card-debt-household/.

22. D. Hollinger, *Choosing the Good: Christian Ethics in a Complex World* (Grand Rapids:
Baker Academic, 2002), 179.

23. Aquinas, ST II-II, Q123, A1.

24. Francis I, *Laudato si'*, 2015, http://w2.vatican.va/content/francesco/en/encyclicals
/documents/papa-francesco_20150524_enciclica-laudato-si.html, sec. 153.

25. P. Sonn and Y. Laythrop, "Raise Wages, Kill Jobs? Seven Decades of Historical Data Find No Correlation between Minimum Wage Increase and Employment Levels," *National Employment Law Project*, May 5, 2016, http://www.nelp.org/publication
/raise-wages-kill-jobs-no-correlation-minimum-wage-increases-employment-levels/.

26. Aquinas, ST II-II, Q141, A1.

27. Aquinas, ST II-II, Q144, A1.

28. A. Smith, *The Theory of Moral Sentiments* (Oxford: Bennett, 2008), 62–71.

29. Smith, *Theory of Moral Sentiments*, 65.

Notes to Chapter 11

1. M. Kosfeld et al., "Oxytocin Increases Trust in Humans," *Nature: International Weekly
Journal of Science*, June 2, 2005, http://www.nature.com/nature/journal/v435/n7042/abs
/nature03701.html.

2. A. Lincoln, *Collected Works*, ed. R. P. Blaser (New Brunswick, NJ: Rutgers University
Press, 1953), 6: 536.

3. P. Tillich, *Dynamics of Faith* (New York: Harper and Row, 1957), 4.

4. R. Edleman, *Edelman Trust Barometer (Executive Summary)* (New York: Daniel J.
Edelman Holdings, 2017), 1.

5. Edelman, *Edelman Trust Barometer*, 6.

6. P. Zak and J. Barraza, "The Neurobiology of Collective Action," *Frontiers in Science*, November 19, 2013, https://www.ncbi.nlm.nih.gov/pmc/articles/PMC3832785/.

7. John Paul II, *Crossing the Threshold of Hope* (London: Random House, 1994), 5.

8. Gallup, Inc., *Gallup-Hope Index 2015* (Washington, DC: Gallup, Inc., 2016), https://www.operationhope.org/images/uploads/Files/OperationHope_Final_2015.pdf, 4.

9. S. Forbes and J. Prevas, "The Price of Arrogance," *Forbes*, June 18, 2009, https://www.forbes.com/2009/06/18/alexander-great-hubris-leadership-power.html.

Notes to Chapter 12

1. L. McMillan, *Snapshot of the Australian Workplace* (Melbourne, Australia: Reventure, 2016), 6.

2. McMillan, *Snapshot*, 23.

3. McMillan, *Snapshot*, 6.

4. McMillan, *Snapshot*, 15.

5. McMillan, *Snapshot*, 20.

6. Mars Incorporated (Mars Catalyst Project), "The Economics of Mutuality" *Responsible Business Forum: Saïd Business School*, May 2016, http://www.sbs.ox.ac.uk/sites/default/files/research-projects/MiB/10-Maua-and-Bloom-Presentation.pdf.

7. R. Yeoman and M. Santos, "Fairness and Organizational Performance: Insights for Supply Chain Management," *Mutuality in Business, Briefing* No. 3, Saïd Business School, University of Oxford. November 11, 2016, http://www.sbs.ox.ac.uk/sites/default/files/research-projects/MiB/Fairness_and_Organizational_Performance_Insights_for_Supply_Chain_Management_MiB_Briefings_No_3_HF241116_0.pdf.

8. S. Webley and E. More, "Does Business Ethics Pay?," (London: Institute of Business Ethics, 2003), 10.

9. For a more exhaustive exploration of the benefits businesses derive from operating ethically, I would point readers to David Gill, *It's about Excellence: Building Ethically Healthy Organizations* (Eugene, OR: Wipf & Stock, 2008).

10. L. McMillan, *Delivering Purpose and Meaning* (Melbourne, Australia: Reventure, 2017), 4.

11. McMillan, *Delivering Purpose*, 14.

12. T. Malloch, *Spiritual Enterprise: Doing Virtuous Business* (New York: Encounter, 2008), 18.

13. EEOC, "Religious Garb and Grooming in the Workplace: Rights and Responsibilities," 2017, https://www.eeoc.gov/eeoc/publications/qa_religious_garb_grooming.cfm.

14. K. Marx, *Capital: A Critical Analysis of Capitalist Production* (Ware, UK: Wordsworth Editions, 2012), 373.

15. J. Dienhart, *Business, Institutions and Ethics* (Oxford: Oxford University Press, 2000), 65.

16. For example, these values are among several listed on the Coca-Cola company's website: http://www.coca-colacompany.com/our-company/mission-vision-values.

17. A complete transcript of the Declaration of Independence can be found at http://www.archives.gov/exhibits/charters/declaration.html.

18. Six Sigma refers to the lean methodology originally created by Motorola Corporation in the 1980s.

19. *Kanban* and *kaizen* are Japanese words meaning "signboard" and "improvement," respectively. Similarly, 5S refers to a popular methodology whose component parts all begin with the letter *s* in both Japanese and English.

20. Triple bottom line (TBL) refers to an accounting principle that measures business performance in terms of "profits, people, and planet." It is often employed by so-called social entrepreneurships and some public agencies.

21. While Weatherford's book predates the emergence of Bitcoin by twelve years, his anticipation of electronically based private currencies now seems rather prophetic.

22. J. Weatherford, *The History of Money* (New York: Three Rivers Press, 1997), 135.

23. Weatherford, *History of Money*, 136.

24. Small amounts of gold coins (up to one hundred dollars) and jewelry (such as wedding rings) were exempted from the policy.

25. Leaving the gold standard was only one part of the president's program, which included other measures to combat unemployment and inflation, including a wage and price freeze and a 10 percent import tariff on certain goods.

26. In 1971, gold traded at $35 per ounce. As of this writing, gold is trading at $1,237 per ounce.

27. Less than 12 percent of America's money is in the form of cash (M0), with the rest existing electronically (M1–M3). See https://www.federalreserve.gov/releases/h6/current/.

28. Weatherford, *History of Money*, 78.

29. For concerns relative to the bond market, see http://www.bbc.com/news/business -39325794.

30. See Museum of American Finance, http://www.moaf.org/exhibits/trading_street /buttonwood-display.

31. G. Berman, "What Drives the Complexity and Speed of Our Markets," Speech to the NATA Summit, April 15, 2014, https://www.sec.gov/news/speech /2014-spch041514geb#_edn4.

32. InvestingAnswers.com, "50 Quotes from the World's Most Controversial Billionaire," October 18, 2013, http://www.investinganswers.com/education/famous-investors /50-quotes-worlds-most-controversial-billionaire-2897.

33. See Suredividend.com.

34. A. Lovins, "This Much I Know," *The Guardian*, March 23, 2008, https://www .theguardian.com/environment/2008/mar/23/ethicalliving.lifeandhealth4.

35. H. Wee, "The Problem with Wall Street Greed Five Years after the Crash," *CNBC*, September 13, 2013, http://www.cnbc.com/id/101022751.

36. P.-Y. Néron, "Rethinking the Very Idea of Egalitarian Markets and Corporations: Why Relationships Might Matter More Than Distribution," *Business Ethics Quarterly* 25, no. 1 (2015): 93–124, doi:10.1017/beq.2015.7.

37. NCEO, "ESOPs by the Numbers," 2017, http://www.nceo.org/articles/esops-by -the-numbers.

38. Knowledge@Wharton, "Why Impact Investing Needs to Go Mainstream," July 26, 2017, http://knowledge.wharton.upenn.edu/article/impact-investing-going-mainstream.

39. P. Heslam, *Transforming Capitalism: Entrepreneurship and the Renewal of Thrift*, (Cambridge, UK: Grove Books, 2010), 9.

40. Heslam, *Transforming Capitalism*, 9–10.

Notes to Chapter 13

1. InvestingAnswers.com, "50 Quotes from the World's Most Controversial Billionaire," October 18, 2013, http://www.investinganswers.com/education/famous-investors/50-quotes-worlds-most-controversial-billionaire-2897.

2. Swan Credit Union, 2016, http://swancreditunion.org.uk/wp-content/uploads/Biz Plan_2016–19_Final.pdf.

3. Swan Credit Union, 2016, http://swancreditunion.org.uk/wp-content/uploads/Biz Plan_2016–19_Final.pdf, 2–3.

4. C. Horst and P. Greer, *Entrepreneurship for Human Flourishing* (Washington, DC: AEI Press, 2014), 64.

5. T. Keller and K. Leary Alsdorf, *Every Good Endeavor: Connecting Your Work to God's Work* (New York: Penguin, 2012), 27.

6. Ironically, research also suggests that constant email communication hurts business productivity as well. See https://hbr.org/2015/03/your-late-night-emails-are-hurting-your-team.

7. A. H. Maslow, "A Theory of Human Motivation," *Psychological Review* 50 (1943): 370–96.

8. A. Smith, *The Theory of Moral Sentiments* (Oxford: Bennett, 2008), 154.

9. P. Fiddes, *Seeing the World and Knowing God: Hebrew Wisdom and Christian Doctrine in a Late-Modern Context* (Oxford: Oxford University Press, 2013), 265.

10. Francis I, *Laudato si'*, 2015, http://w2.vatican.va/content/francesco/en/encyclicals/documents/papa-francesco_20150524_enciclica-laudato-si.html, 48:189–90. Francis includes a citation from Pope John Paul II found in *Compendium of the Social Doctrine of the Church*, 2004.

11. F. McGlaughlin, *The Marketer as Philosopher: Ten Brief Reflections on the Power of Your Value Proposition* (Jacksonville, FL: MECLABS Institute, 2014), 54.

INDEX OF NAMES AND SUBJECTS

INDEX OF SCRIPTURE